THE QUICK & EASY COOKBOOK

Southern Living®

THE QUICK & EASY COOKBOOK

Lee Cannon

Oxmoor House, Inc., Birmingham

Copyright © 1979 by Oxmoor House, Inc.
Book Division of The Progressive Farmer
    Company
Publisher of *Southern Living*®, *Progressive
    Farmer*®, and *Decorating & Craft Ideas*®
    magazines.
P.O. Box 2463, Birmingham, Alabama 35201

Eugene Butler	Chairman of the Board
Emory Cunningham	President and Publisher
Vernon Owens, Jr.	Executive Vice President

Conceived, edited and published by Oxmoor
    House, Inc., under the direction of:

Don Logan	Vice President and General Manager
Gary McCalla	Editor, *Southern Living*
John Logue	Editor-in-Chief
Jean Wickstrom Liles	Foods Editor, *Southern Living*
Ann H. Harvey	Managing Editor
Jerry Higdon	Production Manager

The Quick & Easy Cookbook

Designer and Illustrator: Carol Middleton
Foods Assistants: The *Southern Living* Foods
    Staff
Photography by the *Southern Living* Staff

Library of Congress Catalog Number: 79-88365
ISBN: 0-8487-0509-2

Manufactured in the United States of America
Third Printing 1980

Table of Contents

Introduction

Good food and good friends go together, and one way to maintain close ties with other people is through the ceremony of eating. Although the number of meals eaten away from home is increasing, people still spend more time eating together at home than in any other activity. And the vision of Mom or Grandmother in the kitchen—with company coming—still provides us with warm tender memories.

Our modern life-styles, however, leave little time to fuss around in the kitchen. Today's chefs—men or women, single or married, working in or out of the home or both—simply cannot afford the time to be chained to meal preparation. But because they have a host of other responsibilities, there is no reason to give up the congeniality, hospitality, good health, and satisfaction that eating good food together brings. Time need not be a factor!

If you are one of today's meal managers who feel guilty because you cannot prove your love to family and friends, or even to yourself, by spending long hours in the kitchen, take heart. You can plan and prepare good-tasting, nutritious, professional-looking meals in an hour or less for your family or for those unexpected guests.

In fact, there are so many changes in all areas of food service, and so many new techniques available for reducing time, energy, and money, that you can find a new excitement in meal planning. The Quick & Easy Cookbook is designed to show how to apply these new techniques to produce high-quality meals, and how to use common sense and more practical methods of serving to save time.

The Quick & Easy Cookbook will show you how to get away from commercially prepared convenience foods that add to cost and often are not as nourishing as they should be. You will discover how to make your own biscuit, cake, pudding, and sauce mixes, so that you are always prepared. At the same time, you will learn how to use some "quick foods," frozen or canned, in gourmet dishes.

You will learn new and easier methods of food preparation as well as how to preserve nutritive values and how to experiment with seasonings—all with a limited number of appliances.

You will find out how to make desserts so elegant and easy to prepare that you will be embarrassed to share the recipe. In addition to the compliments you will receive for being a fast, efficient, and marvelous cook, you will save money since most recipes can be prepared from "scratch."

The Quick & Easy Cookbook allows experienced cooks freedom to innovate, adapt, and create. Over 700 recipes and 57 planned meals help to start new traditions, as "quick and easy" is equated with good nutrition and high standards of appearance, taste, and economy.

Look for the hints scattered liberally throughout, from how to separate eggs to how to frost grapes. Today's equivalents and substitutions are also included to give you confidence as you learn new skills.

Good living and good eating go together. When you can prepare interesting, delicious, and nourishing meals in a minimum of time, you will have more of that precious commodity to spend in fun and fellowship with friends and family.

Lee Cannon

Section I

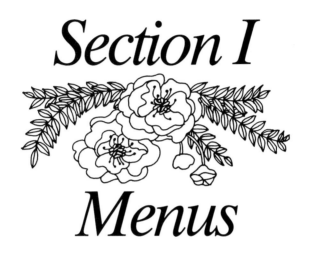

Menus

Brunches for All Occasions

*A*s the name implies, a brunch is defined as a meal between breakfast and lunch, usually served between the hours of 10:00 a.m. and 1:00 p.m.

More substantial than a breakfast, a brunch can include a light dessert. Depending on the customs of the group, cocktails may precede the meals. Because the dishes are easily served, often buffet-style, you may have time to join your guests.

Brunches are a great way to entertain retired people because many do not like to travel after dark and may prefer a full, but not heavy, meal at midday. Also the brunch is a fun method for entertaining before afternoon football games or matinees or even during holidays when early-morning rising is not necessary. Once you have entertained at midday, you will want to make it a habit.

Although these menus can be prepared in an hour or less, a little pre-preparation allows you to assemble and serve them even more quickly.

Any Day Brunch
Brunch for Six

Easy Turkey Tetrazzini
Scalloped Tomatoes
Parmesan Lettuce Salad
Hot Buttered French Bread (*see* Index)
Fruit Compote
Milk   Coffee

 *Prepare tetrazzini and scalloped tomatoes. Put both casseroles in 375° oven at the same time. Combine salad ingredients and refrigerate. Prepare dressing. Arrange fruit compote. Then butter bread and put into oven. Toss salad before serving.*

EASY TURKEY TETRAZZINI

  1 (8-ounce) can sliced mushrooms, drained
  2 tablespoons melted butter
  1 teaspoon salt
⅛ teaspoon pepper
  2 cups cooked diced turkey
  1 (10¾-ounce) can cream of celery soup, undiluted
  1 cup commercial sour cream
  1 (8-ounce) package spaghetti or noodles
½ cup grated Parmesan cheese

Cook mushrooms in butter in medium skillet for 1 minute over low heat. Add salt, pepper, turkey, soup, and sour cream; mix well. Cook spaghetti according to package directions; drain. Alternately layer spaghetti and turkey mixture in a 13- x 9- x 2-inch baking dish. Sprinkle with cheese. Bake at 375° for 25 minutes. Yield: 6 servings.

SCALLOPED TOMATOES

  1 small onion, chopped
¼ cup melted butter or margarine
  2 cups fresh bread cubes
  1 teaspoon salt
½ teaspoon basil
¼ teaspoon pepper
½ teaspoon monosodium glutamate (optional)
  2 (16-ounce) cans tomatoes or 1 to 2 pounds fresh tomatoes, sliced
  1 tablespoon plus 1 teaspoon sugar

Sauté onion in butter in medium saucepan over medium heat. Stir in bread cubes and seasonings.

Place one-fourth of tomato slices and liquid in a 1½-quart casserole; sprinkle with 1 teaspoon sugar and one-fourth of onion mixture. Repeat layering 3 times, ending with onion mixture. Bake at 375° for 30 minutes or until hot and bubbly. Yield: 6 servings.

PARMESAN LETTUCE SALAD

1 head crisp lettuce, torn into bite-size
   pieces
6 green onions with tops, sliced
1 (10-ounce) package frozen green
   peas, thawed
  Garlic salt
  Pepper
¼ cup vegetable oil
2 tablespoons wine vinegar
  Grated Parmesan cheese
  Italian seasoned salad croutons

Combine lettuce, onion, and peas; toss.
Sprinkle with garlic salt and pepper; toss.
Add oil and vinegar; toss. Sprinkle with
Parmesan cheese; top with croutons.
Yield: 6 servings.

FRUIT COMPOTE

1 (8-ounce) can Bing cherries
1 (11-ounce) can mandarin orange
  sections
1 (8-ounce) can pineapple chunks
1 (6-ounce) can green grapes or 1 cup
  seedless green grapes
¼ cup firmly packed brown sugar
1 cup commercial sour cream
  Seedless green grapes (optional)

Drain fruit. (Use juice for fruit punch or
freeze for later use.) Arrange fruit in dessert compotes. Combine brown sugar and
sour cream; top each serving with a dollop
of sour cream mixture. Garnish with green
grapes, if desired. Yield: 6 servings.

Sunday Brunch

Brunch for Six to Eight

Golden Crown Ham on Toasted English Muffins
Old-Time Succotash
Assorted Fresh Fruit—Pink Fruit Dressing
Lime Sherbet
Tea   Coffee

 *While eggs are cooking, dice fruit and refrigerate. Prepare dressing and
hold. Cook succotash while preparing the sauce and ham. Toast muffins
last. Commercial cookies may be served with or instead of sherbet.*

GOLDEN CROWN HAM ON TOASTED ENGLISH MUFFINS

  8 hard-cooked eggs
  ¼ cup plus 2 tablespoons butter or
     margarine
  ¼ cup plus 2 tablespoons all-purpose
     flour
  4 cups milk
  ¾ teaspoon salt
  ¾ teaspoon paprika
  ¼ teaspoon pepper
  2 cups cooked diced ham
  3 or 4 English muffins, split and
     toasted

Separate yolks and whites of hard-cooked eggs; chop egg whites. Melt butter in a heavy saucepan over low heat; add flour, stirring until smooth. Cook 1 minute, stirring constantly. Gradually stir in milk; cook over medium heat, stirring constantly, until thickened and bubbly. Stir in salt, paprika, and pepper. Add chopped egg whites and ham. Press yolks through a sieve. Pour ham mixture over English muffin; sprinkle egg yolk over top of each serving. If mixture is too thick to pour, dilute with milk. Yield: 6 to 8 servings.

OLD-TIME SUCCOTASH

  2 cups sliced celery
  1 cup chopped onion
  2 tablespoons melted butter or
     margarine
  1 (17-ounce) can lima beans, drained
  1 (12-ounce) can whole kernel corn
     Salt and pepper

Sauté celery and onion in butter in a saucepan until tender. Add beans and corn. Heat; season to taste. Yield: 8 servings.

PINK FRUIT DRESSING

  ½ cup wine vinegar
  ½ cup honey
  1 teaspoon dry mustard
  1 teaspoon salt
  ½ teaspoon paprika
  1 cup vegetable oil
     Fresh fruit

Combine first 5 ingredients in container of electric blender; blend until smooth. Remove cap in cover and with blender operating slowly, pour in oil. Serve over fresh fruit. Yield: 1¾ cups.

Cheesy Egg Brunch

Brunch for Six

Cheesy Egg Bake
Baked Tomato Halves
Green Beans with Almonds
Assorted Fresh Fruit—Honey Dressing (*see* Index)
Toasted English Muffins
Vanilla Ice Cream—Coffee-Butterscotch Sauce
Iced Tea   Coffee

 *Cook eggs. Prepare tomato halves and salad dressing. Put tomatoes into oven; complete egg dish and bake. Prepare green beans and fruit salad. Toast English muffins last.*

CHEESY EGG BAKE

- 1 (10½-ounce) can cream of celery soup, undiluted
- 2 tablespoons milk
- 1 small onion, grated
- 2 teaspoons prepared mustard
- 1 cup (4 ounces) shredded Cheddar cheese
- 6 hard-cooked eggs, cut in half lengthwise
- Chopped parsley

Combine first 4 ingredients in saucepan; cook and stir until heated through. Remove from heat; stir in cheese until melted. Pour 1 cup sauce into a 10- x 6- x 2-inch baking dish. Place eggs cut side down in sauce. Spoon remaining sauce around eggs. Bake at 350° about 15 minutes. Sprinkle with chopped parsley. Yield: 6 servings.

Note: Cream of chicken soup may be substituted for cream of celery soup. Swiss cheese may be substituted for Cheddar cheese.

BAKED TOMATO HALVES

- 3 large tomatoes
- 1½ teaspoons salt
- 1 teaspoon prepared mustard
- 1 teaspoon chopped onion
- 1 tablespoon chopped parsley
- 1 tablespoon chopped celery leaves
- 1 teaspoon whole oregano (optional)
- 1 teaspoon butter or margarine

Wash tomatoes; remove stem end and cut crosswise in half. Sprinkle tomatoes with salt and spread with mustard. Combine onion, parsley, celery leaves, and oregano; sprinkle over tomatoes. Dot each half with butter. Bake at 350° for 30 minutes or until tender. Yield: 6 servings.

GREEN BEANS WITH ALMONDS

- 2 (10-ounce) packages frozen French-style green beans or 2 (16-ounce) cans French-style green beans, drained
- ⅓ cup slivered blanched almonds
- ½ cup melted butter or margarine

Cook beans according to package directions. Sauté almonds in butter in small skillet until golden brown. Pour over hot, drained green beans. Yield: 6 servings.

COFFEE-BUTTERSCOTCH SAUCE

- 1 cup firmly packed brown sugar
- ¼ cup light corn syrup
- ¼ cup butter or margarine
- ⅓ cup half-and-half
- 1 teaspoon instant coffee granules

Combine all ingredients in a saucepan; bring to a boil. Boil 2 minutes, stirring constantly. Serve warm over vanilla ice cream. Yield: 1½ cups.

Note: For a Praline Sauce add ½ cup chopped pecans.

CARROT CASSEROLE

1 (5⅓-ounce) can evaporated milk
¼ cup milk
2 eggs, slightly beaten
3 tablespoons sugar
½ teaspoon salt
3 cups coarsely grated carrots
3 tablespoons butter or margarine
   Parsley sprigs

Combine milk, eggs, sugar, and salt in mixing bowl; add carrots. Pour into a greased 1-quart baking dish. Dot with butter. Bake, uncovered, at 350° for 30 to 40 minutes or until set. Garnish with parsley sprigs. Yield: 6 servings.

ASPARAGUS WITH CHEESE SAUCE

2 (14-ounce) cans asparagus spears
½ cup milk
2 cups (8 ounces) diced process cheese
   spread
1 teaspoon salt
1 teaspoon Worcestershire sauce
2 teaspoons prepared mustard
   Paprika or parsley (optional)

Heat asparagus in its own liquid. Combine milk and cheese and slowly heat in a saucepan; stir until well blended. Add salt, Worcestershire sauce, and mustard. Drain asparagus and place in a small serving dish. Top with cheese sauce. Garnish with paprika or parsley, if desired. Yield: 6 servings.

STRAWBERRY COMPOTES

1 to 2 pints strawberries, washed and
   stems removed
1 cup commercial sour cream,
   whipped
   Brown sugar

Alternate layers of strawberries, sour cream, and sprinkling of brown sugar in 6 compotes. Chill until ready to serve. Yield: 6 servings.

New Year's Brunch

Brunch for Four to Six

Blue Cheese Spread   Crackers
Deviled Salmon
Broccoli with Creamy Lemon Sauce
Buttered Celery
Caesar Salad with Avocado
Commercial French Rolls
Chilled Raspberry Dessert
White Wine   Coffee

BLUE CHEESE SPREAD

- 1 (8-ounce) package cream cheese, softened
- ¼ cup crumbled blue cheese
- 1 to 2 tablespoons grated onion
- ½ cup chopped parsley

Combine cream cheese, blue cheese, and onion in a small mixing bowl; beat until smooth. Top with parsley. Serve with crackers. Yield: 1½ cups.

DEVILED SALMON

- 1 medium onion, finely chopped
- 1 tablespoon finely chopped green pepper
- ½ cup melted butter or margarine
- 1 (16-ounce) can salmon, drained
- 1 cup cracker crumbs
- 2 tablespoons lemon juice
- 1 tablespoon Worcestershire sauce
- 1 tablespoon dry mustard
- 2 eggs, slightly beaten
- ½ cup whipping cream
  Butter or margarine
- ¼ cup chopped parsley
  Commercial tartar sauce

Sauté onion and green pepper in butter in small skillet until tender; do not brown or drain. Combine salmon, cracker crumbs, lemon juice, Worcestershire sauce, mustard, eggs, cream, and onion mixture. Put into individual shells or a greased 1½-quart casserole. Dot with additional butter. Bake casserole at 350° for 30 minutes, or individual shells for 20 minutes. Garnish with parsley. Serve with commercial tartar sauce. Yield: 4 to 6 servings.

Note: Crabmeat may be substituted for salmon.

BROCCOLI WITH CREAMY LEMON SAUCE

- 3 (10-ounce) packages frozen broccoli spears
- ¼ cup butter or margarine
- 2 tablespoons all-purpose flour
- ¼ cup lemon juice
- 1 cup boiling water
- ¼ teaspoon salt
  Hot sauce
- ½ cup commercial sour cream
- 1 tablespoon melted butter or margarine

Prepare broccoli according to package directions; drain.

Melt ¼ cup butter in medium saucepan over low heat; add flour, stirring until smooth. Cook 1 minute, stirring constantly. Gradually stir in lemon juice and water; cook over medium heat, stirring constantly, until thickened and bubbly. Stir in salt and hot sauce. Just before serving, add sour cream and 1 tablespoon melted butter. Pour over broccoli. Yield: 6 servings.

Note: Asparagus spears may be substituted for broccoli.

BUTTERED CELERY

**3 to 4 large stalks celery, cut into
 1-inch pieces (about 3 cups)
Butter
Salt and pepper to taste**

Cook celery in boiling salted water until tender, about 10 minutes; drain. Add butter and stir until melted and celery is coated. Season to taste. Yield: 6 servings.

CAESAR SALAD WITH AVOCADO

**½ cup vegetable oil
¼ cup lemon juice
½ teaspoon garlic salt
½ teaspoon Worcestershire sauce
⅛ teaspoon dry mustard
¼ teaspoon pepper
½ cup grated Parmesan cheese
2 quarts torn lettuce (1 large or 2
 small heads)
1 (¾-ounce) can anchovy fillets,
 drained and chopped
1 egg
1 avocado, peeled and diced
1 cup garlic-flavored salad croutons**

Combine oil, lemon juice, garlic salt, Worcestershire sauce, mustard, pepper, and cheese in salad bowl. Add lettuce and anchovies; toss. Break egg onto salad and toss until flecks of yolk disappear. Add avocado and croutons; toss gently. Yield: 6 servings.

CHILLED RASPBERRY DESSERT

**1 (3-ounce) package red
 raspberry-flavored gelatin
½ cup boiling water
1 cup ice cubes
1 (10-ounce) package frozen
 raspberries, thawed
Mint leaves (optional)**

Pour gelatin into blender; add water. Cover and blend 2 minutes to dissolve gelatin. Remove cap from blender top; add ice cubes one at a time. Blend 1 minute. Reserve enough raspberries to garnish top; spoon remaining raspberries into 6 sherbet dishes. Top with gelatin mixture. Garnish top with raspberries and mint, if desired. Chill 5 minutes or until ready to serve. Yield: 6 servings.

Holiday Brunch

Brunch for Six

**Chilled Pineapple Juice
Shrimp and Egg Scramble
Zesty Tomatoes
Green Rice
Toasted English Muffins
Peaches Zanzibar
Tea   Coffee**

 *Begin preparation by simmering the peaches. While they simmer, begin cooking the rice and chop the ingredients for the Scramble. Prepare tomatoes and toast muffins. Finish preparation of Scramble. Broil tomatoes and complete rice.*

SHRIMP AND EGG SCRAMBLE

   2 (4½-ounce) cans shrimp, drained
   3 slices bacon
   ¾ cup chopped green pepper
   ½ cup chopped onion
   ¼ teaspoon salt
   ¼ teaspoon cayenne pepper
   6 eggs, beaten
   ¼ cup half-and-half
   ½ teaspoon Worcestershire sauce

Rinse shrimp with cold water; set aside. Cook bacon until crisp; remove from skillet and reserve drippings. Crumble bacon. Sauté green pepper and onion in reserved drippings until tender. Add seasonings and shrimp; heat. Combine eggs, half-and-half, Worcestershire sauce, and bacon. Add to shrimp mixture and cook until eggs are firm, stirring occasionally. Yield: 6 servings.

GREEN RICE

   2 cups chicken bouillon
   1 to 1½ teaspoons garlic salt
   1 cup uncooked regular rice
   2 tablespoons melted butter or
       margarine
   2 tablespoons cooked, strained,
       chopped spinach
   ½ cup grated Parmesan cheese

Combine bouillon and garlic salt in medium saucepan; bring to a boil. Add rice; reduce heat to low. Cover and cook until rice is tender, 15 to 20 minutes. Add butter and spinach; mix well. Sprinkle with cheese. Cover and cook 2 minutes or until thoroughly heated. Yield: 4 to 6 servings.

ZESTY TOMATOES

   6 tomatoes
       Salt and pepper to taste
   2 tablespoons minced onion
   2 tablespoons minced green pepper
   2 tablespoons chopped parsley
       Grated Parmesan cheese

Cut a slice from top of each tomato; hollow out small well in center. Season with salt and pepper. Combine onion, green pepper, and parsley; put 1 teaspoon of mixture in well and on top of each tomato. Broil 3 minutes. Sprinkle with Parmesan cheese and broil until lightly browned. Yield: 6 servings.

PEACHES ZANZIBAR

   1 (29-ounce) can peach halves
   2 pieces whole ginger
   2 (3-inch) sticks cinnamon
   8 whole allspice
   6 whole cloves
   1 pint vanilla ice cream
       Whipped topping (optional)

Drain peaches, reserving juice. Cut ginger into small pieces; add with other spices to reserved juice. Simmer 15 minutes; strain. Add peaches; chill until ready to use. Put scoop of ice cream in dessert dish. Place 1 peach half over ice cream; spoon juice over peach. Garnish with whipped topping. Yield: 6 servings.

Buffet Meals for Today's Home

*A*t one time buffet service was used only when many guests were expected and very little help in serving was available. This is no longer true; today, buffet service is a preferred method of entertaining for all types of meals, from the very formal to the casual. However, when a buffet service is suggested, it immediately implies a casual, informal, yet very pleasant way to feed friends and family.

There are three types of buffets. All are self-service from a delightfully set buffet or table, differing only in how and when eaten. For example, table service *means that you set a dining table and supply all necessary silverware. The guest serves himself before sitting at the table. You can serve almost any kind of food for this type of buffet.*

The second type, tray service, *requires the guest to fill his plate and carry it on a tray to a convenient seat. When entertaining in this way, serve meat tender enough to cut with a fork; no other silver is required.*

The third type of buffet is plate service. *Individuals serve themselves from the buffet table with only plate and fork in hand, and they find a place to sit or stand while eating. For this buffet, you can only serve foods that can be eaten with a fork, and you must butter all bread.*

A well-organized buffet table with all foods served at the right temperature can provide a pleasant meal for everyone. With some planning ahead these meals can be prepared and served elegantly and quickly.

Quick Chicken Buffet

Buffet Supper for 12

Chicken Oriental
Buttered Peas and Onions
Orange-Almond Fruit Salad
Toasted Whole Wheat Bread
Cake Cubes with Peach Topping
Coffee   Iced Tea

 *This meal will go even more quickly if you have celery and onion chopped and in freezer. Assemble ingredients for Chicken Oriental. While these are sautéing, start peas and onions. Prepare salad dressing and chill. While chicken is cooking, combine cake and topping. Toast bread. During last five minutes of chicken cooking, assemble individual salads. You still have time to set the table and get the dessert dishes ready.*

CHICKEN ORIENTAL

   2 cups thinly sliced celery
   2 medium onions, thinly sliced
   ¼ cup vegetable oil
   ¼ cup cornstarch
   2 (16-ounce) cans bean sprouts,
        drained
   4 chicken bouillon cubes
   ¼ cup honey
   ½ cup soy sauce
   2 cups water
   6 cups cooked chopped chicken
        Hot cooked rice (optional)
        Chow mein noodles

Cook celery and onion in oil in large skillet until crisp-tender. Blend in cornstarch. Stir in bean sprouts, bouillon cubes, honey, soy sauce, and water. Cook over medium heat, stirring occasionally, until mixture is thickened and bouillon cubes are dissolved. Add chicken and simmer 5 minutes. To serve, spoon chicken mixture gently over hot rice, if desired, and sprinkle liberally with chow mein noodles. Yield: 12 servings.

BUTTERED PEAS AND ONIONS

   2 (10-ounce) packages frozen green
        peas
   2 (16-ounce) cans onions, undrained
   1 teaspoon salt
   ½ cup melted butter or margarine
        Pepper
   ¼ cup chopped parsley

Combine peas, onions, and salt in medium saucepan; cook over medium heat until peas are tender; drain. Pour butter over vegetables and season to taste. Sprinkle with parsley. Yield: 12 servings.

ORANGE-ALMOND FRUIT SALAD

    4 cups cottage cheese
    ½ cup toasted slivered almonds
    ¼ cup chopped maraschino cherries
    2 teaspoons grated orange rind
    12 chilled pineapple slices
    12 lettuce cups
       Halved seedless grapes (optional)

Beat cottage cheese until smooth; fold in almonds, cherries, and rind. Place a pineapple slice on each lettuce cup; top with ⅓ cup cheese mixture. Garnish with grapes, if desired. Yield: 12 servings.

CAKE CUBES WITH PEACH TOPPING

    3 cups small cake cubes
    1 (9-ounce) package frozen whipped topping, thawed
    2 (16-ounce) cans sliced peaches, drained

Fold cake into whipped topping. Spoon into individual serving dishes and top with peaches. Yield: 12 servings.

Candlelight Buffet

Buffet Dinner for Twelve

Seafood Mediterranean
Buttered Rice (*see* Index)
Deviled Brussels Sprouts
Grapefruit and Avocado Salad—French Fruit Dressing (*see* Index)
Parmesan Sticks (*see* Index)
Peruvian Pound Cake
Coffee   Wine

Assemble ingredients for seafood dish, but do not cook until last minute. While the rice is cooking, prepare the salad and refrigerate; then prepare the dressing. Combine dessert topping and refrigerate to blend flavors. Cook Brussels sprouts and combine sauce ingredients. Prepare breadsticks and while bread is baking, prepare Seafood Mediterranean. Perk coffee, and assemble dessert just before serving.

SEAFOOD MEDITERRANEAN

6 cloves garlic, crushed
½ cup olive oil
1 cup dry white wine
2 (16-ounce) cans tomatoes
2 teaspoons whole oregano
4 bay leaves
1 tablespoon salt
1 teaspoon pepper
2 pounds shrimp, peeled and deveined
2 pounds crabmeat
1 cup chopped parsley
1 cup chopped chives
Buttered Rice (optional)

Sauté garlic in olive oil. Add wine, tomatoes, oregano, bay leaves, salt, and pepper; mix thoroughly. Cover and simmer 4 to 5 minutes; add shrimp. Cover and simmer 3 minutes until shrimp is pink. Stir in crabmeat, parsley, and chives. Heat thoroughly. Serve on Buttered Rice, if desired. Yield: 12 servings.

DEVILED BRUSSELS SPROUTS

4 (10-ounce) packages frozen Brussels
    sprouts
½ cup melted butter or margarine
1 tablespoon plus 1 teaspoon prepared
    mustard
1 tablespoon plus 1 teaspoon
    Worcestershire sauce
1½ teaspoons salt
    Cayenne pepper to taste

Cook Brussels sprouts according to package directions; drain. Combine remaining ingredients; mix until smooth. Pour over hot Brussels sprouts. Serve immediately. Yield: 12 servings.

For a great dessert, pour cream sherry over a chilled grapefruit.

GRAPEFRUIT AND AVOCADO SALAD

4 large grapefruits
4 ripe avocados
12 lettuce cups
    French Fruit Dressing (*see* Index)

Peel and section grapefruit. Peel avocado and cut each into 12 slices. Arrange grapefruit sections and avocado slices in overlapping fashion on lettuce. Serve with French Fruit Dressing. Yield: 12 servings.

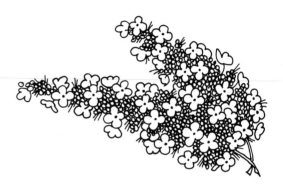

PERUVIAN POUND CAKE

2 cups commercial sour cream
¼ cup lemon juice
2 tablespoons sugar
½ teaspoon vanilla extract
2 (16-ounce) cans sliced peaches,
    drained
    Pound or angel food cake, sliced

Combine sour cream, lemon juice, sugar, and vanilla; chill to blend flavors. Serve peaches over cake; top with sour cream mixture. Yield: 12 servings.
Note: 1 quart of sweetened fresh peaches can be substituted for canned peaches.

Try dusting the top of a fresh cake with powdered sugar instead of using a frosting. Or serve sliced or diced fruit as a topping for cake instead of a rich frosting.

After-the-Game Buffet

Buffet Supper for Twelve

Hungarian Hamburger on Buttered Noodles
Fresh Buttered Okra (*see* Index)
Lettuce, Egg, and Anchovy Salad
Buttermilk Biscuits
Syllabub
Beer   Coffee

Q&E *Start by draining raspberry pulp and cooking eggs. Prepare hamburger, salad, and then biscuits. While biscuits bake, cook okra, boil noodles, and prepare dessert.*

HUNGARIAN HAMBURGER ON BUTTERED NOODLES

- 1 cup chopped onion
- 2 cloves garlic, minced
- ¼ cup melted butter or margarine
- 2 pounds ground beef
- ¼ cup all-purpose flour
- 1 tablespoon plus 1 teaspoon salt
- ½ teaspoon pepper
- 2 (8-ounce) cans sliced mushrooms, drained
- 2 (10½-ounce) cans cream of chicken soup, undiluted
- 1 (16-ounce) carton commercial sour cream, divided
- ¼ cup chopped parsley, chives, or pimiento
  Hot cooked noodles

Sauté onion and garlic in butter in large skillet. Stir in meat, flour, salt, pepper, and mushrooms; cook about 5 minutes, stirring occasionally. Stir in soup. Cover and simmer 10 minutes. Remove from heat; stir 1⅓ cups sour cream into meat mixture, reserving remainder for garnish. Top with reserved sour cream and parsley. Serve on buttered noodles. Yield: 12 servings.

LETTUCE, EGG, AND ANCHOVY SALAD

- 2 cloves garlic
- 2 heads lettuce, torn into bite-size pieces
- 6 hard-cooked eggs, sliced
- 1 (2-ounce) can anchovies, chopped
- 4 tomatoes, peeled and sliced
  Commercial French dressing

Rub salad bowl with garlic; discard garlic. Add lettuce, eggs, anchovies, and tomatoes. Add dressing and toss. Serve immediately. Yield: 12 servings.

BUTTERMILK BISCUITS

4 cups self-rising flour
½ teaspoon soda
1 cup shortening
2 cups buttermilk

Combine flour and soda in mixing bowl. Cut in shortening with pastry blender until mixture resembles coarse meal. Add buttermilk; stir until dough clings together. Turn dough out onto a lightly floured surface; knead lightly about 20 seconds. Pat or roll dough to ½-inch thickness. Cut into rounds with a 2-inch biscuit cutter. Place on a greased baking sheet. Brush top with additional buttermilk, if desired. Bake at 400° for 12 minutes. Yield: 2 dozen.

Note: You may wish to use this quicker method: Roll dough into rectangle; cut with knife into squares. Transfer to baking sheet. Bake as above.

SYLLABUB

2 (10-ounce) packages frozen raspberries, thawed
1 cup Madeira or Port (optional)
2 dozen ladyfingers, split
1 quart whipping cream
¼ cup sugar

Drain raspberries and reserve juice. Add Madeira to juice. Refrigerate pulp and juice separately. Line glass bowl or sherbet dishes with ladyfingers; pour juice over ladyfingers until they are well soaked. Whip cream with sugar until stiff. Fold pulp of raspberries into whipped cream; spoon over ladyfingers. Yield: 12 servings.

Note: Two (9-ounce) cartons whipped topping can be substituted for whipped cream; eliminate sugar.

Hot Sandwich Buffet

Buffet Supper for Six

Broiled Salmon Buns
Oven-Fried Potatoes
Broccoli with Almonds
Hot Slaw
Waikiki Dessert
Lemonade   **Milk**

 *Begin preparation for this meal by getting the potatoes in the oven because they take the longest to cook. Cook eggs and get slaw ready to cook. Cook broccoli. Assemble the salmon buns and ingredients for dessert. Steam slaw; broil salmon. Prepare dessert and store in refrigerator until ready to serve in parfait glasses or compotes.*

BROILED SALMON BUNS

2 (7¾-ounce) cans salmon
6 hard-cooked eggs, chopped
¼ cup plus 2 tablespoons pickle relish
⅔ cup mayonnaise
6 to 8 hamburger buns, split and
    buttered

Drain and flake salmon; combine with remaining ingredients except buns. Spread mixture evenly onto buttered sides of buns. Broil until golden, about 5 minutes. Yield: 6 to 8 servings.

OVEN-FRIED POTATOES

5 potatoes
½ cup melted butter or margarine or
    vegetable oil
Salt to taste

Wash and pare potatoes; cut each into 4 thick slices. Dip slices in butter and arrange in shallow baking pan. Cover pan with foil. Bake at 425° for 10 minutes. Remove foil; continue to bake about 30 minutes or until delicately brown, turning once. Sprinkle with salt. Yield: 6 servings.

BROCCOLI WITH ALMONDS

2 (10-ounce) packages frozen broccoli
    spears
½ cup melted butter or margarine
2 tablespoons lemon juice
½ cup chopped toasted almonds

Cook broccoli according to package directions; drain. Combine butter and lemon juice. Arrange broccoli in bowl; top with butter mixture and sprinkle with almonds. Yield: 6 servings.

HOT SLAW

3 cups water
½ teaspoon salt
2 tablespoons vinegar
3 cups shredded cabbage
1 tablespoon butter or margarine
1 stalk celery, thinly sliced
1 medium onion, thinly sliced
1 small green pepper, thinly sliced
    (optional)
Salt and pepper
Soy sauce (optional)

Put water, salt, and vinegar in a large saucepan; bring to a boil. Add cabbage; cover and cook 5 minutes; drain. Melt butter in large skillet and add vegetables; stir. Cover and steam 5 minutes, stirring occasionally. Season with salt, pepper, and soy sauce, if desired. Yield: 6 servings.

WAIKIKI DESSERT

1 (8-ounce) package cream cheese,
    softened
2 tablespoons sugar
1 cup milk, divided
1 (8½-ounce) can crushed pineapple,
    drained
1 (3½-ounce) package instant vanilla
    pudding and pie filling mix
8 maraschino cherries, chopped

Combine cream cheese, sugar, and ¼ cup milk; mix well. Add remaining milk, pineapple, and pudding mix; beat only 1 minute. Just before serving, spoon into dessert dishes. Garnish with cherries. Yield: 6 servings.
Note: Dessert may be chilled before serving.

Teen Buffet

Buffet Supper for Six to Eight

Skillet Macaroni and Cheese
Stewed Tomatoes
Neapolitan Green Salad
Southern Hot Egg Bread
Fruit Crisp
Iced Tea   **Coffee**

 *Start with the macaroni and cheese dish. While it simmers, start cooking tomatoes. Wash and cube lettuce, and store in refrigerator until ready to use. Prepare dressing. While egg bread bakes, prepare fruit crisp. Do last step of the macaroni; then toss the salad. Check tomatoes and turn heat down to warm. Remove egg bread from oven, turn down temperature, and bake fruit crisp. By the time dessert is to be served, the crisp will be cooked to the peak of perfection.*

SKILLET MACARONI AND CHEESE

½ **cup butter or margarine**
1 **(8-ounce) package elbow macaroni, uncooked**
1 **large onion, chopped**
1 **medium-size green pepper, diced**
2 **teaspoons garlic salt**
½ **teaspoon pepper**
1 **teaspoon whole oregano**
½ **teaspoon dry mustard**
1 **cup water**
1 **tablespoon all-purpose flour**
1 **(13-ounce) can evaporated milk**
2 **tablespoons chopped pimiento**
2 **to 3 cups shredded sharp Cheddar cheese**

Melt butter in a large skillet over low heat; add macaroni, onion, green pepper, garlic salt, pepper, oregano, and mustard. Cook, stirring occasionally, over medium heat for 7 to 8 minutes or until onion becomes transparent. Add water and bring to a boil. Cover and simmer 20 minutes or until macaroni is tender. Sprinkle flour over mixture and blend well. Stir in evaporated milk, pimiento, and cheese. Simmer 5 minutes or until cheese is completely melted, stirring occasionally. Serve hot. Yield: 6 to 8 servings.

STEWED TOMATOES

2 **(16-ounce) cans tomatoes, undrained**
¼ **cup butter or margarine**
2 **teaspoons sugar**
Salt and pepper to taste
Croutons

Place tomatoes in a saucepan. Cook over high heat until tomatoes steam; reduce heat to simmer and cook for 5 minutes. Add butter, sugar, salt, and pepper. Keep covered until ready to serve; top each serving with crisp croutons. Yield: 6 servings.

Combine dry ingredients; add eggs, milk, and shortening. Mix well. Pour into a greased 8-inch square pan; bake at 425° for 20 to 30 minutes. Serve hot. Yield: 9 servings.

Note: Eliminate soda, baking powder, and salt if self-rising cornmeal is used.

NEAPOLITAN GREEN SALAD

　1　**large head lettuce**
　¼　**cup plus 2 tablespoons vegetable oil**
　3　**tablespoons wine vinegar**
1½　**teaspoons prepared mustard**
　5　**anchovy fillets, mashed**
　　Crushed Italian pepper

Tear lettuce into chunks in salad bowl. Mix remaining ingredients for dressing. Just before serving, toss lettuce with dressing. Yield: 6 servings.

FRUIT CRISP

　⅓　**cup all-purpose flour**
　½　**teaspoon ground cinnamon**
　½　**cup firmly packed brown sugar**
　1　**cup quick-cooking oats, uncooked**
　5　**cups fresh sliced peaches or any
　　　fruit**

Combine flour, cinnamon, brown sugar, and oats; mix with fruit. Put into a greased 8-inch baking pan. Bake at 375° for about 30 minutes or until fruit is tender and top is browned. Yield: 6 servings.

Note: Frozen and thawed or canned and drained fruit can be substituted for fresh fruit.

SOUTHERN HOT EGG BREAD

　2　**cups cornmeal**
　¼　**teaspoon soda**
　2　**teaspoons baking powder**
　1　**teaspoon salt**
　2　**eggs, beaten**
　2　**cups sour milk or buttermilk**
　2　**tablespoons melted shortening or
　　　vegetable oil**

To store onions, put them in a loosely woven bag (or basket or crate) so that there will be good air circulation. Store in a cool, dark, dry, well-ventilated place. Do not refrigerate until the onion is cut; then place in a plastic bag or plastic bowl, in the refrigerator where it will keep for several days. Chopped onion can be placed in a shallow pan and frozen. After freezing, put loosely into a jar from which the onion can be scooped.

Pre-Dance Buffet

Buffet Supper for Six to Eight

Chicken à la King Supreme
Cold Vegetable Medley
Cranapple Muffins
Blueberries au Cointreau
Rhine Wine   Coffee

 *Assemble ingredients for chicken dish. Prepare vegetable medley and refrigerate in serving dishes. Mix pudding for dessert and chill. While muffins bake, prepare chicken. Complete dessert before serving.*

CHICKEN À LA KING SUPREME

```
  2  chicken bouillon cubes
  1  cup boiling water
  1  cup chopped celery
  3  tablespoons chopped green pepper
  ¼  cup melted butter or margarine
  ¼  cup all-purpose flour
  1  cup milk
  1  egg yolk
  ¼  cup chopped pimiento
  2  tablespoons capers
  3  cups cooked chopped chicken
1½  teaspoons salt
  1  tablespoon Worcestershire sauce
     Hot sauce to taste
     Sliced almonds
     Chow mein noodles
```

Dissolve bouillon cubes in boiling water; set aside. Sauté celery and green pepper in butter in large skillet over low heat. Add flour, stirring until smooth. Cook for 1 minute, stirring constantly. Gradually stir in bouillon and milk; cook over medium heat, stirring constantly, until thickened and bubbly. Beat egg yolk and add a little of the sauce; then slowly add this mixture to remaining sauce. Add next 6 ingredients. Add almonds just before serving over chow mein noodles. Yield: 6 to 8 servings.

Note: Chicken may be served in pastry shells.

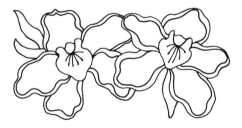

For an award-winning dessert topping mix 1 cup commercial sour cream and ½ cup brown sugar. Let the mixture stand in refrigerator for about an hour; then mix again to make sure the sugar is completely dissolved. Serve on top of sliced peaches, baked apples, or warm blueberry pie.

COLD VEGETABLE MEDLEY

1 (16-ounce) can green peas, drained
1 (16-ounce) can whole kernel corn, drained
1 (14-ounce) can artichoke hearts, drained and quartered
1 large onion, sliced into thin rings
1 medium-size green pepper, cut into strips (optional)
1 (8-ounce) bottle commercial creamy Italian dressing
1 tomato, cut into wedges
1 to 2 cups torn lettuce
    Imitation bacon
    Seasoned croutons

Combine peas, corn, artichoke, onion, and green pepper, if desired; add dressing. Just before serving, stir in tomato and lettuce. Top with bacon and croutons. Leftover salad will keep for several days in refrigerator. Yield: 6 to 8 servings.

CRANAPPLE MUFFINS

1 (8¼-ounce) can crushed pineapple
1 egg
¼ cup milk
⅓ cup sugar
2 cups biscuit mix
2 tablespoons melted margarine
½ cup chopped fresh cranberries

Drain pineapple, reserving ¼ cup syrup. Combine reserved syrup, egg, milk, sugar, biscuit mix, and margarine; beat vigorously for 30 seconds. Fold in pineapple and cranberries. Fill greased muffin pans two-thirds full. Bake at 400° for 15 minutes or until muffins are slightly browned. Serve warm. Yield: 16 muffins.

BLUEBERRIES AU COINTREAU

1 (3¼-ounce) package instant vanilla pudding and pie filling
⅛ teaspoon salt
1 tablespoon Cointreau
3 cups fresh blueberries or 1 (16-ounce) can blueberries, drained
    Powdered sugar
    Whipped cream (optional)

Prepare pudding according to package directions; add salt and Cointreau. Fill sherbet glasses with pudding; top with blueberries. Sprinkle with powdered sugar. Serve with whipped cream, if desired. Yield: 6 servings.

Salads are a valuable part of the menu since they help introduce those foods high in mineral and vitamin content that should be included in the daily diet as well as contribute color, contrasting textures, and flavor. Salads may be served as a first course, an accompaniment to the main dish, a main dish, or a dessert.

Friday Night Buffet

Buffet Supper for Six

Oysters Baked in Cream-Style Corn
Spinach with Peppers
Apple-Raisin Slaw
Commercial Dinner Rolls
Fudge Pie
White Wine   Coffee

 *While oysters are baking, start spinach and peppers. While peppers are cooking, prepare slaw and store in refrigerator. Mix fudge pie and place in refrigerator until ready to bake. If pie is warm, serve in compotes. Heat rolls along with pie.*

OYSTERS BAKED IN CREAM-STYLE CORN

1 pint fresh oysters, well drained
2 eggs, beaten
1 cup cracker crumbs
½ cup milk
⅓ cup melted butter or margarine
½ teaspoon salt
1 (17-ounce) can cream-style corn
Parsley sprigs

Combine all ingredients; pour into a greased 1-quart baking dish. Bake at 350° about 35 minutes or until mixture sets. Oysters will be tough if they are cooked too long. Garnish with parsley sprigs. Yield: 6 servings.

Put old bread in blender to make bread-crumbs, or toast bread in oven until very dry and roll with rolling pin to make bread-crumbs. Store in airtight jar until needed.

SPINACH WITH PEPPERS

2 green peppers, cut into strips
1 tablespoon minced pimiento
3 tablespoons minced onion
¼ cup plus 2 tablespoons melted butter or margarine
3 (10-ounce) packages frozen spinach, thawed and drained
1 teaspoon salt
2 tablespoons lemon juice
Chopped pimiento

Sauté green pepper, pimiento, and onion in butter in a large skillet until tender. Add spinach and salt; heat thoroughly. Add lemon juice before serving. Garnish with chopped pimiento. Yield: 6 servings.

Start a fun weekend with this quick, mouth-watering Friday Night Buffet planned around Oysters Baked in Cream-Style Corn.

Overleaf: A hearty meal for hearty appetites, this Saturday Luncheon, page 38, is a favorite served before a fall football game.

APPLE-RAISIN SLAW

1½ teaspoons lemon juice
2 unpeeled apples, diced
½ cup seedless raisins
3 cups shredded cabbage
1 cup mayonnaise
Lettuce leaves

Sprinkle lemon juice over apples; toss well. Mix in raisins and cabbage. Add mayonnaise. Toss and arrange in lettuce-lined bowl. Serve immediately. Yield: 6 servings.

FUDGE PIE

½ cup butter or margarine
¼ cup plus 2 tablespoons cocoa
1 cup sugar
2 eggs, slightly beaten
¼ cup all-purpose flour
Dash of salt
1 teaspoon vanilla extract
Whipped cream or ice cream (optional)

Melt butter in medium saucepan; remove from heat. Add cocoa, sugar, eggs, flour, salt, and vanilla; beat well. Pour into a well-greased 9-inch piepan. Bake at 350° for 15 minutes; cool. Serve plain or topped with whipped cream or ice cream, if desired. If served warm, spoon into compotes. If chilled, cut as pie wedges. Yield: 6 servings.

Italian Buffet

Buffet Supper for Six

Mock Lasagna
Brussels Sprouts in Lemon Butter
Italian Salad
Parmesan Sticks (*see* Index)
Ice Cream de Menthe
Chianti   Coffee

Prepare lasagna completely. Cook noodles while making the sauce. Prepare salad and refrigerate. Prepare dressing, but do not toss until just before serving. Cook Brussels sprouts; put bread in oven seven minutes before lasagna is done. Assemble dessert just before serving.

MOCK LASAGNA

- 1 (8-ounce) package wide noodles, uncooked
- 1 pound ground beef
- 1 tablespoon melted butter or margarine
- 1 (15-ounce) can tomato sauce
- 1 (3-ounce) package cream cheese, softened
- ¼ cup commercial sour cream
- 1 (8-ounce) carton cottage cheese
- 1 small onion, chopped
- 1 small green pepper, chopped
- 2 tablespoons melted butter or margarine

Cook noodles according to package directions; drain. Brown beef in 1 tablespoon butter in medium skillet; stir in tomato sauce. Remove from heat and set aside. Combine cream cheese, sour cream, cottage cheese, onion, and green pepper. Layer half the noodles in a greased 2-quart casserole; cover with cheese mixture; top with remaining noodles. Pour 2 tablespoons melted butter over noodles; pour beef-sauce mixture on top. Bake at 350° for 30 minutes or until hot. Lasagna may be made ahead of time and reheated. Yield: 6 to 8 servings.

ITALIAN SALAD

- ½ head lettuce, chopped
- ½ bunch curly endive, coarsely chopped
- 1 (2-ounce) can anchovy fillets, drained
- 3 tomatoes, peeled and diced
- 1 teaspoon garlic salt
- ½ cup vegetable oil
- ¼ cup lemon juice or wine vinegar
- ½ cup grated Parmesan cheese
- ½ teaspoon pepper
  Italian-flavored croutons

Place lettuce, endive, anchovies, and tomatoes in salad bowl. Sprinkle with garlic salt. Pour on vegetable oil, lemon juice, cheese, pepper, and croutons. Toss lightly. Correct seasoning. Yield: 6 servings.

BRUSSELS SPROUTS IN LEMON BUTTER

- 2 (10-ounce) packages frozens Brussels sprouts
- ¼ cup melted butter or margarine
- 1 tablespoon lemon juice
  Salt and pepper

Cook Brussels sprouts according to package directions; drain. Combine butter and lemon juice; pour over Brussels sprouts. Season to taste. Yield: 6 servings.

ICE CREAM DE MENTHE

Pour 2 tablespoons of crème de menthe on each serving of vanilla ice cream.

Whenever pasta (macaroni, spaghetti, noodles, etc.) are cooked and not drained, all water soluble nutrients are saved.

Sunday Evening Buffet

Buffet Supper for Four

Broiled Chicken, Modified
Buttered Broccoli (*see* Index)
Brown Potatoes
Ambrosia Salad
Breadsticks
Iced Tea   Coffee

 *Start chicken first; then prepare potatoes. Prepare salad ingredients and refrigerate. Cook broccoli and prepare breadsticks. Prepare tea and refrigerate. Dinner can be served as soon as chicken is done.*

BROILED CHICKEN, MODIFIED

¼ cup melted butter or margarine
1 tablespoon lemon juice (optional)
1 (2- to 2½-pound) broiler-fryer
   chicken, quartered
Salt and pepper

Combine butter and lemon juice, if desired; brush over chicken halves. Season with salt and pepper. Place skin side down on a rack that stands 3 to 4 inches above the bottom of a shallow baking pan. (Elevate a cake cooling rack on custard cups placed in baking pan.) Bake at 425° about 1 hour (20 or 30 minutes per pound). Chicken does not have to be turned as it browns evenly during cooking. Serve immediately. Yield: 4 servings.

Keep bananas at room temperature because they turn brown when refrigerated.

BROWN POTATOES

4 potatoes, cooked
⅓ cup butter or margarine
   Salt and pepper

Thinly slice potatoes. Melt butter in large skillet; add potatoes and brown over medium heat. Season to taste. Yield: 4 servings.

Note: Garlic salt or onion salt can be used as seasoning.

Use only enough water to create steam and prevent sticking when cooking vegetables. They will retain more vitamins and taste better, and they will require less energy to cook.

AMBROSIA SALAD

2 bananas, sliced
¾ cup diced oranges
½ cup seedless grapes
¼ cup chopped dates
3 tablespoons lemon juice
¼ cup whipping cream, whipped
1 tablespoon mayonnaise
  Lettuce
¼ cup shredded coconut

Combine bananas, oranges, grapes, and dates; sprinkle with lemon juice and chill. Combine whipped cream and mayonnaise. Stir into fruit that has been drained of juice that accumulates. Serve on crisp lettuce and garnish with coconut. Yield: 4 to 6 servings.

BREADSTICKS

Remove crust from bread and cut each slice into 4 strips. Spread softened butter or margarine on each breadstick. Put on a baking sheet; toast at 450° or until lightly browned.

If the dish you are preparing qualifies, make more than is necessary for one meal. Freeze extra food in foil-lined baking dish. When frozen, remove frozen food, wrap, and store in freezer. This makes cooking time pay dividends.

A Dozen Dollar Stretchers:

Add bits of snappy cheese to chopped, cooked vegetables heated with milk to make a tasty, satisfying soup. Bits of leftover meat tastes good in soups, too. (Wrap cooked leftover meats and vegetables tightly and use promptly.)

Serve macaroni and cheese for a main dish. You can add hard-cooked egg to this mixture.

Use cheese sauce or cream sauce for leftover meat and vegetables. Serve over toast or rice.

Use ground beef in loaves, patties, meatballs, and in meat sauce over spaghetti. Serve creamed dried beef over boiled or baked potatoes.

Buy less expensive cuts of meat to cook slowly in some liquid, as with a pot roast.

Choose beef, lamb, or pork liver instead of calves' liver.

Brown eggs may be less expensive than white but have the same nutritive value.

Use dried peas and beans in casserole dishes with tomatoes and ground beef or pork.

Use tomato juice instead of orange juice at times.

Buy fresh fruits and vegetables in season if they are less expensive than frozen or canned.

Use leftover vegetable juices to flavor soup; use leftover juice from canned fruit in gelatins and fruit sauces for cake or ice cream.

Split leftover biscuits or rolls; butter or sprinkle with cheese, and brown under broiler. Refreshen slightly stale bread by toasting.

Luncheons and Late Night Suppers

*L*uncheons and late night suppers have a major characteristic in common: the meals are always light. They should be well planned and attractive to the eye, enhanced as both are by the noonday sun or midnight hour. Another bonus is that menus included here require no help but yourself in the kitchen.

Luncheons are usually more conservative than late night suppers. Each place must be accounted for since guests are generally seated at a festive table.

A late night supper can be a very festive occasion. These menus, although light, are interesting and varied, yet more substantial than a casual snack supper. You must plan these carefully so that very little is left to do at the time of serving. However, some can be prepared as an impromptu meal for the late evening hour.

Springtime Luncheon

Luncheon for Four to Six

Quick Creamed Turkey
Sautéed Green Peppers
Commercial Spiced Crabapples
Chef's Asparagus Salad—Lemon-Caper Dressing (*see* Index)
Toasted French Bread Fingers (*see* Index)
Peach Ambrosia
White Wine   Coffee

 *If using puffed pastry, prepare first. Start heating sauce for turkey. While peppers cook, combine dessert ingredients and refrigerate. Prepare bread fingers, salad, and complete turkey.*

QUICK CREAMED TURKEY

1 (8-ounce) package cream cheese
1 (10¾-ounce) can cream of
   mushroom soup, undiluted
1 (4½-ounce) can mushrooms, drained
   (optional)
2 cups chopped cooked turkey
   Garlic salt to taste
   Pepper to taste
   Pimiento strips

Melt cream cheese in top of double boiler over hot water or over low heat, stirring constantly. Add soup and mushrooms, if desired; stir until blended. Add turkey and stir until mixture is hot. Season with garlic salt and pepper. Serve in puffed pastry shells, on toast, or over hot rice. Garnish with pimiento strips. Yield: 4 to 6 servings.

Check this! A whole chicken is usually a better buy than chicken pieces.

SAUTÉED GREEN PEPPERS

5 green peppers, sliced into rings
2 tablespoons melted butter or
   margarine
1 teaspoon salt
⅛ teaspoon pepper
1 teaspoon Worcestershire sauce

Sauté green pepper in butter in a covered skillet over low heat for 15 minutes. Remove cover and cook until brown. Season with salt, pepper, and Worcestershire sauce. Yield: 4 to 6 servings.

When cooking turkey or chicken, use large birds. Leftovers can be packaged in family-size portions (sliced or cubed), labeled, and frozen for future use.

CHEF'S ASPARAGUS SALAD

2 (14½-ounce) cans asparagus spears
 or 2 (10-ounce) packages frozen
 asparagus spears
6 lettuce cups
 Lemon-Caper Dressing (*see* Index)
3 hard-cooked eggs, sliced
 Paprika

Cook frozen asparagus spears according to package directions. Drain asparagus and chill. Place 3 to 5 asparagus spears in each lettuce cup. Cover with approximately 2 tablespoons Lemon-Caper Dressing. Top each with 3 egg slices; sprinkle with paprika. Yield: 6 servings.

PEACH AMBROSIA

2 pounds (about 8 medium) fresh
 peaches or 2 (16-ounce) cans
 sliced peaches
1 cup sliced bananas
2 tablespoons sugar
2 tablespoons lemon juice
⅓ cup flaked coconut

Peel and slice peaches. Combine peaches, bananas, sugar, and lemon juice; chill. Spoon into serving dish. Top with flaked coconut. Yield: 6 to 8 servings.

Bridge Luncheon
Luncheon for Four

Shrimp Wiggle
Mixed Vegetable Sauté
Blue Cheese Deviled Eggs
Mock Apricot-Filled Danish Pastry
Iced Tea   Coffee

 *Chop vegetables while eggs cook. Prepare Danish pastry and bake. Stuff eggs and store in refrigerator. Sauté vegetables. The main dish is the last thing to prepare: make white sauce and add shrimp. A delightful but simple meal.*

SHRIMP WIGGLE

White Sauce (recipe follows)
1½ cups cooked and peeled shrimp
½ teaspoon celery salt
1 teaspoon chopped parsley
Saltine crackers or hot cooked rice

Combine first 4 ingredients in a saucepan; heat thoroughly and serve over saltine crackers or rice. Yield: 4 servings.

White Sauce:

¼ cup butter
¼ cup all-purpose flour
1 teaspoon salt
1 teaspoon pepper
2 cups milk

Melt butter in heavy saucepan over low heat; add flour, stirring until smooth. Cook 1 minute, stirring constantly. Add salt and pepper. Gradually stir in milk; cook over medium heat, stirring constantly, until thickened and bubbly. Yield: 2 cups.

Note: You may use White Sauce Mix (*see* Index) to equal 2 cups.

MIXED VEGETABLE SAUTÉ

3 green peppers cut into wide strips
3 medium onions, sliced
3 stalks celery, sliced
3 tablespoons vegetable oil
1 (8-ounce) can mushrooms, drained (stems and pieces)
½ teaspoon monosodium glutamate (optional)
Salt and pepper to taste

Sauté pepper, onion, and celery in oil until tender. Cover and simmer for 5 minutes. Add mushrooms and seasonings. Yield: 6 servings.

BLUE CHEESE DEVILED EGGS

8 hard-cooked eggs
⅓ cup crumbled blue cheese
⅓ cup commercial sour cream
¾ teaspoon vinegar
Chopped pimiento
Lettuce cups

Peel eggs and cut lengthwise. Remove yolks and set aside whites. Mash yolks with cheese; blend in sour cream and vinegar. Fill egg white with yolk mixture. Garnish with pimiento. Cover and chill. Serve in lettuce cups. Yield: 4 servings.

MOCK APRICOT-FILLED DANISH PASTRY

1 (8-ounce) can refrigerator crescent rolls
2 tablespoons melted butter or margarine
½ cup apricot preserves
Sugar

Unroll package of crescent roll dough on a lightly greased 15½- x 12-inch baking sheet. Shape dough into a rectangle, pressing perforations together with fingertips. Brush with melted butter. Spread preserves lengthwise down center of rectangle in a 3-inch strip. On long sides of rectangle, make cuts toward the center 1½ inches long and 1 inch apart. Fold strips of dough to center to cover filling. Sprinkle with sugar. Bake at 375° for 12 to 15 minutes. Cut in strips. Serve hot. Yield: 6 to 8 servings.

Unless flower arranging is one of your skills, it is best to use three or five brightly colored blossoms in a simple container to give your table a distinctive atmosphere.

Autumn Day Luncheon

Luncheon for Six

Hot Turkey or Chicken Sandwiches
Buttered Peas and Carrots
Wilted Lettuce Salad
Strawberries Romanoff
Iced Tea   Coffee

 *Wash lettuce, hull strawberries, and refrigerate. Assemble sandwiches. While baking the sandwiches, cook egg, cook vegetables, and finally prepare salad dressing to heat and pour on at the last minute. Complete dessert at serving time.*

HOT TURKEY OR CHICKEN SANDWICHES

- 6 slices white bread
- 6 or more slices turkey or chicken
- 1 (10½-ounce) can cream of chicken soup, undiluted
  - About 1½ cups (6 ounces) shredded Cheddar cheese

Remove crusts from bread. Arrange bread in a 13- x 9- x 2-inch baking dish. Top each slice with turkey or chicken. Spoon soup over each and top with cheese. Bake at 375° for 15 minutes. Yield: 6 servings.

Cooking time for young poultry can be less than for an older bird, but the broth may not be as rich and flavorful. Add common spices or herbs to flavor the broth when cooking or add some chicken bouillon cubes.

BUTTERED PEAS AND CARROTS

- 2 (10-ounce) packages frozen peas and carrots
- 1 teaspoon salt
- 2 tablespoons butter or margarine

Break blocks of peas and carrots into a 1-quart pan. Add salt. Cover tightly and cook on medium heat 10 minutes. Stir. Reduce heat to very lowest and cook 6 minutes. Add butter; cover. Turn off heat. Keep covered until butter melts or vegetables are ready to serve. Yield: 6 servings.

When wrapping food for the freezer, think before you wrap. How are you going to use it? If a sweet roll is to be warmed up before serving, wrap it in foil. If a casserole is to be reheated, put the mixture in a foil pan or a freezer-to-oven dish.

WILTED LETTUCE SALAD

> 1 head iceberg lettuce or 1 bunch leaf
> lettuce, torn into bite-size pieces
> ½ cup chopped green onions with tops
> 4 slices bacon
> ¼ cup cider vinegar
> 1 teaspoon sweet basil or any salad
> herb
> 2 tablespoons half-and-half or
> commercial sour cream
> 1 hard-cooked egg, sliced

Combine lettuce and onion in salad bowl. Cook bacon until crisp; remove from skillet; reserve drippings. Cut bacon into small pieces. Add vinegar, basil, and half-and-half to bacon drippings; heat to boiling. Add bacon; pour over lettuce. Garnish with egg slices. Yield: 6 servings.

STRAWBERRIES ROMANOFF

> 2½ cups fresh or frozen strawberries
> 1 cup orange juice
> 2 ounces Kirsch, Curacao, or white
> Port (optional)
> 1 cup sweetened whipping cream,
> whipped, or 2 cups whipped
> topping

Combine strawberries, orange juice, and liqueur; chill. Whip cream. Combine whipped cream and strawberries lightly before serving in sherbet glasses. Yield: 6 to 8 servings.

Saturday Luncheon

Luncheon for Twelve

Meat Cakes with Quick Mushroom Sauce
Buttered Rice
Quick Corn Sauté
Peas and Cheese Salad
Hot Buttered French Bread (*see* **Index**)
Cherry Chiffon Parfait
White Wine   **Coffee**

 *Start with the meat cakes; while they cook, combine sauce and hold until ready to heat and serve. Next, cook the rice; then prepare bread and put into the oven. It would be better to mix and refrigerate salad to allow flavors to blend before serving. At this point, prepare the luscious-looking parfait and refrigerate. Sauté corn last.*

MEAT CAKES WITH QUICK MUSHROOM SAUCE

    2 pounds ground beef
    1 pound ground pork
 1½ cups quick-cooking oats, uncooked
 1½ teaspoons salt
  ½ teaspoon pepper
    1 teaspoon sage
  ½ teaspoon garlic powder
    3 eggs
    1 medium onion, finely chopped
    1 teaspoon Worcestershire sauce
    1 cup milk
      Quick Mushroom Sauce

Combine all ingredients except Quick Mushroom Sauce in large mixing bowl in order listed; mix well. Pack into well-greased 2-inch muffin pans. Bake at 350° for 20 minutes or until done. Place meat cakes in Sauce; cover skillet tightly and heat about 8 minutes. Yield: 10 to 12 servings.

Quick Mushroom Sauce:

    1 (10¾-ounce) can cream of
       mushroom soup, undiluted
  ½ cup milk

Combine soup and milk in large skillet; heat. Yield: about 1½ cups.

BUTTERED RICE

    2 cups uncooked rice
    4 cups water
    2 teaspoons salt
  ⅔ cup butter or margarine

Combine rice, water, and salt in a 1-quart saucepan. Place over high heat; bring to a vigorous boil and stir several times; cover tightly. Reduce heat as low as possible and cook for 14 minutes; turn off heat and add butter. Lift grains of rice gently with a fork until butter is melted and mixed in. Cover and allow rice to steam 3 to 4 minutes. Serve hot. Yield: 12 servings.

QUICK CORN SAUTÉ

    1 cup sliced onion
  ½ cup melted butter or margarine
    4 (17-ounce) cans whole kernel corn,
       drained
    2 cups diced green pepper
    1 tablespoon plus 1 teaspoon sugar
  ⅔ teaspoon dried basil leaves
 1½ teaspoons salt
  ¼ teaspoon pepper

Sauté onion in butter in large skillet for 1 minute. Add remaining ingredients; cook and stir for 5 minutes. Yield: 12 servings.

PEAS AND CHEESE SALAD

    3 (10-ounce) packages frozen green
       peas, partially cooked and drained
    3 cups (12 ounces) diced Cheddar
       cheese
  ¾ cup chopped dill pickle
 1½ cups mayonnaise
 1½ teaspoons prepared mustard
    1 tablespoon vinegar
      Salt and pepper
   12 lettuce cups or leaves

Combine peas, cheese, and pickle in large mixing bowl. Combine mayonnaise, mustard, and vinegar. Add mayonnaise mixture to vegetable mixture; toss. Season to taste. Chill until ready to serve on lettuce cups. Yield: 12 servings.

To help fruit keep its shape add sugar before cooking. This makes the fruit less able to absorb moisture. However, firm varieties should be cooked in water instead of syrup; add sugar during the last cooking minutes.

CHERRY CHIFFON PARFAIT

    2 cups whipping cream or 4 cups
        whipped topping
    ⅛ teaspoon salt
    ¾ cup sugar
    2 teaspoons vanilla extract
    2 cups commercial sour cream
    2 (22-ounce) cans cherry pie filling

Whip cream; add salt, sugar, and vanilla. Fold in sour cream. Alternate layers of whipped cream mixture and cherry pie filling in parfait glasses. Chill until ready to serve. Yield: 12 servings.

Note: If whipped topping is used, eliminate salt, sugar, and vanilla.

Informal Luncheon

Luncheon for Four

Gazpacho Salad
Liver Stroganoff
Commercial French Rolls
Quick Peach Parfait
Iced Tea   Coffee

 *Prepare gazpacho and refrigerate. While the stroganoff is simmering and the noodles cooking, prepare dessert and refrigerate. Split and butter rolls. If you do not want to heat oven, broil rolls just before serving.*

GAZPACHO SALAD

    2 large tomatoes, peeled and coarsely
        chopped
    1 small cucumber, peeled and coarsely
        chopped
    ½ medium onion, finely chopped
        (optional)
    ½ green pepper, chopped
    1 cup tomato juice
    1 tablespoon wine vinegar
    ½ teaspoon salt
    ⅛ teaspoon pepper

Combine all ingredients in large bowl. Cover and refrigerate to blend flavors before serving. Will keep 2 or 3 days in refrigerator. Serve in cups or in salad or soup bowls. Serve with crackers or thin French bread slices. Yield: 4 servings.

Since meat is usually the major item in the food budget, it is one of the best places to look for savings. The less expensive cuts of meat, with appropriate cooking methods, can be as appetizing and delicious as the more costly ones.

LIVER STROGANOFF

 1 medium onion, sliced
 ¼ cup melted butter or margarine
 1 pound liver
 ¼ cup all-purpose flour
 ½ teaspoon salt
 ¼ teaspoon pepper
 ½ cup milk
 1 (10½-ounce) can onion soup,
    undiluted
 ½ cup commercial sour cream
    Hot buttered noodles

Sauté onion in butter in medium skillet; remove onion and set aside. Cut liver into thin strips. Combine flour, salt, and pepper; dredge liver in flour mixture and brown in drippings in skillet about 10 minutes. Combine milk and remaining flour mixture; add with onion and soup to liver. Cover and simmer 20 minutes, stirring occasionally. Stir in sour cream; serve immediately over hot buttered noodles. Yield: 4 servings.

Note: Chicken livers may be used. Cream of mushroom soup may be substituted for onion soup.

QUICK PEACH PARFAIT

 1 (3¾-ounce) package instant vanilla
    pudding
 1 (4½-ounce) container frozen
    whipped topping, thawed
    Sweetened sliced peaches

Prepare vanilla pudding as directed on package. Fold in whipped topping; layer in parfait glasses with peaches. Yield: 4 servings.

Ladies' Day Luncheon

Luncheon for Four to Six

Hot Chicken Salad Pinwheel
Buttered Asparagus (*see* Index)
Commercial Spiced Peaches
Cucumber in Yogurt Dressing
Alaskan Pie
Iced Tea   Coffee

 *Prepare first part of dessert and freeze. While Chicken Salad Pinwheel bakes, prepare cucumbers and dressing and heat asparagus. Beat egg whites and complete pie just before serving.*

HOT CHICKEN SALAD PINWHEEL

1½ cups chopped cooked chicken
¼ cup chopped celery
¼ cup chopped green pepper
¼ cup chopped onion
½ cup green peas, drained
Salt and pepper to taste
⅓ cup mayonnaise
1 (8-ounce) can crescent dinner rolls
¼ cup shredded sharp Cheddar cheese
4 slices cooked bacon, crumbled, or ¼ cup imitation bacon
1 egg, beaten
1 (10½-ounce) can asparagus tips, drained

Combine first 7 ingredients; mix well, and set aside. Separate crescent rolls into triangles. Arrange 4 triangles on a greased baking sheet with the points outward and the bases forming a square in the center of the pan. Arrange remaining 4 triangles over the first 4 triangles with the points outward and the bases forming a second square at a 45° turn over the first square. Press overlapping part of triangles slightly to mesh bases and form a 2-inch circle in the center of the pan.

Spoon chicken mixture onto crescent pinwheel, forming a ring. Sprinkle with cheese and bacon. Bring points of triangles over the chicken mixture and secure tips under the edges of the circle, stretching triangles slightly as necessary. Brush with beaten egg. Bake at 350° for 25 minutes or until crust is golden brown. Remove to serving platter. Heat asparagus, if desired, and arrange in center of pinwheel. Yield: 4 to 6 servings.

Every time you open the door to the oven the temperature drops from 25 to 30 degrees. That's why you have an oven window—so you don't have to waste that energy when you open the door.

CUCUMBER IN YOGURT DRESSING

1½ teaspoons salt
2 or 3 cucumbers, unpeeled and thinly sliced
2 tablespoons chopped parsley
¾ teaspoon dillweed
½ teaspoon garlic salt
½ cup plain yogurt
Parsley (optional)

Sprinkle salt over cucumbers; toss. Chill 30 minutes, tossing occasionally. Combine chopped parsley, dillweed, garlic salt, and yogurt. Drain cucumber well; stir in yogurt dressing. Garnish with additional parsley, if desired. Yield: 4 to 6 servings.

ALASKAN PIE

1 quart flavored ice cream, softened
1 baked 9-inch pastry shell
Meringue (recipe follows)

Spoon ice cream into pastry shell; spread to edge and level top. Freeze until serving time. Preheat oven to 425°. When ready to serve, cover completely with meringue. Bake 3 to 4 minutes or until meringue is lightly browned. Serve immediately. Yield: 6 to 8 servings.

Meringue:

3 egg whites
¼ teaspoon cream of tartar
6 tablespoons sugar

Beat egg whites until foamy. Add cream of tartar and beat until soft peaks form. Add sugar, 1 tablespoon at a time. Continue beating until shiny peaks form. Yield: meringue for one 9-inch pie.

Note: Completed pie may be frozen and served as desired. Drizzle with chocolate syrup, if desired, after baking meringue.

After-the-Theater Supper

Supper for Six

Grapefruit Juice
Cajun Panned Oysters
Sesame Spinach
Sautéed Mushrooms
Lettuce Wedges—Thick Roquefort Dressing
Cherry Chocolate Cream
Coffee

 *Prepare all ingredients for sautéed mushrooms. Make salad dressing and dessert. Toast seeds and bread. Oysters, mushrooms, and spinach can be cooked last. You will have lots of time to visit with guests.*

CAJUN PANNED OYSTERS

  2 pints oysters
½ cup butter or margarine
¼ cup dry white wine
  2 tablespoons lemon juice
  2 teaspoons Worcestershire sauce
  1 teaspoon salt
¼ to ½ teaspoon hot sauce
   Toast points

Drain oysters. Melt butter in large skillet over low heat; add oysters and cook about 5 minutes or until edges begin to curl. Add wine, lemon juice, Worcestershire sauce, salt, and hot sauce; heat. Serve over toast points. Yield: 6 servings.

SESAME SPINACH

  6 tablespoons sesame seeds
  3 (10-ounce) packages frozen chopped
    spinach, thawed and well drained
½ cup butter or margarine
  1 teaspoon salt
⅛ teaspoon pepper

Toast seeds in 350° oven until brown. Combine with remaining ingredients and heat just until hot in saucepan. Do not overcook. Yield: 6 to 8 servings.

SAUTÉED MUSHROOMS

  1 pound fresh mushrooms or 2
    (8-ounce) cans sliced mushrooms
½ cup chopped onion
¼ cup melted butter or margarine
  1 teaspoon salt
¼ teaspoon pepper

Rinse, pat dry, and slice fresh mushrooms (makes about 5 cups), or drain canned mushrooms; set aside. Sauté onion in butter in a large skillet for 2 minutes. Add mushrooms, salt, and pepper; sauté for 3 minutes. Yield: 6 servings.
Note: For variation, add 1 cup diced tomato and 1 teaspoon basil leaves, crumbled along with mushrooms; sauté as above.

THICK ROQUEFORT DRESSING

½ medium onion, chopped
1 cup mayonnaise
1 clove garlic, minced
¼ cup chopped parsley
½ cup commercial sour cream
¼ cup wine vinegar
1 tablespoon lemon juice
1 cup blue cheese
⅔ teaspoon salt
¼ teaspoon pepper

Combine all ingredients and blend with beater or in blender. Chill and use within 1 or 2 days. Serve over lettuce wedges. Yield: 1 pint.

CHERRY CHOCOLATE CREAM

1 cup whipping cream
1 teaspoon cocoa
2 cups coarsely broken chocolate wafers
½ cup cherry preserves

Combine whipping cream and cocoa; whip. Reserve ¼ cup whipped cream; set aside. Combine remaining cream with chocolate wafers. Put 2 tablespoons of wafer mixture in each of 6 sherbet glasses. Top with 1 tablespoon cherry preserves. Add remaining wafer mixture. Top with remaining whipped cream. Garnish each serving with 1 teaspoon cherry preserves. Yield: 6 servings.

Sportsman's Late Night Feast

Supper for Six

Blue Cheese　　　　Crackers
Oriental Steak Sandwiches
Buttered Rutabagas or Skillet Scalloped Potatoes
Marinated Cucumber and Onion Slices
Mixed Fruit
Beer　　　　Coffee

 *Combine sauce and marinate beef slices. While potatoes cook, prepare marinade for salad. Prepare mixed fruit and chill until ready to serve. Wrap buns in foil and heat in oven. When all is ready, cook beef slices and serve hot.*

ORIENTAL STEAK SANDWICHES

1 pound beef (cut from rib roast or sirloin tip)
Oriental Sauce
2 tablespoons vegetable oil
Buns or French rolls

Cut beef into ¼-to ⅓-inch-thick slices. Marinate beef slices in Oriental Sauce for 15 minutes. Heat oil in 10-inch skillet; add beef and cook quickly, turning once. Serve on heated buns or French rolls. Yield: 6 servings.

Oriental Sauce:

½ cup soy sauce
⅓ cup sherry
1 clove garlic, crushed
1 teaspoon ground ginger
½ teaspoon brown sugar

Combine all ingredients and mix well. Yield: about 1 cup.

BUTTERED RUTABAGAS

1½ pounds rutabaga, peeled and cut into 1-inch cubes (about 1 large rutabaga)
1 teaspoon salt
¼ cup butter or margarine
Salt and pepper to taste

Place rutabaga in saucepan with water to cover. Add 1 teaspoon salt; bring to a boil. Cook 15 to 20 minutes or until tender; drain. While hot, add butter and stir until melted. Check seasonings. Serve hot. Yield: 6 servings.

SKILLET SCALLOPED POTATOES

4 to 5 medium potatoes, peeled and thinly sliced
1 small onion, chopped
3 tablespoons melted butter or margarine
1 cup boiling water
1 (13½-ounce) can evaporated milk
½ teaspoon salt
⅛ teaspoon pepper

Sauté potatoes and onion in butter in large skillet over low heat for 3 to 4 minutes or until most of butter is absorbed. Add water and milk; continue cooking over low heat until potatoes are tender and sauce thickens, about 25 to 30 minutes, stirring occasionally. Add salt and pepper. Serve hot. Yield: 6 servings.

MARINATED CUCUMBER AND ONION SLICES

3 cucumbers, sliced
1 large onion, sliced
1 cup commercial sour cream
2 to 3 tablespoons vinegar or lemon juice
1 teaspoon salt
½ teaspoon white pepper

Place cucumber and onion in covered container. Combine sour cream, vinegar, salt, and pepper; pour over slices. Marinate until ready to serve. Will keep several days in refrigerator. Yield: 6 servings.

MIXED FRUIT

2 oranges
2 grapefruits
¼ pound seedless grapes
1 apple, unpeeled
2 tablespoons lemon juice
¼ cup sugar
2 tablespoons pink chablis (optional)
3 maraschino cherries, halved

Peel and section oranges and grapefruits. Cut each section in half. Halve grapes. Cut apple into cubes. Combine all fruit except cherries; add lemon juice, sugar, and chablis, if desired. Chill until ready to serve. Serve in compote. Top with cherry half. Yield: 6 servings.

Light Late Supper

Supper for Six

Baked Cheese Sandwiches
Succotash
Fruit Salad with Poppy Seed Dressing
Chocolate Pudding
Tea **Coffee**

 *Prepare dessert first and refrigerate. Assemble sandwiches and bake. Prepare salad and dressing while succotash is heating.*

BAKED CHEESE SANDWICHES

12 slices bread
   Prepared mustard
 6 slices Swiss cheese
 4 eggs
 2 cups milk
 1 teaspoon salt
 1 tablespoon Worcestershire sauce
 6 tomato slices
 2 cups (8 ounces) shredded Cheddar
   cheese

Spread bread with mustard. Place 6 slices bread mustard-side up in a greased 13- x 9- x 2-inch baking pan. Top with Swiss cheese, folded in half. Cover with remaining bread slices. Combine eggs, milk, salt, and Worcestershire sauce; mix well. Pour over sandwiches. Top with tomato slices. Sprinkle with Cheddar cheese. Bake at 375° for 25 minutes or until puffed. Yield: 6 servings.

Note: Dish may be stored in refrigerator overnight and baked next day.

SUCCOTASH

1 (16-ounce) can stewed tomatoes
1 (17-ounce) can lima beans, drained
1 (12-ounce) can whole kernel corn,
   drained
2 tablespoons butter or margarine
   Salt and pepper
2 tablespoons cornstarch (optional)

Drain tomatoes, reserving 2 tablespoons liquid; set aside. Combine tomatoes, beans, corn, and margarine in large saucepan; heat. Season with salt and pepper. Thicken vegetables with cornstarch, if desired. Dissolve cornstarch in reserved tomato liquid; stir into heated mixture. Cook until thick. Yield: 6 to 8 servings.

Process cheese is a mixture of fresh and aged natural cheeses pasteurized. Process cheese will melt easily when heated.

FRUIT SALAD WITH POPPY SEED DRESSING

1 (11-ounce) can mandarin orange
    sections, drained
1 grapefruit, sectioned
1 avocado, sliced
    Lettuce
    Poppy Seed Dressing

Arrange orange and grapefruit sections and avocado slices on bed of lettuce. Top with Poppy Seed Dressing before serving. Yield: 6 servings.

Poppy Seed Dressing:

¼ cup plus 1 tablespoon sugar
½ teaspoon dry mustard
1 teaspoon grated onion or ½
    teaspoon onion juice
½ teaspoon paprika
½ teaspoon salt
3 tablespoons lemon juice
½ cup vegetable oil
1 teaspoon poppy seeds

Combine first 6 ingredients in container of electric blender. Cover and blend at low speed for 5 seconds. Remove center cap and add oil. Blend at high speed about 15 seconds or until mixture is thick and smooth. Stir in poppy seeds. Yield: ¾ cup.

CHOCOLATE PUDDING

1 cup sugar
½ cup cocoa
¼ cup plus 2 tablespoons all-purpose
    flour
    Dash of salt
½ cup cold milk
2 eggs, beaten
2 cups milk, scalded
1 tablespoon butter or margarine
1 teaspoon vanilla extract
    Whipped topping

Combine sugar, cocoa, flour, and salt in large bowl; mix thoroughly. Add cold milk and eggs; mix well. Add to scalded milk in a 2-quart saucepan. Cook, stirring constantly, over low heat until mixture thickens. Add butter and vanilla. Pour into serving dishes. Top with whipped topping. Yield: 6 servings.

Note: Pudding may be poured into a baked 9-inch pastry shell.

Latin Supper

Supper for Six

Mexican Sausage Casserole
Fresh Spinach Salad with Zesty Dressing (*see* Index)
Parmesan Sticks
Elegant Applesauce Compote
Tea   Coffee

 *Assemble the Mexican dish and while it is cooking, prepare the dessert and refrigerate. Wash spinach leaves and refrigerate. Make dressing in blender and toss just before serving. Bake Parmesan Sticks so they will be hot at serving time.*

MEXICAN SAUSAGE CASSEROLE

2 pounds pork sausage
1 medium onion, chopped
1 small green pepper, chopped
1 clove garlic, crushed
2 (16-ounce) cans tomatoes
1¾ cups buttermilk
2 cups elbow macaroni, uncooked
1 tablespoon sugar
1 to 1½ tablespoons chili powder
1½ teaspoons salt
½ teaspoon pepper

Brown sausage, onion, green pepper, and garlic in large skillet; drain. Add tomatoes, buttermilk, macaroni, sugar, and seasonings; stir. Cover and simmer for 25 minutes or until macaroni is cooked. Yield: 6 servings.

Note: One pound sausage and 1 pound ground beef may be substituted for 2 pounds sausage. Any leftover Mexican Sausage Casserole can be placed in a casserole, topped with shredded sharp Cheddar cheese, and heated until cheese melts.

PARMESAN STICKS

6 slices bread
½ cup cornflake crumbs
1 (1½-ounce) can grated Parmesan cheese
¼ teaspoon garlic salt
¼ cup melted butter or margarine

Trim crust from bread; cut each slice of bread into 4 strips. Combine crumbs, cheese, and garlic salt. Dip bread sticks in butter; roll in crumb mixture. Bake at 425° for 7 minutes. Yield: 6 servings.

Note: This recipe may be doubled easily to serve 12.

ELEGANT APPLESAUCE COMPOTE

½ cup honey
1 cup sweetened whipped cream or whipped topping
1 (28-ounce) can applesauce
    Grated sweet chocolate or finely chopped candied fruit

Spoon 1 tablespoon of honey in each of 8 sherbet dishes. Add a 1-inch layer of whipped cream. Spoon on a thick layer of applesauce; top with whipped cream and grated chocolate or candied fruit. Chill. Yield: 8 servings.

Seated Dinners

*W*hen the term seated dinner *is mentioned, one tends to think of the very formal dinner composed of five to seven courses. This is not really the case in the modern American home, for today's hostesses have become their own cooks who depend only on their own imaginations. Through the years many changes in meal service have taken place. Now, for even the most formal guest meal, the menu can still be simple and practical, composed of as few as two or four courses. You may or may not choose to add a touch of elegance by using the best china, silver, and linens the family has. The guests are seated at the dining tables and served by the hostess, another family member, or even one hired person.*

The seated dinner can be as casual as a family dinner or as formal as a special guest meal, complete with place cards and several varieties of wine. These meals will appeal to the hostess who enjoys entertaining elegantly only a few people at one time.

Spring Lamb Dinner

Dinner for Four to Six

Spinach Soup
Broiled Lamb Chops with Mint Sauce
Buttered Asparagus
Hominy and Tomatoes
Pitted Black Olives—Celery Sticks
Grape and Nut Salad
Quick English Muffins
Lemon Sherbet
Rosé   Coffee

 *Prepare soup, mint sauce, salad, and celery sticks. Hominy, asparagus, and muffins can be cooked on range while lamb chops broil.*

SPINACH SOUP

 1 (10-ounce) package frozen chopped
    spinach
 1 (10¾-ounce) can cream of chicken
    soup, undiluted
 1 soup can milk
 1 teaspoon Worcestershire sauce
    Dash of hot sauce
 1 teaspoon chervil or chopped parsley
    Salt and pepper to taste
    Commercial sour cream

Cook spinach according to package directions; drain. Combine spinach, soup, milk, Worcestershire sauce, hot sauce, and chervil in container of electric blender; blend until smooth. Add seasonings. Serve hot or cold topped with sour cream. Yield: 4 to 6 servings.

The large dinner napkin is 22 to 24 inches square. For economy in laundering and use of material, it is being replaced by a 15-inch square.

BROILED LAMB CHOPS WITH MINT SAUCE

 4 to 6 (1-inch thick) lamb chops
    Salt to taste
    Mint Sauce

Broil chops 3 to 4 inches from heat for 5 to 7 minutes. Salt; turn chops and cook 5 to 7 minutes or to desired degree of doneness. Salt; do not overcook. Serve with Mint Sauce. Yield: 4 to 6 servings.

 Mint Sauce:

 ½ cup cider vinegar
 ½ cup powdered sugar
 ¼ to ½ cup fresh mint leaves, finely
    chopped

Heat vinegar and sugar; pour over mint. Let stand at least 1 hour. Add more sugar if a sweeter sauce is desired. Yield: 1 cup.

Never allow a flower arrangement on a dinner table to obstruct the view across the table.

BUTTERED ASPARAGUS

24 fresh asparagus spears
½ teaspoon salt
3 tablespoons melted butter or margarine

Wash asparagus; remove scales and cut off tough bottoms. Place asparagus in saucepan and barely cover with boiling water. Add salt; cover and cook 10 to 20 minutes after water returns to boil or until tender. Drain; add butter and serve hot. Yield: 4 to 6 servings.

Note: If canned asparagus is used, heat, drain, and add butter.

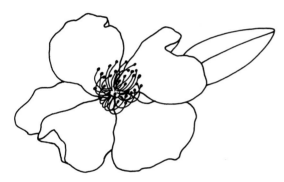

HOMINY AND TOMATOES

1 (29-ounce) can hominy, drained
2 (16-ounce) cans tomatoes, drained
2 tablespoons butter or margarine
1 teaspoon garlic salt
¼ teaspoon pepper
¼ cup grated Parmesan cheese

Combine hominy and tomatoes in a large saucepan; add butter, garlic salt, and pepper. Bring to a boil; lower heat and simmer until mixture reaches desired thickness, stirring occasionally. Stir in cheese before serving. Yield: 4 to 6 servings.

GRAPE AND NUT SALAD

2 (3-ounce) packages cream cheese, softened
2 tablespoons mayonnaise
1 tablespoon powdered sugar
2 tablespoons milk
1 pound seedless grapes
¼ to ½ cup chopped walnuts or pecans
Lettuce cups

Combine cream cheese, mayonnaise, powdered sugar, and milk; mix until smooth. Pour over grapes and walnuts. If dressing is too thick, add more milk. Chill before serving. Serve in lettuce cups. Yield: 4 to 6 servings.

QUICK ENGLISH MUFFINS

Canned buttermilk biscuits
Cornmeal

Separate each biscuit and flatten out to size and shape of an English muffin. Dredge each in cornmeal. Heat greased skillet over medium heat. Brown biscuits 7 minutes on each side. Spread with butter, jelly, or preserves.

Lamb is naturally delicate, tasty, and tender because it's from animals usually less than one-year-old. Lamb is also quite nutritious.

Even the breast, riblets, neck, or shank make excellent and tender lamb dishes when braised slowly. These cuts are not only tasty but are often good buys. Most lamb cuts, including shoulder cuts, are tender and can be oven roasted, broiled, or pan-broiled. Lamb's tenderness is a big reason for its popularity and versatility.

Elegant but Quick Dinner

Dinner for Six

Quick and Tangy Crab
Parsleyed Potatoes
Glazed Carrots
Celery Sticks and Ripe Olives
Toasted French Bread Fingers
Easy Peach Shortcake
White Wine   Coffee

 *While crab is baking, boil water and pour over pared potatoes. Cook frozen carrots while making the glaze. Prepare celery sticks. Broil bread fingers. You will still have time to sip white wine with your guests. Assemble peach shortcake just before serving.*

QUICK AND TANGY CRAB

  1 cup commercial sour cream
  ⅓ cup grated Parmesan cheese
  1 tablespoon lemon juice
  ¼ cup grated onion
  ½ teaspoon salt
  1 or 2 dashes hot sauce
  2 (6½-ounce) cans crabmeat, drained
     and flaked
  2 tablespoons melted butter
  ¾ cup fine breadcrumbs
    Paprika
    Parsley (optional)

Preheat oven to 350°. Combine sour cream, cheese, lemon juice, onion, salt, and hot sauce; stir until blended. Add crabmeat. Spoon into a greased 1-quart casserole or 6 individual shells. Combine butter and crumbs; sprinkle on crabmeat mixture. Sprinkle with paprika. Bake at 350° for 20 minutes for individual shells or 30 minutes for casserole. Top with sprig of parsley before serving, if desired. Yield: 6 servings.

PARSLEYED POTATOES

  6 medium potatoes
  ¼ cup melted butter or margarine
    Finely chopped parsley

Pare potatoes. Cook in boiling salted water to cover until tender, 10 to 20 minutes. Transfer potatoes to serving dish. Pour butter over potatoes; sprinkle with parsley. Yield: 6 servings.

Onions offer outstanding nutritive value. They are a good source of calcium and vitamins A and C. They contain iron, riboflavin, thiamine, and niacin, have a high percentage of water, and supply essential bulk. They are low in calories and have only a trace of fat.

GLAZED CARROTS

- ¼ cup butter or margarine
- 3 tablespoons orange juice
- 1½ tablespoons sugar
- 6 whole cloves
- ¼ teaspoon salt
- 4 cups cooked carrots or 3 (10-ounce) packages frozen carrots, cooked

Combine butter, orange juice, sugar, cloves, and salt in medium saucepan. Cook until butter is melted and sugar is dissolved. Pour over hot carrots. Yield: 6 servings.

TOASTED FRENCH BREAD FINGERS

- 1 (8-ounce) loaf French bread
- 1 cup melted butter or margarine

Cut French bread in half lengthwise. With kitchen shears, cut each half crosswise into fingers. Dip cut sides in butter. Lightly toast under broiler. (Bread can be prepared ahead and reheated in aluminum foil.) Yield: about 6 servings.

EASY PEACH SHORTCAKE

Sliced peaches
Slices of angel food or pound cake
Thawed frozen whipped topping

Spoon peaches over slices of cake. Top with whipped topping.

Entertaining the Boss Supper

Supper for Four to Six

Spinach Dip   Crackers
Seasoned London Broil
Baked Tomato Slices
Onion-Cheese Bake
Lettuce Wedges—Thick Roquefort Dressing (*see* Index)
Commercial Crescent Rolls
Pineapple Upside-Down Cake
Rosé   Coffee

Marinate steak and let it stand until the last minute before cooking. Since the cake takes the longest time to bake, mix and place in oven first. Then prepare Onion-Cheese Bake and tomato slices, putting them into the oven as soon as possible. While all are baking, prepare Spinach Dip. Enjoy it with the wine while waiting for the meat to broil.

SPINACH DIP

- 1 (10-ounce) package frozen chopped spinach, cooked and drained
- ½ cup chopped green onions (include tops)
- ½ cup chopped parsley
- 1 cup mayonnaise
  Garlic salt to taste
  Hot sauce to taste
- ½ teaspoon monosodium glutamate (optional)

Combine all ingredients. Serve at room temperature with crackers. Yield: about 2½ cups.

SEASONED LONDON BROIL

- 1 (0.7-ounce) envelope Italian or blue cheese salad dressing mix
- 2 tablespoons vegetable oil
- 1 tablespoon dry white wine
- 1½ to 2 pounds flank steak

Combine salad dressing mix, oil, and wine. Score steak in crisscross pattern on both sides, being careful not to cut more than ⅛-inch deep. Place on broiler rack and spread both sides of steak with the seasoned oil mixture; let stand 20 minutes. Broil steak 2 inches from heat for 2 minutes. Turn and broil 3 minutes longer or until of desired doneness. Cut diagonally across grain of meat into thin slices. Yield: 4 to 6 servings.

Note: Seasoned London Broil may also be grilled over a charcoal grill about the same length of time.

BAKED TOMATO SLICES

- 6 tomatoes
  Salt and pepper
  Brown sugar
- ¼ cup finely chopped green pepper (optional)
  Butter or margarine
  Rye bread or toast

Wash tomatoes; cut in ½-inch slices. Place on greased cookie sheet. Sprinkle with salt, pepper, and brown sugar. Cover top of each slice with green pepper, if desired. Place ¼ teaspoon butter on each slice. Bake at 350° for 20 minutes.

Serve on rounds of rye bread or toast. Yield: 6 servings.

Note: Tomato slices make a pretty garnish around meat platter.

ONION-CHEESE BAKE

- 2 (16-ounce) cans small white onions, drained
- 1 (10¾-ounce) can cream of mushroom soup, undiluted
- 1 cup (4 ounces) shredded Cheddar cheese, divided
- 1 cup cheese cracker crumbs, divided
- ¼ teaspoon pepper

Put onions in a greased 1½-quart casserole. Combine soup, ½ cup cheese, ½ cup crumbs, and pepper. Pour over onions. Sprinkle with remaining ½ cup cheese and top with remaining ½ cup cracker crumbs. Bake at 350° for 25 to 30 minutes. Yield: 6 servings.

PINEAPPLE UPSIDE-DOWN CAKE

1 **(9-ounce) package white or yellow cake mix**
2 **tablespoons butter or margarine**
¼ **cup firmly packed brown sugar**
Canned pineapple slices, drained
Maraschino cherries, drained
Chopped pecans (optional)

Prepare cake batter according to package directions; set aside in mixing bowl. Melt butter in a 9-inch pan. Add brown sugar and stir until mixture is syrupy. Make a layer of pineapple slices, centering each with a maraschino cherry. Sprinkle with chopped pecans, if desired. Add cake batter. Bake at 325° for 30 minutes or until cake springs back to the touch. Invert cake on serving plate. Yield: 6 servings.

Spring Get-Together Dinner

Dinner for Four

Iced Shrimp—Festive Cocktail Sauce
Lamb Chops In Wine
Maitre d'Hotel Potatoes
New-Style Buttered Peas
Lettuce Wedges with Vinaigrette Dressing
Hot Buttered French Bread
Ice Cream Topped with Raspberries
Rosé   Coffee

To prepare this meal in an hour, use commercially-cooked shrimp, canned potatoes, and frozen raspberries thawed at room temperature. Prepare French bread and put in slow oven; prepare cocktail sauce and salad dressing, chilling until ready to serve. Put potatoes and peas on to cook; begin chops; then peel tomatoes by dipping in hot water. Cut lettuce wedges and chop celery, onion, and parsley. Drain potatoes and season while hot. Now you are ready to assemble all dishes.

FESTIVE COCKTAIL SAUCE

    1 cup chili sauce
    ½ cup finely chopped celery
    1½ tablespoons lemon juice
    1½ tablespoons horseradish
    ½ teaspoon salt

Combine all ingredients and blend well.
Serve with chilled boiled shrimp or crab
claws. Yield: about 1¾ cups.

LAMB CHOPS IN WINE

    4 (¾-inch thick) lamb chops
    2 tablespoons vegetable oil
    4 whole tomatoes, peeled
      Salt and pepper
    ¾ cup dry red wine
    4 teaspoons butter or margarine

Brown lamb chops in oil in large skillet.
Add tomatoes; season to taste with salt
and pepper. Cover and cook 5 minutes.
Add wine and cook 5 minutes more. Top
each tomato with 1 teaspoon butter. Serve
immediately. Yield: 4 servings.

MAITRE D'HOTEL POTATOES

    4 potatoes
    ¼ cup plus 2 tablespoons melted butter
      or margarine
    ¼ teaspoon paprika
    ¼ teaspoon salt
    ⅛ teaspoon pepper
    ¼ cup minced parsley
    1½ tablespoons lemon juice

Cook potatoes in boiling salted water in a
large covered saucepan for 20 to 30 minutes or until tender (depends upon size of
potatoes); drain. Peel potatoes and set,
uncovered, in warm place. Combine butter, paprika, salt, pepper, and parsley;
heat in small saucepan. Add lemon juice.
Add sauce to potatoes just before serving.
Yield: 4 servings.
  Note: Can substitute 2 (16-ounce) cans
small whole potatoes, heated in can liquid,
and drained. Add sauce as above.

NEW-STYLE BUTTERED PEAS

    1 (10-ounce) package frozen green
      peas, thawed
    ¼ cup butter or margarine
    ½ teaspoon salt
    ½ teaspoon pepper

Combine all ingredients in saucepan.
Cover; heat until peas are hot and butter is
melted. Season to taste. Yield: 4 servings.
  Note: Peas will be crisp-tender.

*Less tender cuts of beef are often a good
buy. Such cuts include shoulder arm chuck
roasts, bottom round and eye-of-round
roasts, and brisket. Cook these with moist
heat. The most tender cuts are no more
nutritious than less tender cuts.*

*In most cases the term "London Broil" is
used for flank steak. This is definitely a less
tender cut of beef, but it can be marinated
to help tenderize and flavor it; then broiled
and sliced very thin on the diagonal to
make a delicious entree.*

LETTUCE WEDGES WITH VINAIGRETTE DRESSING

1¼ cups olive oil
¼ cup plus 1 tablespoon vinegar
   Salt and freshly ground pepper to taste
2 tablespoons chopped parsley
1 tablespoon chopped onion
1 hard-cooked egg, finely chopped
2 tablespoons sweet pickle relish
   Lettuce wedges

Combine first 8 ingredients; mix well. Serve over lettuce wedges. Yield: 2¼ cups.

HOT BUTTERED FRENCH BREAD

½ cup butter or margarine
2 teaspoons parsley flakes
1 (1-pound) loaf French or Italian Bread

Melt butter; add parsley flakes. Cut bread diagonally into thin slices, almost to the bottom. Brush butter mixture between slices and over the top of bread. Wrap in aluminum foil. Bake at 350° for 15 minutes or until hot. Yield: 8 servings.

Surprise Company Dinner
Dinner for Four

Clam Dip   Crackers
Chinese Pepper Steak
Rice Pilaf
Green Beans and Broccoli with Water Chestnuts (*see* Index)
Assorted Fresh Fruit—Orange Mayonnaise Dressing
Commercial Bread Slices
Peppermint Dessert
Rosé   Coffee

While pepper steak is cooking, prepare clam dip and refrigerate. Cook vegetables and pilaf. Now prepare dessert topping and salad.

CLAM DIP

1 (8-ounce) can minced clams
1 (16-ounce) carton creamed cottage cheese
Hot sauce to taste
Garlic salt to taste
½ teaspoon monosodium glutamate (optional)

Drain clams; reserve juice. Put cottage cheese in container of electric blender; add only enough clam juice to blend to a smooth consistency. Add hot sauce, garlic salt, and monosodium glutamate, if desired. Stir in clams. Serve with crackers. Yield: about 2½ cups.

CHINESE PEPPER STEAK

2 tablespoons vegetable oil or drippings
1 pound beef chuck, cut into thin strips
2 tablespoons minced onion
2 cloves garlic, minced
½ cup sliced celery
2 large green peppers, cut into strips
2 tablespoons chopped pimiento
½ cup beef consommé or beef stock
¼ teaspoon salt
¼ teaspoon pepper
1 tablespoon cornstarch
2 tablespoons water
1 tablespoon soy sauce

Heat oil; add beef and brown slowly. Add onion, garlic, celery, green pepper, pimiento, consommé, salt, and pepper. Cover and simmer 20 minutes. Combine cornstarch, water, and soy sauce. Stir a small portion of hot mixture into cornstarch mixture; add to remaining hot mixture to thicken. Simmer 5 minutes. Serve hot with Rice Pilaf. Yield: 4 servings.

RICE PILAF

1 (10½-ounce) can beef consommé, undiluted
1 (10½-ounce) can onion soup, undiluted
½ cup butter or margarine
1 (4-ounce) can mushrooms, drained
1½ cups instant rice, uncooked

Combine consommé, onion soup, butter, and mushrooms in a saucepan; bring to a boil. Stir in rice. Cover and remove from heat; let stand for 5 minutes. Fluff with fork and serve. Yield: 4 to 6 servings.

ORANGE MAYONNAISE DRESSING

1 tablespoon plus 1 teaspoon instant orange-flavored breakfast drink
1 cup mayonnaise

Combine breakfast drink and mayonnaise; let stand 5 minutes. Stir before serving. Serve over assorted fresh fruits. Yield: 1 cup.

PEPPERMINT DESSERT

3 to 4 chocolate-covered toffee candy bars
1 cup whipping cream
Sponge cake, sliced
Peppermint ice cream

Crush candy bars. Whip cream; fold in candy. Chill until serving time. Top each cake slice with a scoop of ice cream. Top with whipped cream mixture. Yield: 4 to 6 servings.

Colorful Company Dinner

Dinner for Six

Chilled Vegetable Juice with Celery Stirrers
Broiled Pork Chops with Crabapple Peaches
Asparagus with Hot Wine Mayonnaise
Buttered Summer Squash
California Green Salad
Seasoned Breadsticks (*see* Index)
Blueberry Crumble
Rosé **Coffee**

 *Prepare Blueberry Crumble. While it bakes, prepare celery stirrers, squash, asparagus, and hot mayonnaise. While chops broil, prepare salad and refrigerate. Toast breadsticks. Add dressing to salad when ready to serve dinner.*

BROILED PORK CHOPS WITH CRABAPPLE PEACHES

1 (16-ounce) can cling peach halves
1 (16-ounce) jar spiced crabapples
6 (1¼- to 1½-inch thick) loin pork
    chops
    Salt and pepper
    Parsley sprigs

Drain peaches and crabapples; reserve peach juice. Place pork chops on rack in broiler pan. Place pan 6 to 7 inches from heat. Broil 15 to 17 minutes on first side; season with salt and pepper. Turn chops and broil second side 15 minutes, basting with peach juice. During last 5 minutes of broiling, place a crabapple in each peach half and arrange on broiler rack with chops. Continue broiling until chops are browned and peaches and crabapples are heated through, brushing fruit and chops with peach juice. Place chops and fruit in serving dish. Garnish with parsley sprigs. Yield: 6 servings.

ASPARAGUS WITH HOT WINE MAYONNAISE

3 (10-ounce) packages frozen
    asparagus spears
    Hot Wine Mayonnaise

Cook asparagus spears according to package directions. Drain thoroughly. Place warm asparagus in flat serving dish, and top with Hot Wine Mayonnaise. Yield: 6 servings.

Hot Wine Mayonnaise:

1 tablespoon instant minced onion
¼ cup Sauterne
2 tablespoons parsley flakes
1 tablespoon lemon juice
¾ cup mayonnaise

Combine onion and wine; let stand 10 minutes. Add remaining ingredients. Heat over hot, but not boiling, water. Yield: 1 cup sauce.

BUTTERED SUMMER SQUASH

1½ pounds yellow squash, washed and
    sliced
1 teaspoon salt
1 medium onion, chopped
3 tablespooons butter or margarine

Place squash in medium saucepan with
tight lid. Cover with water; drain water off
completely. Add salt and onion. Cover
and cook over medium heat about 3 to 4
minutes. Do not lift cover. Reduce heat to
lowest temperature; simmer 6 minutes.
Remove cover; add butter. Replace cover;
turn off heat. Keep covered until butter
melts or ready to serve. Yield: 6 servings.

CALIFORNIA GREEN SALAD

1 large head iceberg lettuce
  Garlic salt
  Freshly ground pepper
  Commercial Italian dressing
2 avocados, peeled and diced

Tear lettuce into bite-size pieces in salad
bowl. Add garlic salt and pepper. Toss
lightly with dressing to coat the leaves.
Add avocado. Toss lightly and serve at
once. Yield: 6 servings.

BLUEBERRY CRUMBLE

2 (16-ounce) packages frozen
    blueberries, thawed
⅓ cup sugar
1 tablespoon lemon juice
½ cup quick-cooking oats, uncooked
½ cup all-purpose flour
½ cup firmly packed brown sugar
1 teaspoon ground cinnamon
¼ cup butter or margarine

Combine blueberries, sugar, and lemon
juice; place in buttered 8-inch square baking dish. Combine oats, flour, brown
sugar, and cinnamon; cut in butter until
mixture resembles coarse meal. Spread
over fruit mixture. Bake at 350° for 30 to
35 minutes. Serve warm, plain or with
cream. Serve leftovers cold topped with
whipped cream or ice cream. Yield: 6 servings.
Note: Any fruit can be substituted for
blueberries.

*Dehydrated vegetable flakes may be used
for flavoring in place of fresh vegetables in
equivalent amounts such as: 2 sprigs of
parsley equal 1 teaspoon dehydrated flakes.
One-half medium stalk of celery equals one
tablespoon dehydrated flakes.*

*This Colorful Company Dinner described above
combines tantalizing flavor with pleasing color. Fea-
turing Broiled Pork Chops with Crabapple Peaches,
the menu is perfect for a seated dinner party.*

*Overleaf: A delicious and cosmopolitan meal to in-
trigue guests features Catfish Parmesan, Turkish
Pilaf, and Sweet-Sour Green Beans. The menu and
recipes for this Baked Fish Casual Supper are on
page 64.*

Festive Fish Dinner

Dinner for Six

Festive Fish Fillets
Stir-Fried Carrots and Mushrooms
Grapefruit and Apple Salad
Pumpernickel Parmesan
Vanilla Ice Cream—Quick Chocolate Sauce
White Wine   Coffee

 *Section grapefruit and slice apples (cover apples with grapefruit juice to keep from browning); refrigerate. Mix up dressing; prepare chocolate sauce; spread bread. While fish and bread are baking, stir-fry vegetables.*

FESTIVE FISH FILLETS

  2 pounds fish fillets, fresh or frozen
  ½ cup commercial French dressing
1½ cups crushed cheese crackers
  2 tablespoons melted butter or
      margarine
      Paprika

Thaw frozen fillets. Skin fillets and cut into serving-size portions. Dip fish in dressing and roll in cracker crumbs. Place on a well-greased cookie sheet. Drizzle butter over fish. Sprinkle with paprika. Bake at 500° for 10 to 12 minutes or until fish flakes easily when tested with a fork. Yield: 6 servings.

Cooked fresh vegetables are great served with Parmesan Butter. Combine ½ cup melted butter with ¼ cup grated Parmesan cheese, 1 tablespoon lemon juice, and ½ teaspoon leaf oregano.

STIR-FRIED CARROTS AND MUSHROOMS

  2 tablespoons butter or margarine
  2 tablespoons vegetable oil
  5 large carrots, peeled and thinly
      sliced
  ½ pound mushrooms, thinly sliced
  5 green onions with tops, thinly sliced
  1 tablespoon lemon juice
  ¼ teaspoon salt
  ¼ teaspoon pepper

Heat butter and oil in large skillet until bubbly; add carrots, mushrooms, and onion. Cook and stir about 8 minutes or until vegetables are tender. Stir in lemon juice, salt, and pepper. Yield: 6 servings.

Candles are not an accepted practice for breakfast or luncheon tables. Save them for evening meals or parties.

GRAPEFRUIT AND APPLE SALAD

2 large grapefruits
2 large apples, unpeeled
  Shredded lettuce
  French Fruit Dressing (*see* Index) or
  Pink Fruit Dressing (*see* Index)

Peel and section grapefruit. Wash, core, and cut each apple into 12 slices. Arrange sections of grapefruit and 4 slices of apples half-moon fashion on a bed of shredded lettuce. Serve with French Fruit Dressing or Pink Fruit Dressing. Yield: 6 servings.

PUMPERNICKEL PARMESAN

¾ cup grated Parmesan cheese
⅓ cup mayonnaise
2 tablespoons finely chopped onion
5 slices pumpernickel bread, cut in
  half diagonally

Combine cheese, mayonnaise, and onion; spread on bread. Place on cookie sheet; heat before serving. Yield: 6 servings.

QUICK CHOCOLATE SAUCE

2 cups sugar
¼ cup cocoa
¼ cup butter or margarine
1 (13½-ounce) can evaporated milk
2 teaspoons vanilla extract

Combine sugar and cocoa in a saucepan; stir over low heat for 2 minutes. Add butter and evaporated milk. Turn up heat and bring to a boil. Boil 1 minute. Remove from heat; add vanilla. Serve over vanilla ice cream. Refrigerate leftovers. Yield: 3 cups.

Baked Fish Casual Supper

Supper for Six

Catfish Parmesan—Tartar Sauce
Dill Pickle Sticks
Bermuda Onion Slices
Turkish Pilaf
Sweet-Sour Green Beans
Commercial Hard Rolls
Peaches in Wine Sauce
Iced Tea   Coffee

 *Thaw fish early in the day. While catfish bakes prepare the tartar sauce and pilaf. As pilaf simmers, cook the green beans. Slice onion, heat the rolls, and prepare beverages. The peach dessert is best prepared just before serving.*

CATFISH PARMESAN

  6 skinned, pan-dressed catfish, fresh
     or frozen
  1 cup dry breadcrumbs
  ¾ cup grated Parmesan cheese
  ¼ cup chopped parsley
  1 teaspoon paprika
  ½ teaspoon whole oregano
  ¼ teaspoon leaf basil
  2 teaspoons salt
  ½ teaspoon pepper
  ½ cup melted butter or margarine
    Lemon wedges
    Parsley sprigs

Thaw frozen fish. Clean, wash, and dry fish. Combine breadcrumbs, Parmesan cheese, parsley, paprika, oregano, basil, salt, and pepper. Dip catfish in butter and roll in crumb mixture. Arrange fish in a well-greased 13- x 9- x 2-inch baking dish. Bake at 375° about 25 minutes or until fish flakes easily when tested with a fork. Garnish with lemon wedges and parsley. Yield: 6 servings.

TARTAR SAUCE

  1 cup mayonnaise
  1 tablespoon chopped onion
  ¼ cup sweet pickle relish
  1 tablespoon lemon juice

Combine all ingredients; mix until well blended. Yield: 1¼ cups.

TURKISH PILAF

  2 cups instant rice, uncooked
  ¼ cup butter or margarine
  1 (16-ounce) can tomatoes, chopped
  2 beef bouillon cubes
  1 cup boiling water
  1 medium onion, sliced
  1 clove garlic, minced
  1 teaspoon salt
  1 teaspoon sugar
  ¼ teaspoon pepper
  1 bay leaf

Brown rice in butter in medium saucepan. Add remaining ingredients. Bring to a boil; reduce heat. Cover and simmer 15 to 17 minutes, stirring occasionally. Remove bay leaf before serving. Yield: 6 servings.

SWEET-SOUR GREEN BEANS

  4 slices bacon
  1 cup finely diced onion
  2 (15½-ounce) cans cut green beans,
    undrained
  2 tablespoons sugar
    Dash of pepper
  ¼ cup vinegar

Cut bacon in ½-inch pieces. Partially cook bacon in medium skillet; add onion and cook until onion is lightly browned. Drain beans and add liquid to bacon and onion; cook down to about ½ cup liquid. Add remaining ingredients to liquid. Heat and serve. Yield: 6 servings.

PEACHES IN WINE SAUCE

1 (29-ounce) can peach halves
3 tablespoons butter or margarine
2 tablespoons lemon juice
⅓ cup firmly packed brown sugar
⅓ cup rosé
½ cup whipping cream
1 tablespoon cornstarch

Drain peaches, reserving 2 tablespoons juice; set aside. Melt butter in an 8-inch skillet over medium heat; add lemon juice and peaches. Turn peaches over to coat with butter. Sprinkle with brown sugar; add wine. Cover and simmer about 5 minutes until peaches are lightly glazed. Stir in cream and allow to simmer several minutes. Combine reserved peach liquid and cornstarch; stir until blended and sauce is thickened. Serve peaches warm with sauce. Yield: 4 to 6 servings.

Dinner for a Relaxed Evening

Dinner for Six

Sweet-Sour Peachy Pork Chops
Mashed Sweet Potatoes
Lettuce and Tomato Wedges—Cottage Cheese Dressing
Commercial Rolls
Easy Hot Apple Betty
Red Wine   Coffee

 *Start cooking sweet potatoes. Prepare dessert and bake. While chops cook, prepare dressing and lettuce. Complete salad at serving time. Mash the potatoes while still hot and just before serving.*

SWEET-SOUR PEACHY PORK CHOPS

12 pork chops, thinly sliced
   Salt and pepper
1 (16-ounce) can sliced peaches
¼ cup firmly packed brown sugar
⅓ cup soy sauce
2 tablespoons white vinegar
2 to 3 tablespoons cornstarch
¼ cup water

Sprinkle pork chops lightly with salt and pepper; place in large skillet. Drain peaches, reserving syrup. Set peaches aside. Combine syrup, brown sugar, soy sauce, and vinegar; pour over chops. Cover and cook 15 minutes over medium heat. Remove cover and cook 5 minutes longer. Remove pork chops from skillet and place on a serving platter.

Skim any fat from liquid in pan. Combine cornstarch and water; mix until smooth. Add a little of hot juice from skillet to cornstarch mixture. Gradually stir cornstarch mixture into broth; cook until sauce is clear and thickened. Add pork chops and peaches. Keep hot until ready to serve. Yield: 6 servings.

COTTAGE CHEESE DRESSING

½ cup cottage cheese
⅛ teaspoon salt
1½ teaspoons lemon juice
1½ to 2 tablespoons mayonnaise
¼ teaspoon celery seeds

Beat cottage cheese until smooth; add remaining ingredients and mix well. Serve on salad greens and tomato wedges. Yield: ⅔ cup.

MASHED SWEET POTATOES

6 medium-size sweet potatoes, pared
1 teaspoon salt
¼ cup butter or margarine
¼ cup milk
Salt and pepper to taste

Cut potatoes in half; place in large saucepan. Add enough water to cover; add 1 teaspoon salt and bring to a boil. Cook potatoes until tender; drain. Mash potatoes; add butter and milk while hot. Season. Yield: 6 servings.

EASY HOT APPLE BETTY

1 (28-ounce) can applesauce
2 bananas, sliced
1 cup firmly packed light brown sugar
⅓ cup melted butter or margarine
½ cup graham cracker crumbs
Cream or vanilla ice cream

Combine first 5 ingredients; pour into a greased 1½-quart shallow baking dish. Bake at 325° for 35 minutes. Serve warm with cream or vanilla ice cream. Yield: 6 servings.

Neapolitan Dinner

Dinner for Six

Beef Balls Italiano
Special Chef Salad
Hot Cheese Garlic Bread
Chilled Fruit in Wine
Dry Red Wine   Coffee

While beef balls bake, prepare dessert and chill. Make salad dressing. Assemble salad ingredients, slice and butter bread, and cook vermicelli. Broil bread just before serving. You may have time left to sip Lambrusco or a dry red wine before dinner is served.

BEEF BALLS ITALIANO

2 slices rye or whole wheat bread,
    crumbled
½ cup hot milk
1 egg
1 pound ground beef
1½ teaspoons garlic salt
½ teaspoon pepper
2 teaspoons parsley flakes
2 (10½-ounce) cans tomato soup,
    undiluted
½ cup wine
1 teaspoon whole oregano
1 teaspoon fennel seeds
1 teaspoon whole thyme
1 (8-ounce) package vermicelli, cooked
    (optional)

Combine bread, milk, egg, ground beef,
garlic salt, pepper, and parsley flakes in a
large bowl. Work mixture well with hands;
shape into 10 to 12 large meatballs. Place
in shallow 2-quart baking dish. Combine
soup, wine, oregano, fennel, and thyme;
pour over meatballs. Bake at 350° for 30
minutes. Serve over vermicelli, if desired.
Yield: 6 servings.

SPECIAL CHEF SALAD

1 head lettuce, torn into bite-size
    pieces
¼ cup Swiss cheese strips
¼ cup sliced radishes
1 or 2 tomatoes, cut into wedges
    Chopped parsley
1 teaspoon dry mustard
1 teaspoon seasoned salt
½ teaspoon paprika
¼ teaspoon garlic juice
¼ cup wine vinegar
½ cup olive oil

Toss lettuce, cheese, radishes, tomatoes,
and parsley in salad bowl. Chill. Combine

mustard, salt, paprika, and garlic juice in a
mixing bowl and mix well; add vinegar.
Add olive oil very slowly, beating constantly until all oil is added. Add dressing
to vegetables just before serving. Yield: 6
servings.

HOT CHEESE GARLIC BREAD

½ cup butter or margarine, softened
½ teaspoon garlic salt
⅓ cup grated Parmesan cheese
1 teaspoon Worcestershire sauce
¼ teaspoon cayenne pepper
1 (1-pound) loaf French bread

Whip butter; blend in garlic salt, cheese,
Worcestershire sauce, and cayenne pep-
per. Slice French bread into ¼-inch slices.
Butter both sides of each slice. Broil 1
minute on each side or toast in oven.
Yield: 6 to 8 servings.
Note: Bread may be wrapped in foil and
heated on the grill.

CHILLED FRUIT IN WINE

½ cup sugar
½ cup water
½ cup Burgundy or Bordeaux wine
1 pint strawberries
1 pint blueberries
1 pint red raspberries

Combine sugar, water, and wine in saucepan; bring to a boil. Lower heat and simmer 5 minutes. Put strawberries,
blueberries, and raspberries in a glass
bowl; pour wine syrup over fruit and chill
until ready to serve. Yield: 6 to 8 servings.

Steak-in-a-Bag Supper

Supper for Six

Consommé with Okra   Sesame Crackers
Steak-in-a-Brown Bag
Whipped Potatoes Paprika
French Peas
Mexican Tomato and Onion Salad
Yorkshire Pudding
Fresh Fruit with Lime Sauce
Rosé   Coffee

While the steak is cooking in the bag, put on potatoes, peas, and consommé. (Cook consommé gently.) Prepare fruit and sauce and refrigerate. Assemble salad and refrigerate. Mix oil and vinegar; whip potatoes. Ten minutes before steak is finished, put Yorkshire pudding in the oven. When steak is removed, turn oven to 400° to complete baking Yorkshire pudding. Serve immediately. Transfer steak from bag to platter, serving meat juices separately to dress up the already pretty potatoes.

CONSOMMÉ WITH OKRA

  4 (10½-ounce) cans beef consommé
  2 (10-ounce) packages frozen sliced
      okra
      Salt and pepper to taste
  ½ cup sherry
      Sesame crackers

Pour consommé into 2-quart saucepan; bring to a boil. Add okra and cook until okra is tender. Season with salt and pepper. Add sherry. Serve with sesame crackers. Yield: 6 servings.

Food cooks just as fast in gently boiling water as it does when the water boils hard.

STEAK-IN-A-BROWN BAG

  3 tablespoons garlic spread
      concentrate
  2 tablespoons vegetable oil
  2 teaspoons Worcestershire sauce
  1 teaspoon seasoned salt
  1½ teaspoons pepper
  1 (2½- to 3½-pound) sirloin steak, cut
      2 inches thick
  1 cup coarse breadcrumbs or cracker
      crumbs

Make a paste of garlic spread, oil, Worcestershire sauce, salt, and pepper; spread mixture over steak on all sides. Press crumbs firmly on both sides of steak. Place steak in a brown bag and close with a skewer. Bake at 375° for 40 minutes for rare (approximately 15 minutes per pound). Yield: 4 to 6 servings.

WHIPPED POTATOES PAPRIKA

6 medium potatoes, peeled and cubed
1 (3-ounce) package cream cheese,
  softened
¼ cup butter or margarine
Salt and pepper to taste
Milk
Paprika

Cook potatoes in boiling, salted water until tender; drain. Add cream cheese, butter, salt, pepper, and enough milk for desired consistency; beat with mixer until smooth and fluffy. Sprinkle with paprika. Yield: 6 servings.

FRENCH PEAS

Lettuce leaves
2 (10-ounce) packages frozen green
  peas
½ teaspoon salt
¼ teaspoon pepper
¼ teaspoon ground nutmeg
¼ teaspoon sugar
¼ cup butter

Line bottom and sides of heavy saucepan with washed lettuce leaves; add peas. Sprinkle with salt, pepper, nutmeg, and sugar. Add butter. Cover with lettuce leaves. Cover and cook over low heat for 25 minutes or until tender. Discard lettuce. Yield: 6 servings.

MEXICAN TOMATO AND ONION SALAD

1 head lettuce, coarsely torn
3 tomatoes, peeled and sliced
3 onions, thinly sliced
  Salt and pepper to taste
¼ cup vegetable oil
2 tablespoons wine vinegar

Layer one-third of lettuce, tomatoes, and onion in salad bowl; sprinkle with salt and pepper. Repeat layers. Chill until ready to serve. Combine oil and vinegar; pour over salad. Yield: 6 servings.

YORKSHIRE PUDDING

1 cup all-purpose flour
½ teaspoon salt
2 eggs
1 cup milk
¼ cup plus 2 tablespoons beef
  drippings or butter

Combine flour and salt; set aside. Beat eggs; add milk. Add egg mixture to dry ingredients. Pour beef drippings in an 8-inch square pan; heat in oven at 375° or until sizzling. Pour pudding batter over drippings. Turn oven to 400° and bake for 20 minutes or until brown and puffy. Serve immediately. Yield: 6 servings.

FRESH FRUIT WITH LIME SAUCE

⅓ cup fresh lime juice
⅓ cup sugar
⅛ teaspoon salt
1 teaspoon vanilla extract
3 cups diced melon and cantaloupe

Combine first 4 ingredients; toss lightly with melon. Chill until serving time. Serve in sherbet glasses. Yield: 5 to 6 servings.

Fit for Company

*C*ompany is coming to dinner! Such a situation can be the cause of a real family crisis until you realize that it should mean nothing more than a simple, well-planned, home-cooked meal with a relaxed, congenial hostess. With good planning, such a meal can be attractive and delicious, while belying the small amount of time spent in its preparation.

The first step is to have a so-called "emergency menu" planned with the food always available in the pantry or freezer. Select dishes that involve a minimum number of pots and pans so that clean up is almost instant. A centerpiece of lighted candles in various holders placed on a flat mirror can provide your table with instant glamour. The reflection of the candlelight will give the table and food a warm company feeling.

Wipe out the trauma of "company" and extend hospitality to your family and friends with these easy and unique ideas for company meals.

Cool Evening Supper

Supper for Six

Tuna Divan
Broiled Tomato Slices
Apple, Celery, and Coconut Salad
Hot Cherry Dumplings
Iced Tea   Coffee

 *Prepare tuna and dessert. While these are cooking, prepare salad and refrigerate until ready to serve. When oven is free, broil tomatoes. Toast bread and cut into triangles just before serving.*

TUNA DIVAN

- 2 (10-ounce) packages frozen broccoli spears
- 2 (6½- or 7-ounce) cans tuna, drained and flaked
- 1 tablespoon lemon juice
- 1 (10¾-ounce) can Cheddar cheese soup, undiluted
- 1 tablespoon crushed wheat germ or buttered breadcrumbs

Cook broccoli according to package directions; drain well. Combine tuna, lemon juice, and soup in medium bowl. Arrange broccoli in an 8-inch square baking dish or shallow casserole. Spoon tuna mixture over broccoli and sprinkle with wheat germ. Bake at 350° for 25 minutes or until hot and bubbly. Serve with buttered toast triangles. Yield: 6 servings.

When recipes call for thawed fruits or vegetables, put the fruit in the refrigerator the night before or early that morning.

BROILED TOMATO SLICES

- Tomatoes
- Salt
- Pepper
- Sugar
- Dillweed
- Butter or margarine

Wash tomatoes; remove stem end. Cut into thick slices or halves. Sprinkle each with salt, pepper, sugar, dillweed, and dot with butter. Broil 3 to 5 minutes. Serve hot.

Whip cream, and mound on waxed paper-lined baking sheet. Freeze until firm. Transfer mounds to freezer container. Cover. When ready to use, place mound on dessert. Let stand for 20 minutes before serving.

APPLE, CELERY, AND COCONUT SALAD

- 3 apples, unpeeled and diced
- 1 cup diced celery
- ½ cup flaked coconut
- 1 tablespoon lemon juice
- 1 tablespoon sugar
- ¼ cup vegetable oil
- ¼ cup orange juice
  Salt to taste
  Paprika
  Lettuce leaves
  Currant or plum jelly

Combine apples, celery, and coconut. Combine lemon juice and sugar; sprinkle over fruit. Combine oil, orange juice, salt, and paprika; add to fruit. Chill. Line a salad bowl with lettuce leaves and pile chilled salad in center. Top with jelly. Yield: 6 servings.

HOT CHERRY DUMPLINGS

- 2 (17-ounce) cans red sour pitted cherries, undrained
- 1 cup water
- ¾ cup sugar, divided
- 2 tablespoons cornstarch
- ¼ teaspoon salt
  Few drops red food coloring (optional)
- 1¾ cups biscuit mix
- ⅔ cup milk
  Whipped cream or whipped topping (optional)

Combine cherries and water in a 2-quart saucepan; bring to a boil. Combine ½ cup sugar, cornstarch, and salt; stir into cherry mixture. Cook, stirring constantly, until thick and clear. Add food coloring, if desired. Combine ¼ cup sugar and biscuit mix; stir in milk. Drop by spoonfuls on hot cherry mixture. Cover tightly and cook gently over medium heat about 15 minutes or until dumplings are firm. Serve hot dumplings in compote; pour cherry mixture over dumplings, and top with whipped cream, if desired. Yield: 6 servings.

Early Informal Dinner

Dinner for Six

Oysters Creole on Toast
Buttered Spinach
Grapefruit Sections—Sour Cream-Ginger Dressing
Cup Custard
Hot Tea   Coffee

Section grapefruit, mix dressing, and refrigerate both. While custard and spinach are cooking, prepare oyster dish. Have coffee perking and water boiling for hot tea.

OYSTERS CREOLE ON TOAST

¼ cup plus 2 tablespoons chopped
    onion
2 tablespoons melted butter or
    margarine
¼ cup plus 2 tablespoons all-purpose
    flour
2 cups tomato juice
2 pints oysters, drained
¼ cup chopped parsley
½ teaspoon hot sauce
1 teaspoon salt
    Buttered toast

Sauté onion in butter until tender; blend in flour until smooth. Add tomato juice and cook until thick, stirring constantly. Add oysters, parsley, hot sauce, and salt; simmer about 5 minutes or until edges of oysters begin to curl. Serve on toast. Yield: 6 servings.

BUTTERED SPINACH

2 (10-ounce) packages frozen spinach
2 tablespoons butter or margarine
½ teaspoon ground nutmeg
    Salt and pepper to taste

Cook spinach according to package directions; drain. Add butter, nutmeg, salt, and pepper. Yield: 6 servings.
    Note: An alternate method is to heat thawed spinach; add butter, nutmeg, salt, and pepper. Continue to heat until butter is melted. Yield: 6 servings.

Don't leave fresh fruit in direct sunlight. Let fruits ripen in indirect light in the open air at room temperatures. When fully ripe, refrigerate and use as soon as possible.

SOUR CREAM-GINGER DRESSING

2 tablespoons chopped crystallized
    ginger
1 cup commercial sour cream

Gently fold ginger into sour cream. Chill thoroughly before serving to blend flavors. Serve over grapefruit sections or assorted fresh fruit. Yield: 1 cup.

CUP CUSTARD

5 cups water
5 eggs
¼ cup plus 2 tablespoons sugar
1½ teaspoons vanilla extract
¼ teaspoon salt
3 cups milk, scalded
⅛ teaspoon ground nutmeg

Bring water to boil in a covered 10-inch skillet. Beat eggs, sugar, vanilla, and salt together. Gradually add scalded milk to egg mixture. Pour mixture into six (6-ounce) custard cups. Sprinkle with nutmeg. Set custard cups in boiling water; cover skillet. Cook over low heat 10 to 15 minutes or until knife inserted in center comes out clean. Yield: 6 servings.

New Orleans Jazzy Dinner

Dinner for Six

Cheese Tray   Assorted Crackers
Jambalaya
Buttered Broccoli
Green Salad
Buttermilk Biscuits (*see* Index)
Bananas Flambé
White Wine   Coffee

Prepare Jambalaya and broccoli. While they cook, assemble the salad and dressing. Combine just before serving. Prepare biscuits for baking. Begin cooking bananas and biscuits at the same time. While guests are eating, turn bananas to simmer, and the bananas will be ready for flaming just in time for dessert.

JAMBALAYA

- 6 slices bacon, chopped
- 1 medium onion, chopped
- ½ cup chopped celery
- ½ cup chopped green pepper
- 1 (28-ounce) can tomatoes, undrained and chopped
- ¼ cup uncooked regular rice
- 1 tablespoon Worcestershire sauce
- ½ teaspoon salt
- Dash of pepper
- 2 (6-ounce) cans crabmeat, drained and flaked

Cook bacon in large skillet until lightly browned. Add onion, celery, and green pepper; cook until tender. Add tomatoes, rice, and seasonings. Cover and simmer for 20 to 25 minutes or until rice is tender, stirring occasionally. Add crabmeat; heat thoroughly. Yield: 6 servings.

Note: You may substitute the following for crabmeat: 1 cup cooked chopped ham and 1 (4½-ounce) can shrimp; or 2 cups cooked chopped chicken; or 1 cup cooked chopped ham and 1 cup cooked chopped chicken.

BUTTERED BROCCOLI

- 2 (10-ounce) packages frozen broccoli spears
- ¼ cup melted butter or margarine

Cook broccoli according to package directions and drain. Add melted butter; turn into hot serving dish. Yield: 6 servings.

GREEN SALAD

- ⅓ cup vegetable oil
- 3 tablespoons wine vinegar
- 1 clove garlic, quartered
- ½ teaspoon sweet basil
- ¼ teaspoon garlic salt
- ¼ teaspoon dry mustard
  Pepper
- 1 large head iceberg lettuce, coarsely torn
- ½ cup chopped green onion
- 1 (10-ounce) package frozen green peas, thawed

Combine oil, vinegar, garlic, basil, garlic salt, mustard, and pepper in jar with tight lid. Shake vigorously and set aside until ready to serve. Place lettuce, onion, and peas in salad bowl. Remove garlic from dressing. Add dressing to greens and toss just before serving. Yield: 6 servings.

Note: Do not cook peas.

BANANAS FLAMBÉ

- ¼ cup plus 2 tablespoons butter or margarine
- 1 cup dark corn syrup
- ½ teaspoon ground nutmeg
- ¼ cup plus 2 tablespoons light rum, divided
- 4 medium bananas
- 1 quart vanilla ice cream

Melt butter in medium skillet over low heat; add syrup, nutmeg, and 2 tablespoons rum. Slowly bring mixture to a boil. Reduce heat and simmer uncovered 10 minutes, stirring occasionally. Peel bananas and cut diagonally into large chunks; add to sauce mixture. Gently simmer bananas 6 to 8 minutes or until tender, spooning syrup over bananas several times during cooking.

In small saucepan heat remaining rum; ignite. Pour over bananas. Serve flaming over ice cream. Yield: 6 servings.

Note: If flaming is not desired, add all of rum to melted butter.

Chinese Chicken Supper

Supper for Four

Chinese Chicken Walnut
Buttered Rice (*see* **Index**)
Beets Russé
Spinach Salad
Mayonnaise Biscuits
Orange-Date Mallow
Hot Tea   **Coffee**

 *Prepare chicken and heat beets. Cook eggs while preparing dressing and salad. Refrigerate. Mix dressing and hold. Start cooking rice. Put bananas in oven and prepare biscuits. As soon as you remove bananas from oven, increase temperature and bake biscuits.*

CHINESE CHICKEN WALNUT

3 tablespoons peanut oil
1½ cups uncooked coarsely chopped
   chicken (preferably white meat)
1 tablespoon butter or margarine
¾ cup coarsely broken walnuts
2 tablespoons soy sauce
1 tablespoon lemon juice
2 cups hot cooked rice
Parsley

Heat oil in 8-inch skillet over medium heat until sizzling hot. Add chicken and quickly stir until chicken begins to brown. Add butter and nuts. Cook, uncovered, about 15 minutes, stirring often. Turn off heat. Add soy sauce and lemon juice; stir to coat chicken with sauce. Serve with rice. Garnish with parsley. Yield: 4 servings.

BEETS RUSSÉ

2 (16-ounce) cans beets, cubed or
   sliced
½ cup commercial French dressing
½ cup minced green onion with tops
1 cup commercial sour cream

Heat beets; drain. Stir in French dressing. Place in serving dish and sprinkle with onion. Top with sour cream. Yield: 4 to 6 servings.

SPINACH SALAD

⅔ cup vegetable oil
¼ cup lemon juice
1 teaspoon salt
½ teaspoon sugar
¼ teaspoon dry mustard
⅛ teaspoon ground pepper
¾ pound fresh spinach, torn into
   bite-size pieces
1 (8-ounce) can sliced mushrooms,
   drained
2 hard-cooked eggs, finely chopped

Combine oil, lemon juice, salt, sugar, mustard, and pepper in a jar with tight-fitting lid. Mix thoroughly and chill until ready to serve. Place spinach in large salad bowl. Arrange mushrooms in center. Sprinkle with egg. Just before serving, mix dressing well and pour lightly over spinach. Toss well. Serve immediately. Yield: 4 to 6 servings.

MAYONNAISE BISCUITS

2 cups self-rising flour
¼ cup mayonnaise
1 cup milk

Combine flour and mayonnaise in mixing bowl; blend mayonnaise into flour with a fork until mixture resembles coarse meal. Add milk; blend all ingredients well. Fill greased muffin pans one-half full. Bake at 425° for 10 minutes. Yield: 12 biscuits.

ORANGE-DATE MALLOW

2 (11-ounce) cans mandarin orange
   sections
¼ pound pitted dates, quartered
1 cup miniature marshmallows
½ cup pecan halves
⅔ cup whipped topping
¼ cup toasted coconut or graham
   cracker crumbs

Drain orange sections, reserving 2 tablespoons juice for later use. Combine orange sections, dates, marshmallows, and pecans; toss lightly. Blend whipped topping and reserved orange juice. Mix lightly with fruit mixture. Chill. Garnish each serving with coconut. Yield: 6 servings.

Note: To toast coconut, sprinkle on a baking sheet. Heat at 300° until light golden brown in color. Stir several times to obtain an even brown color.

Oyster Dinner

Dinner for Six

Pan-Broiled Oysters on Toast
Brown Sweet Potatoes
Italian Broccoli
Cooked Carrot Relish
Peaches and Dumplings
Iced Tea　　　　　Coffee

 *Prepare relish and refrigerate. While dumplings are cooking, cook sweet potatoes and broccoli. Broil oysters last as you toast bread.*

PAN-BROILED OYSTERS ON TOAST

½ cup butter or margarine
2 pints oysters, drained
　Salt or garlic salt to taste
　Pepper
2 tablespoons dry sherry wine
1 tablespoon steak sauce (optional)
　Hot buttered toast
　Paprika

Melt butter in medium skillet over low heat; add oysters to hot butter. Simmer until edges of oysters are curled. Turn and simmer on other side. Season with salt, pepper, sherry, and steak sauce, if desired. Serve on toast. Sprinkle paprika over top; baste with oyster liquor in skillet. Yield: 6 servings.

If green vegetables are overcooked, the green chlorophyll pigment turns into an olive brown color, the texture becomes soft and mushy, and the flavor is strong.

BROWN SWEET POTATOES

6 cooked sweet potatoes
½ cup butter or margarine
　Salt and pepper (can use garlic or
　　onion salt)

Cut sweet potatoes into thin slices. Melt butter in medium skillet; add potatoes and brown over medium heat. Season to taste. Yield: 6 servings.
　Note: Any type of potato may be cooked by this method.

Appetites really soar at the mere mention of Jambalaya. Recipes for this New Orleans Jazzy Dinner are on page 75.

Overleaf: Chianti and candlelight enhance this elegant Roman Supper which features Linguine in Clam Sauce and Italian Peas.

ITALIAN BROCCOLI

⅓ cup butter, margarine, or olive oil
1 clove garlic, crushed
2 (10-ounce) packages frozen broccoli
    spears, thawed and drained
½ cup grated Parmesan or Romano
    cheese

Melt butter in large skillet; add garlic and broccoli and sauté until tender. Arrange broccoli on hot platter; sprinkle with cheese. Serve very hot. Yield: 6 servings.

COOKED CARROT RELISH

1 pound carrots, sliced and cooked, or
    1 (16-ounce) can carrots, drained
1 bunch green onions with tops, sliced
2 tablespoons lemon juice
1 cup commercial sour cream

Combine all ingredients; chill thoroughly before serving. Serve as a relish or meat accompaniment. Yield: 6 servings.

PEACHES AND DUMPLINGS

1 (29-ounce) can sliced peaches,
    undrained
2 cups biscuit mix
⅓ cup sugar
½ teaspoon apple pie spice
⅔ cup milk

Heat peaches and syrup to boiling in a large saucepan. Combine biscuit mix, sugar, apple pie spice, and milk; drop dough by spoonfuls onto boiling fruit. Cook, uncovered, for 20 minutes. Serve warm. Yield: 6 to 8 servings.

Roman Supper

Supper for Four to Six

Cheese
Linguine in Clam Sauce
Italian Peas
Tomato, Onion, and Cucumber in Italian Dressing
Hot Garlic French Bread
Peach Melba
Chianti   Coffee

Combine salad ingredients and refrigerate. Slice and butter bread. Prepare Melba sauce and refrigerate. While linguine is cooking, prepare peas and clam sauce. Heat bread in oven.

LINGUINE IN CLAM SAUCE

    3 cloves garlic, minced
    ½ cup melted butter or margarine
    4 (4-ounce) cans sliced mushrooms,
        drained
    2 (6½-ounce) cans minced clams,
        drained
    ½ cup chopped parsley
    ½ teaspoon salt
    1 teaspoon pepper
    8 ounces linguine or spaghetti, cooked
        and drained
        Grated Parmesan cheese

Sauté garlic in butter in large skillet over low heat for 1 minute. Add mushrooms and cook 5 minutes. Stir in clams, parsley, salt, and pepper. Heat thoroughly. Combine linguine and mushroom mixture, toss well, and heat until hot. Top with Parmesan cheese. Yield: 4 to 6 servings.

ITALIAN PEAS

    2 (10-ounce) packages frozen green
        peas
    4 slices bacon
    ¼ cup minced onion
    1 tablespoon water
    2 tablespoons butter or margarine
    ¼ cup shredded lettuce
    ½ teaspoon salt
    1 teaspoon chopped pimiento

Cook peas according to package directions. Dice bacon and cook in medium skillet until crisp; remove bacon and reserve drippings. Cook onion in bacon drippings until soft; remove and drain. Drain skillet. Put water and butter in skillet; add peas and lettuce; cook until lettuce is wilted, about 10 minutes. Add bacon, onion, and salt. Add pimiento just before serving. Yield: 4 to 6 servings.
Note: Two (16-ounce) cans green peas can be substituted for frozen green peas.

TOMATO, ONION, AND CUCUMBER IN ITALIAN DRESSING

    6 tomatoes, peeled and sliced
    1 onion, sliced
    2 cucumbers, sliced
    ¼ cup commercial Italian dressing

Combine all vegetables in salad bowl; add Italian dressing. Refrigerate until ready to serve. Yield: 4 to 6 servings.

HOT GARLIC FRENCH BREAD

    1 (8-ounce) loaf French bread
    ½ cup butter or margarine, softened
    1 teaspoon garlic salt

Slice French bread into ½-inch slices. Butter one side of each slice. Sprinkle with garlic salt. Wrap in aluminum foil; heat. Yield: 6 servings.

PEACH MELBA

    1 (10-ounce) package frozen
        raspberries, thawed and drained
    3 tablespoons sugar
    1½ pints vanilla ice cream
    1 (29-ounce) can peach halves,
        drained
        Whipped cream (optional)

Puree raspberries and sugar in a blender. Spoon ice cream into dessert dishes; top each with a peach half, round side up; cover with raspberry puree. Serve with whipped cream, if desired. Yield: 4 to 6 servings.
Note: Melba sauce can be served with other canned or fresh fruits.

Hurry-Up Suppers

Regardless of the time required to prepare a meal, every cook wants her family and guests to feel that she has done something very special. Elaborate use of time is no indication of a job well done. A quick and simply prepared meal can still convey the impression that this is a good meal which has been prepared especially for "you." A bit of colorful garnish and a sparkling glass of wine immediately say "I care." A sincere display of personal care in preparing and serving the food will never reveal the secret that this was a "hurry-up meal."

In these menus, the names of many of the dishes may be familiar, but in many cases unnecessary steps in preparation have been eliminated without changing the fun of eating.

Busy Day Supper

Supper for Six

Simplified Arroz con Pollo
Green Peas Bayou
Pear Crunch Salad
Beer Muffins
French Cream Tarts with Fruit
Milk   Coffee

 *Get the Arroz con Pollo into the skillet. While it cooks, prepare celery filling for salad; mix beer muffins and bake. Clean fresh berries and prepare French cream tarts. While all of this is going on, cook peas and complete pear salads. You will have plenty of time to prepare beverages and a pretty table.*

SIMPLIFIED ARROZ CON POLLO

  2 medium-size green peppers, diced
  2 medium onions, chopped
  ½ cup vegetable oil
  2 cups uncooked regular rice
  1 tablespoon salt
  ½ teaspoon pepper
  8 chicken bouillon cubes
  4 cups boiling water
  2 cups cooked chopped chicken

Sauté green pepper and onion in oil in large skillet until tender. Add rice, salt, and pepper; stir until rice is evenly coated with oil. Dissolve bouillon cubes in boiling water. Add chicken and bouillon to rice mixture. Bring to a boil; reduce heat. Cover and cook for 15 to 25 minutes until rice is tender. Yield: 6 servings.

GREEN PEAS BAYOU

  2 (10-ounce) packages frozen green
    peas
  ¼ cup boiling water
    Salt and pepper to taste
    Bouquet garni of 6 sprigs parsley,
    1 bay leaf, and 1 large mint leaf
  3 tablespoons butter or margarine
  ¾ cup whipping cream (optional)
    Finely chopped mint

Combine peas, water, salt, pepper, and bouquet garni in large saucepan; cook until peas are tender, about 12 to 15 minutes. Add butter and cream, if desired. Heat mixture just to boiling. Discard bouquet garni; pour mixture into a warm serving dish and sprinkle with mint. Yield: 6 servings.

PEAR CRUNCH SALAD

6 fresh pears
2 tablespoons lemon juice
1 cup chopped celery
½ cup chopped walnuts
¼ cup chopped ripe olives
½ cup mayonnaise
  Crisp salad greens

Core pears and trim tops. Sprinkle 1 teaspoon lemon juice over each pear. Combine celery, walnuts, olives, and mayonnaise; fill pears with celery mixture. Serve on salad greens. Yield: 6 servings.

Note: Pears can be halved and each half topped with celery mixture.

BEER MUFFINS

3 cups biscuit mix
1 tablespoon sugar
1 (12-ounce) can beer (at room
  temperature)

Combine all ingredients; mix gently. Batter will be lumpy. Do not overmix. Fill greased muffin pans two-thirds full. Bake at 400° for 15 minutes. Yield: 2 dozen muffins.

The edible wax on fruits and vegetables makes the product attractive to the consumer and rightly so. The wax coat slows spoilage so the fruit or vegetable keeps longer, and waxing also highlights skin.

FRENCH CREAM TARTS
WITH FRUIT

1 (8-ounce) package cream cheese,
  softened
1 cup powdered sugar
½ pint whipping cream, whipped, or 1
  cup whipped topping
1 teaspoon vanilla extract
6 baked pastry shells (optional)
  Fruit such as strawberries,
  blueberries, pineapple,
  raspberries, or cherries

Combine cream cheese and powdered sugar; beat until fluffy. Fold in whipped cream and vanilla. Spoon into pastry shells, if desired, or dessert dishes. Top cream cheese mixture with fruit. Yield: 6 servings.

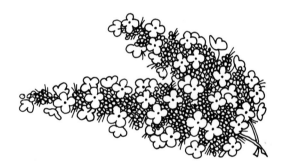

To be a truly efficient meal manager, you need to budget your time as you budget your money. Try these suggestions:

Plan menus a week in advance.

Have a bulletin board handy to record needed items.

Make a major trip to the market once a week. Perishables can be purchased quickly as needed.

Keep a record of good menus, recipes, and brand names that you like. This saves time in planning later.

On a rainy day or free evening prepare mixes and store them properly. This will save one-half the time and energy during final preparation stages.

Informal Family Supper

Supper for Four to Six

Cottage Pie
Peas and Water Chestnuts
Easy Waldorf Salad with Cheese Dressing
Quick Biscuit Braid (*see* Index)
Mystery Cupcakes
Tea   Coffee

 *For this almost total oven meal, preheat the oven to 350°. Prepare the Cottage Pie and bake. Put the cupcakes into the oven at the same time, followed by the peas. Next braid the biscuits and bake during the last ten minutes. While they bake, prepare the Waldorf salad and dressing.*

COTTAGE PIE

> 2 tablespoons butter or margarine
> 1 pound ground beef
> 1 medium onion, chopped
> 1 medium-size green pepper, chopped (optional)
> 2 cups instant mashed potatoes
> 1 teaspoon salt
> ¼ teaspoon pepper
> 1 cup (4 ounces) shredded Cheddar cheese

Melt butter in medium skillet over medium heat; add beef, onion, and green pepper, if desired. Cook until beef is no longer pink and onion and green pepper are tender. Prepare mashed potatoes according to package directions; season with salt and pepper. Spoon meat mixture into a 1½-quart baking dish. Cover with thick layer of potatoes; top with cheese. Bake at 350° for 20 to 25 minutes, or until heated through and cheese is melted. Yield: 4 to 6 servings.

PEAS AND WATER CHESTNUTS

> 1 (17-ounce) can green peas
> 1 chicken bouillon cube
> ½ cup sliced water chestnuts
> 2 tablespoons butter or margarine
> 1 (3½-ounce) can French-fried onion rings

Drain peas, reserving liquid. Heat reserved liquid and dissolve bouillon cube in it; add peas, water chestnuts, and butter. Place in a shallow baking dish; top with onion rings. Bake at 350° for 20 minutes. Yield: 4 to 6 servings.

Linen napkins, desirable as they are, have become luxuries to be used on special occasions. Paper napkins are now acceptable for family use at all meals—Happy Day!

EASY WALDORF SALAD WITH CHEESE DRESSING

- 3 large unpeeled apples, diced
- ½ cup coarsely chopped pecans or walnuts
- 1 cup sliced celery
  Lettuce leaves
  Cheese Dressing

Combine apples, nuts, and celery. Serve on lettuce. Top with spoonful of Cheese Dressing. Yield: 6 servings.

Cheese Dressing:

- 1 (3-ounce) package cream cheese, softened
- 2 to 4 tablespoons orange juice
- 2 tablespoons chopped almonds (optional)
- ¼ cup chopped raisins (optional)

Combine cream cheese and orange juice; stir until smooth. Blend in almonds and raisins, if desired. Yield: about ¾ cup.

To chop sticky foods such as dates, raisins, and marshmallows, cut with kitchen shears dipped in cold water.

MYSTERY CUPCAKES

- ¼ cup butter or margarine
- ⅔ cup firmly packed brown sugar
- 1 egg, slightly beaten
- 1½ cups all-purpose flour
- 2 teaspoons baking powder
- ⅛ teaspoon salt
- ⅔ cup milk
  Filling (recipe follows)

Cream butter and sugar until fluffy; beat in egg. Sift dry ingredients; add alternately with milk to creamed mixture. Place paper cups in muffin pans. Add small amount of batter. Add 1 tablespoon of filling; add more batter and top with filling. Bake at 350° for 25 minutes. Yield: 1 dozen cupcakes.

Filling:

- ½ cup firmly packed brown sugar
- 2 teaspoons ground cinnamon
- 1 tablespoon all-purpose flour
- ½ cup chopped nuts
- 2 tablespoons butter or margarine, melted

Combine all ingredients in small bowl; mix well. Yield: about 1¼ cups.

Cabbage and Beef Supper
Supper for Six to Eight

Unstuffed Cabbage and Beef
Buttered Noodles
Colorful Vegetable Salad
Commercial Brown-and-Serve Rolls
Curried Fruit Medley
Milk   Coffee

 *While cooking curried fruit, prepare Unstuffed Cabbage and Beef; marinate vegetable salad. Cook noodles according to package directions just to al dente. Put brown-and-serve rolls in oven while you bake the fruit.*

UNSTUFFED CABBAGE AND BEEF

- 3 cups shredded cabbage
- 1 pound ground beef
- 1 cup uncooked regular rice
- 1 small onion, chopped
- 1 egg
- 2 teaspoons salt
- ½ teaspoon pepper
- ½ teaspoon thyme
- 1 tablespoon brown sugar
- ⅔ cup hot water
- 1 (15-ounce) can tomato sauce
- 1 tablespoon lemon juice or vinegar

Place cabbage in large baking dish. Combine beef, rice, onion, egg, salt, pepper, and thyme. Shape into 6 to 8 patties and arrange on cabbage. Dissolve brown sugar in hot water in saucepan; add tomato sauce and lemon juice. Heat to boiling and pour over meat. Cover and bake at 400° for 30 minutes or until rice is tender. Yield: 6 to 8 servings.

COLORFUL VEGETABLE SALAD

- 1 (16-ounce) can diced carrots, drained
- 1 (16-ounce) can diced beets, drained
- 1 (16-ounce) can cut green beans, drained
- 1 (17-ounce) can green peas, drained
- 2 large onions, thinly sliced
- 1 (8-ounce) bottle commercial Italian salad dressing

Layer half of vegetables in a salad bowl. Repeat layers. Add salad dressing. Cover tightly and chill until ready to serve. Yield: 12 servings.

Note: Salad will keep for several days in refrigerator.

CURRIED FRUIT MEDLEY

- 1 (16-ounce) can pear halves, drained
- 1 (16-ounce) can peach halves, drained
- 1 (16-ounce) can pineapple slices, drained
- ¼ cup melted butter or margarine
- 1 cup firmly packed brown sugar
- 1 tablespoon curry powder
- ¼ teaspoon salt
- Commercial sour cream (optional)

Arrange fruit in a 2-quart baking dish. Combine butter, sugar, curry powder, and salt in a small saucepan; heat until sugar is dissolved. Pour over fruit. Bake at 350° for 25 to 30 minutes. Serve hot topped with a dollop of sour cream, if desired. Yield: 6 to 8 servings.

If a family is limited to one set of dishes, a satisfactory plan is to select a good grade of earthenware with a variety of colors in the decoration; or select a plain one, so that a variety of colored linens, glassware, and flowers can be used with it.

Seaside Supper

Supper for Six

Fish Chowder
Confetti Slaw
Baked Hushpuppies
Angel Food Cake with Sour Cream Topping
Tea   Coffee

 *Prepare slaw and dressing and chill. Mix hushpuppy batter. While the chowder and hushpuppies cook, prepare dessert and refrigerate until ready to serve.*

FISH CHOWDER

 1 **pound fish fillets, fresh or frozen**
 2 **(10½-ounce) cans minestrone soup, undiluted**
1⅓ **cups water**
 1 **(8-ounce) can tomato sauce**
 ½ **teaspoon salt**
 ¼ **teaspoon basil**
 ¼ **teaspoon ground oregano**
   Dash of pepper
 1 **tablespoon chopped parsley**

Thaw frozen fillets. Skin fillets and cut into ½-inch pieces. Combine all ingredients in large skillet; simmer 10 to 15 minutes or until fish flakes easily when tested with a fork. Yield: 6 servings.

Dairy products right from the refrigerator are great for quick meals. Fresh vegetables and fruits complement such dairy products as cottage cheese, yogurt, sour cream, or natural cheese; use for tasty snacks, salads, main dishes, or desserts.

CONFETTI SLAW

½ **small head cabbage, shredded**
2 **medium carrots, shredded**
1 **apple, cored and chopped**
½ **green pepper, chopped**
1 **green onion with top, sliced, or ¼ cup chopped onion**
  Dressing (recipe follows)

Combine first 5 ingredients in large bowl. Make dressing. Add to slaw and mix lightly. Cover and chill until ready to use. Yield: 6 servings.

Dressing:

1 **cup mayonnaise**
¼ **cup sugar**
¼ **teaspoon salt**
  Dash of pepper
¼ **cup vinegar**

Combine mayonnaise, sugar, salt, and pepper in a small bowl. Stir in vinegar. Yield: ¾ cup.

BAKED HUSHPUPPIES

½ cup cornmeal
½ cup all-purpose flour
½ teaspoon sugar
1½ teaspoons baking powder
½ teaspoon salt
Dash of cayenne pepper
⅓ cup milk
1 egg, beaten
¼ cup chopped onion
2 tablespoons melted shortening or vegetable oil

Combine dry ingredients; add remaining ingredients and stir only until blended. Place about 1 tablespoon batter into well-greased 1½-inch muffin pans. Bake at 425° for 15 to 20 minutes or until done. Yield: about 2 dozen.

Note: Freeze leftover hushpuppies for another meal.

ANGEL FOOD CAKE WITH SOUR CREAM TOPPING

1 angel food tube cake
1 cup commercial sour cream
Fresh berries (strawberries, raspberries, etc.)
Brown sugar

Cut cake in half horizontally. (Freeze one layer for later use.) Frost remaining half with sour cream. Garnish with berries. Sprinkle cake generously with brown sugar before serving. Yield: 6 servings.

Prepare your favorite sheet cake. Cut enough servings for one meal, wrap, and freeze. If unfrosted, toppings or frosting can be varied. Instant dessert!

Hong Kong Chicken Supper
Supper for Four to Six

Hong Kong Chicken
Tomato Pudding
Corn-Butterbean Salad
Broiled Grapefruit
Tea   Coffee

 *Assemble ingredients for chicken. While tomato pudding bakes, prepare salad and grapefruit. Complete chicken. Broil grapefruit just before serving.*

HONG KONG CHICKEN

  ¼ cup soy sauce
  1 tablespoon dry sherry
  1 teaspoon salt
  1 teaspoon cornstarch
  ¼ teaspoon garlic powder
  1 tablespoon sugar
  ¼ teaspoon ground ginger
  ⅛ teaspoon pepper
  3 cups uncooked chicken, cut into
      1-inch pieces
  ⅓ cup vegetable oil, divided
  2 green peppers, cut into ½-inch
      cubes
  1 (8½-ounce) can sliced bamboo
      shoots, drained
  2 tablespoons honey
  ½ cup cashew nuts
      Chow mein noodles

Combine soy sauce, sherry, salt, cornstarch, garlic powder, sugar, ginger, and pepper in a large bowl; reserve 2 tablespoons mixture for later use. Add chicken and toss gently to coat pieces well. Drain chicken.

Heat 2 tablespoons vegetable oil in a skillet over medium heat. Add chicken; cook uncovered, stirring constantly, until chicken is browned on all sides, about 5 to 7 minutes. Remove chicken from skillet with a slotted spoon and place on platter; cover. Drain skillet; add remaining vegetable oil to skillet; heat. Stir in green pepper, bamboo shoots, and 2 tablespoons reserved soy sauce mixture. Cook, uncovered, until green pepper is crisp-tender, about 3 to 4 minutes.

Return chicken to skillet and stir gently to combine with vegetable mixture. Add honey and cook, uncovered, 2 to 3 minutes longer. Add cashews. Serve on chow mein noodles. Yield: 6 servings.

Check your refrigerator and each shelf as well as your freezer for proper temperature: below 45° for your refrigerator and 0° or below for your freezer.

TOMATO PUDDING

  1 (10-ounce) can tomato puree
  ¼ cup boiling water
  3 tablespoons light brown sugar
  ½ teaspoon salt
  2 cups (1-inch) white bread cubes
  ¼ cup melted butter or margarine

Combine tomato puree and water in a saucepan. Add sugar and salt; boil 5 minutes. Place bread in a 1-quart casserole. Pour butter over bread. Add tomato mixture. Cover and bake at 350° for 30 minutes. Yield: 4 to 6 servings.

CORN-BUTTERBEAN SALAD

  1 (16-ounce) can whole kernel corn,
      drained
  1 (16-ounce) can butterbeans, drained
  1 medium onion, chopped
  1 green pepper, chopped (optional)
  ½ cup mayonnaise
  ¼ cup sandwich and salad sauce
  2 tablespoons lemon-pepper marinade
  1 teaspoon monosodium glutamate
      (optional)
  1 teaspoon salt
  ¼ teaspoon pepper

Combine all ingredients. Yield: 6 servings.
Note: This salad is a delicious stuffing for tomatoes.

BROILED GRAPEFRUIT

  3 medium grapefruits
  6 tablespoons powdered sugar
  1½ teaspoons ground cinnamon
      Mace or angostura bitters

Cut grapefruits in half; separate sections. Sprinkle each grapefruit half with 1 tablespoon powdered sugar, ¼ teaspoon cinnamon, and dash of mace. Place under broiler and cook until lightly brown. Serve immediately. Yield: 6 servings.

Curried Eggs Supper
Supper for Six

Curried Eggs on Rice
Polka Dot Vegetables
Tomato Salad with Bacon Dressing
Hot Beer Bread
Candied Apples with Almond Topping
Milk   Coffee

 *Prepare bread while cooking eggs. Assemble and simmer dessert. While cooking curry sauce, heat vegetables. Mix up salad dressing but do not pour on salad until last minute. Complete details while waiting for bread to finish baking.*

CURRIED EGGS ON RICE

  6 to 8 hard-cooked eggs
  2 chicken bouillon cubes
  ¾ cup boiling water
  2 tablespoons butter or margarine
  2 tablespoons all-purpose flour
  ¼ cup evaporated milk
  1 teaspoon curry powder
  ½ teaspoon salt
    Dash of pepper
    Hot cooked rice
  ¼ cup chopped chutney (optional)

Cut eggs in half lengthwise. Dissolve bouillon cubes in boiling water; set aside. Melt butter in a medium saucepan over low heat; add flour, stirring until smooth. Cook 1 minute, stirring constantly. Gradually stir in bouillon and milk; cook over medium heat, stirring constantly, until thickened and bubbly. Stir in curry powder, salt, and pepper. Add eggs to sauce and heat. Serve over rice; top with chutney, if desired. Yield: 6 servings.

POLKA DOT VEGETABLES

  ⅓ cup chopped onion
  ¼ cup melted butter or margarine
  2 tablespoons Worcestershire sauce
  2 teaspoons sugar
  ¼ teaspoon salt
    Dash of pepper
  1 (17-ounce) can green peas, drained
  1 (12-ounce) can whole kernel
    vacuum-packed corn

Sauté onion in butter in large saucepan. Add remaining ingredients and heat thoroughly. Yield: 6 servings.

To mince parsley and other herbs, form into a tight bunch. Hold the herbs firmly in one hand, and cut with kitchen shears or on a board with sharp knife.

TOMATO SALAD WITH BACON DRESSING

- 1 large green pepper, chopped
- 2 or 3 tomatoes, coarsely chopped
- ½ cup chopped onion
  Lettuce cups
- 4 slices bacon
- 1 teaspoon chili powder
- ¼ teaspoon salt
- ⅓ cup vinegar

Combine green pepper, tomato, and onion; arrange in lettuce cups. Dice bacon and fry slowly until crisp. Add chili powder, salt, and vinegar to bacon in skillet. Heat to boiling. Pour over salad and serve immediately. Yield: 6 servings.

Note: Same dressing can be used with potato or other vegetable combinations.

HOT BEER BREAD

- 3 cups self-rising flour
- 3 tablespoons sugar
- 1 (12-ounce) can beer (at room temperature)
- 2 teaspoons melted butter or margarine (optional)

Mix all ingredients. Pour batter into buttered loafpan. Bake at 350° for 50 minutes. Brush top with melted butter, if desired. Yield: 1 loaf.

CANDIED APPLES WITH ALMOND TOPPING

- ¼ cup apricot jam
- 3 tablespoons sugar
- ½ cup water
- ¼ cup apple juice
- 1 tablespoon grated orange rind
- 6 medium apples
  Whipped cream or whipped topping
  Chopped almonds

Combine apricot jam, sugar, water, apple juice, and orange rind in large saucepan; heat 5 minutes. Cut apples in half; remove cores and peel. Place apples in hot syrup; cover and cook slowly until apples are tender but not mushy. Add additional apple juice if more liquid is needed. Remove apples to dessert dishes; spoon remaining syrup over them. Top each with whipped cream mixed thickly with chopped almonds. Serve warm or cold. Yield: 6 servings.

Soup and Salad, Anytime Meal

Supper for Ten to Twelve

Fresh Vegetable and Beef Soup
Lettuce Wedges with Ranch-Type Dressing
Cheese Drop Biscuits
Chocolate Fluff Topping on Angel Food Cake (*see* Index)
Milk   Coffee

 *Assemble all ingredients for soup. While meat browns, chop already washed, fresh vegetables. Add all ingredients to meat and simmer. While simmering soup, prepare biscuits, whipped topping, salad, and dressing. Put biscuits in oven when soup is about half cooked. Freeze leftover soup for another quick and easy meal.*

FRESH VEGETABLE AND BEEF SOUP

1 pound lean ground beef
4 beef bouillon cubes
2 cups water
4 cups diced fresh tomatoes, peeled, or 2 (16-ounce) cans tomatoes, undrained
2 cups cubed fresh potatoes or 1 (16-ounce) can potatoes, undrained and cubed
1 cup diced celery
7 green onions, chopped
1 cup sliced carrots
1 (16-ounce) can whole kernel corn, undrained
1 cup fresh snap beans or 1 (16-ounce) can cut green beans, undrained
1 (16-ounce) can sliced yellow squash, undrained (optional)
1 tablespoon salt
2 teaspoons garlic powder
½ teaspoon dried basil (optional)
¼ teaspoon pepper

Brown beef in large saucepan; add bouillon cubes, water, vegetables, and seasonings. Bring to boiling point. Cover and simmer 20 minutes or until vegetables are tender. Serve hot. Yield: 4 quarts or 12 servings.
Note: If using fresh vegetables, additional water may be necessary.

Refrigerate lard, butter, margarine, drippings, and opened containers of cooking and vegetable oils.

LETTUCE WEDGES WITH RANCH-TYPE DRESSING

1 cup mayonnaise
¾ cup buttermilk
2 tablespoons lemon juice
1 tablespoon seasoned salt
Hot sauce to taste
Lettuce wedges

Combine first 5 ingredients in a jar; shake thoroughly. Will keep at least 1 week in refrigerator. Serve on lettuce wedges. Yield: about 2 cups.
Note: Crushed garlic or crumbled blue cheese may be added for variety.

CHEESE DROP BISCUITS

2 cups all-purpose flour
½ teaspoon salt
2 teaspoons baking powder
¾ cup shredded Cheddar cheese
¼ cup shortening
¾ cup milk

Combine flour, salt, and baking powder; cut in cheese and shortening. Add milk all at once and stir carefully until dry ingredients are damp. Stir vigorously until mixture forms a soft dough that clings to bowl. Drop from teaspoon onto greased baking sheet. Bake at 425° for 12 to 15 minutes. Yield: 12 large biscuits.

Stove-Top Supper

Supper for Six to Eight

Skillet-Style Pasta Figioli
Green Slaw
Commercial Hard Rolls
Quick Applesauce Dessert
Milk   Coffee

 *Prepare pasta dish. While it cooks, mix dressing and refrigerate until ready to combine with slaw. Shred cabbage and refrigerate. Prepare dessert and refrigerate until ready to serve.*

SKILLET-STYLE PASTA FIGIOLI

  1 pound pork sausage or ground beef
  1 medium onion, diced
  1 clove garlic, crushed
  1 small green pepper, diced (optional)
  1 (16-ounce) can tomatoes
  1 cup buttermilk
  1 cup elbow macaroni, uncooked
  1 (16-ounce) can kidney beans
1½ teaspoons sugar
1½ teaspoons chili powder
  1 teaspoon salt
¼ teaspoon crushed red pepper
  1 teaspoon fennel seeds (optional)
½ teaspoon ground oregano
½ teaspoon thyme

Brown meat, onion, garlic, and green pepper, if desired, in large skillet; drain. Add remaining ingredients; stir. Cover; place on high heat until steaming. Reduce heat to low and simmer 25 minutes or until macaroni is cooked. Yield: 6 to 8 servings.

In many dishes ½ pound sausage plus ½ pound ground beef can be substituted for 1 pound sausage or beef.

GREEN SLAW

½ cup mayonnaise
  3 tablespoons chopped onion
  3 tablespoons sweet pickle relish
  1 tablespoon lemon juice or lime juice
  1 teaspoon salt
  3 cups shredded green cabbage
    Lemon or lime wedges

Combine mayonnaise, onion, relish, lemon juice, and salt; chill to blend flavors. Add cabbage and toss lightly. Serve with lemon or lime wedges. Yield: 6 to 8 servings.

QUICK APPLESAUCE DESSERT

  3 cups applesauce, chilled
  3 pralines, crumbled
½ cup coarsely chopped pecans
    Frozen whipped topping, thawed
    Toasted coconut (optional)

Spoon applesauce into shallow dessert dishes. Top each with pralines, pecans, a dollop of whipped topping, and coconut, if desired. Yield: 6 to 8 servings.

Sunday Night Supper

Supper for Six

Jiffy Chicken or Turkey Pie
Vegetable Medley Salad
Orange-Apricot Dessert
Hot Tea   Coffee

 *Prepare chicken pie. While it bakes, prepare salad and refrigerate until ready to serve. Prepare dessert just before serving.*

JIFFY CHICKEN OR TURKEY PIE

  1 **medium onion, chopped**
  2 **tablespoons melted butter or**
      margarine
  2 **tablespoons all-purpose flour**
  1 **(10½-ounce) can cream of chicken**
      soup, undiluted
  1 **(10½-ounce) can chicken noodle**
      soup, undiluted
  2 **cups cooked chopped chicken or**
      turkey
  ½ **teaspoon salt**
  ¼ **teaspoon pepper**
  1 **teaspoon poultry seasoning**
  1 **(8- to 10-ounce) can refrigerated**
      biscuits

Sauté onion in butter; blend in flour and stir until frothy. Add soup; heat until thickened. Add chicken and seasonings. Heat thoroughly. Pour into a greased shallow 3-quart casserole. Arrange biscuits on top. Bake at 400° for 10 to 12 minutes or until biscuits are brown. Yield: 6 servings.

Put fresh fruits in refrigerator to prevent fast spoilage.

VEGETABLE MEDLEY SALAD

  1 **cup diced carrots, cooked**
  ½ **cup diced beets, cooked (optional)**
  1 **cup green peas, cooked**
  ¼ **cup chopped onion**
  1 **cup raw cauliflowerets, sliced**
  1 **cup mayonnaise**
      Lettuce

Combine all vegetables; stir in mayonnaise. Serve on lettuce. Yield: 6 servings.

ORANGE-APRICOT DESSERT

  2 **(11-ounce) cans mandarin orange**
      sections
  2 **(8-ounce) cartons apricot-flavored**
      yogurt
      Whipped topping
      Nuts

Drain oranges; combine with apricot yogurt. Place in glass bowl and garnish with whipped topping and nuts. Serve immediately. Yield: 6 to 8 servings.

In the Holiday Spirit

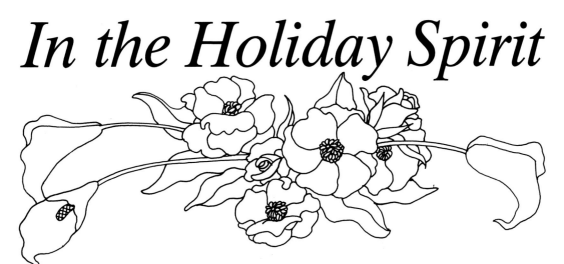

*H*oliday meals do not have to be a tremendous burden to the meal manager. Today, the elaborate holiday meal is becoming the unusual instead of the usual. Huge portions which often result in wasted food at holiday time have no place in the modern home. Let's not forget that holiday meals can mean a cozy little meal with a few close friends or one served in a grand manner of entertaining. The choice is yours. These simple, easy, yet festive meals can be garnished in the holiday motif and dressed up with colorful linens and table decorations. Again, the crystal-clear sparkle of a filled wine glass immediately creates a holiday spirit. The fact that you did not spend unnecessarily long, tedious hours of work need not show if the climate of the party is right.

Mardi Gras Celebration

Dinner for Six

Deviled Cottage Dip—Celery and Carrot Sticks
Braunschweiger Log—Assorted Crackers
Chinese Shrimp and Rice
Beets a l'Orange
Hungarian Cabbage
New Apple Salad
Commercial Hard Rolls
Skillet-Style Peach Cobbler
Sherry   Tea   Coffee

 *Assemble ingredients for shrimp and rice. Prepare dip, celery, carrot sticks, braunschweiger log, and apple salad; refrigerate. Marinate beets in sauce; then prepare the cabbage. At this point begin cooking the peach cobbler. Before preparing the shrimp and rice, enjoy the hors d'oeuvres and sherry.*

DEVILED COTTAGE DIP

1½ cups cottage cheese
1 (2¼-ounce) can deviled ham
2 tablespoons sliced green onions or ½ teaspoon instant minced onion
1 teaspoon paprika
Celery and carrot sticks

Combine cottage cheese, ham, onion, and paprika; beat until smooth. Chill. Serve with celery and carrot sticks. Yield: 1¾ cups.

BRAUNSCHWEIGER LOG

1 pound braunschweiger
2 tablespoons chili sauce
2 tablespoons mayonnaise or salad dressing
½ teaspoon sweet basil
½ cup chopped or slivered nuts

Combine braunschweiger, chili sauce, mayonnaise, and basil. Shape mixture into a 7½-inch long log. Roll in nuts. Serve with assorted crackers. Yield: about 2 cups.

Placing the napkin at the left of the fork is correct. Be sure open edges are toward the plate unless the napkin is monogrammed. If that is the case, show off the design to the best advantage.

Not all table decorations need be live flowers. Candles on a dinner table create a party atmosphere and their light brings out the gleam of silver and glass.

CHINESE SHRIMP AND RICE

- 2 tablespoons chopped onion
- 2 (4½-ounce) cans shrimp, undrained
- 2 cups uncooked instant rice
- 2 tablespoons vegetable oil
- 2 eggs
- 2 beef bouillon cubes
- 1 cup boiling water
- 1 (4-ounce) can sliced mushrooms, undrained
- 1 (16-ounce) can green peas, undrained
- 1 tablespoon soy sauce

Sauté onion, shrimp, and rice in oil in medium skillet until onion is cooked, but not browned; remove from heat. Scramble eggs and cut into small strips; add eggs to sautéed mixture. Dissolve bouillon cubes in boiling water. Bring bouillon, mushrooms, peas, and soy sauce to a boil in a medium saucepan. Stir in rice mixture. Cover and let stand 5 minutes. Stir before servings. Yield: 6 servings.

BEETS A L'ORANGE

- 1 (16-ounce) jar small whole beets
- 1½ tablespoons cornstarch
- 1 teaspoon grated orange rind
- ⅓ cup orange juice
- 3 tablespoons lemon juice
- 2 tablespoons sugar
- ¼ cup butter or margarine

Drain beets, reserving ½ cup liquid. Dissolve cornstarch in reserved liquid; add orange rind, orange juice, lemon juice, and sugar. Cook, stirring constantly, over medium heat until thickened and translucent. Add beets and butter. Heat. Yield: 6 servings.

HUNGARIAN CABBAGE

- 2 slices bacon
- 1 pound cabbage, coarsely shredded
- ¾ teaspoon salt
  Dash of pepper
- 2 tablespoons vinegar (optional)
- 2 tablespoons water

Cook bacon in medium skillet until crisp; remove from skillet. Crumble bacon, and set aside. Add cabbage, salt, pepper, vinegar, if desired, and water to bacon drippings in skillet. Cover and cook over low heat, stirring occasionally. Cabbage should be tender but crisp. Transfer cabbage to serving dish and top with bacon. Serve hot. Yield: 6 servings.

Out of cream and need some desperately for a recipe? In a pinch you can substitute 3 tablespoons of butter and ⅞ cup milk for each cup of cream. This is for cooking only. Don't try it in coffee!

For a holiday dinner, scoop out an orange (remove membranes from the shell) and spoon sweet potato mixture into the shell. Place in a shallow baking pan and bake for 20 minutes until tops are lightly browned.

NEW APPLE SALAD

2 apples, unpeeled
⅓ cup raisins
⅓ cup chopped nuts
½ cup chopped celery
½ cup mayonnaise
½ teaspoon salt
1 avocado
  Lettuce cups

Core and dice apples. Add next 5 ingredients; toss lightly. Cut avocado lengthwise into halves; remove seeds and skin. Dice avocado; fold gently into salad mixture just before serving in lettuce cups. Yield: 6 servings.

If you are in a hurry, substitute 1 (10½-ounce) can of any cream soup diluted with ¼ cup of milk for 2 cups cream sauce.

SKILLET-STYLE PEACH COBBLER

1 (28-ounce) can sliced peaches, undrained
3 tablespoons butter or margarine
1 teaspoon lemon juice
1 cup biscuit mix
2 tablespoons sugar
2 tablespoons butter or margarine
⅓ cup milk
  Vanilla ice cream or whipped topping

Combine peaches, butter, and lemon juice in a 10-inch skillet. Cover and cook over medium heat until simmering. Combine biscuit mix and sugar; cut in butter until mixture resembles coarse meal. Add milk to make a soft dough. Spoon dough into simmering fruit mixture. Cover and cook until dough is thoroughly baked, 12 to 15 minutes. Serve warm topped with vanilla ice cream or whipped topping. Yield: 6 servings.

Traditional Easter Feast

Dinner for Six

Ham with Apricot Sauce
Elegant Broccoli
Carrots in Bouillon
Citrus and Avocado Salad with Date Dressing
Sweet Potato Biscuits
Hawaiian Fluff Topping on Chiffon Cake
Wine   **Coffee**

 *Start cooking eggs for the broccoli immediately; blend ingredients for salad dressing and refrigerate. While browning ham, slice onions. As onions cook, grate the carrots. As ham simmers, put on broccoli and carrots, combine sauce for broccoli, and prepare biscuit mixture. Mix topping for cake using whipped topping for this meal. Refrigerate until dessert time. Slice avocado and section fresh grapefruit or use canned grapefruit sections. Wash and dry lettuce cups and assemble salads. Put biscuits in oven while thickening the ham sauce. Pour wine and you are ready to serve.*

HAM WITH APRICOT SAUCE

    1 (1½-pound) boneless cooked ham
        slice, cut into 6 pieces
    2 tablespoons vegetable oil
 1½ cups sliced onion
    1 (12-ounce) can apricot nectar
 1½ teaspoons cornstarch
  ¼ cup water

Brown ham in hot oil; remove from skillet. Add onion and cook until tender; stir in nectar. Return ham to skillet. Cover and simmer 15 minutes, basting occasionally. Remove ham to serving platter. Dissolve cornstarch in water; add to sauce. Cook, stirring constantly, until thickened and translucent. Serve over warm ham. Yield: 6 servings.

ELEGANT BROCCOLI

    3 (10-ounce) packages frozen broccoli
        spears
  ½ cup butter or margarine
    2 hard-cooked eggs, sieved
 1½ tablespoons white vinegar
    1 teaspoon lemon juice
    1 teaspoon prepared mustard
  ¼ teaspoon cayenne pepper

Cook broccoli according to package directions; drain. Combine butter, eggs, vine-gar, lemon juice, mustard, and cayenne pepper in a mixing bowl; beat until smooth. Place broccoli on serving plate; top with sauce. Sauce is also good with asparagus. Yield: 6 servings.

CARROTS IN BOUILLON

    6 to 8 carrots
    2 cups water or enough to cover
    4 to 5 chicken bouillon cubes

Coarsely grate carrots. Place in a 1½-quart saucepan and cover with water; add bouillon cubes. Bring to a boil; reduce heat to low and cook gently until carrots are tender and bouillon dissolved, about 8 to 10 minutes. Do not overcook. Reserve leftover juice for soups or casseroles. Yield: 6 servings.

CITRUS AND AVOCADO SALAD WITH DATE DRESSING

- 1 cup commercial sour cream
- ½ cup finely chopped dates
- ½ teaspoon grated orange rind
- 2 tablespoons orange juice
- ¼ teaspoon salt
- 3 avocados, peeled and sliced
- 2 large grapefruits, peeled and sectioned
- 1 (11-ounce) can mandarin orange sections, drained
  Lettuce cups

Combine sour cream, dates, orange rind, juice, and salt. Store in refrigerator until ready to use. Arrange avocados, grapefruit, and orange sections on lettuce cups; top with dressing. Yield: 6 servings.

SWEET POTATO BISCUITS

- 1 cup all-purpose flour
- 1 tablespoon baking powder
- ½ teaspoon salt
- 3 tablespoons butter, margarine, or shortening
- 1 cup cooked, mashed sweet potatoes
  About ¼ cup milk

Does that favorite recipe of Grandmother's call for sour milk? Just substitute the same amount of today's buttermilk right from the carton, or pour 1 tablespoon of lemon juice or vinegar in a measuring cup and add enough milk to make 1 cup. Let stand 5 minutes before using.

Both fresh broccoli and asparagus cook better if stood on end. An ordinary coffee can helps hold the vegetable upright.

Combine dry ingredients; cut in butter until mixture resembles coarse meal. Add sweet potatoes and mix well. Gradually add enough milk to make a soft dough. Turn dough out onto floured surface, and knead lightly 3 or 4 times. Roll dough to ⅓-inch thickness; cut into rounds with a 2-inch biscuit cutter. Place on a baking sheet. Bake at 450° for 12 to 15 minutes. Serve hot. Yield: about 12 biscuits.

HAWAIIAN FLUFF TOPPING ON CHIFFON CAKE

- 2 cups whipping cream or 4 cups whipped topping
- ¼ cup plus 2 tablespoons powdered sugar
- ¾ cup well-drained crushed pineapple
- ½ cup flaked coconut
- ½ cup chopped, toasted, blanched almonds
- ½ cup maraschino cherries, quartered
  Plain chiffon cake

Beat whipping cream until stiff; blend in sugar. Fold in pineapple, coconut, almonds, and cherries. Serve on wedges of cake. Yield: 6 to 8 servings.

Note: If whipped topping is used, eliminate powdered sugar.

Graduation Patio Supper

Outdoor Supper for Six

Snappy Beefburgers
Boiled Potatoes
Spinach Italian-Style
Tomato Wedges with Sour Cream Herb Dressing
Vanilla Ice Cream—Peanut Butter-Fudge Sauce
Milk   Cold Sodas

 *Marinate spinach in Italian dressing. Prepare meat patties and refrigerate until ready to grill. Start cooking the potatoes and cook eggs. Combine salad dressing and pour over tomato wedges. Separate, wash, and dry lettuce cups. While grilling beef patties, prepare fudge sauce, heat spinach, and drain and butter potatoes.*

SNAPPY BEEFBURGERS

  1 **cup seasoned stuffing mix**
  1 **teaspoon salt**
  2 **medium onions, finely chopped**
  1 **cup milk**
  ¼ **teaspoon pepper**
  2 **pounds lean ground beef**
  2 **tablespoons Worcestershire sauce**
  ¼ **cup sugar**
  ¼ **cup red wine**
  2 **tablespoons vinegar**
  1 **cup catsup**
     Sesame seed buns (optional)

Combine first 6 ingredients; shape into patties. Combine next 5 ingredients in saucepan; heat. Cook patties on grill until browned on both sides and to desired degree of doneness, brushing often with sauce. Serve on buns, if desired. Yield: 6 servings.

Note: Patties may be cooked in skillet: brown patties, add sauce, and simmer 10 minutes.

BOILED POTATOES

Select 6 potatoes of uniform size. Wash thoroughly, leave the skins on, and cook in a small amount of boiling salted water until tender when pierced with a fork.

Drain; shake pan gently over low heat to dry potatoes. Cut a crisscross gash on potato top and squeeze until potato pops up through the skins. Place a pat of butter in opening; sprinkle with pepper or paprika. Yield: 6 servings.

Note: Potatoes may be pared before or after cooking, if desired.

For a lush lime cooler beat ½ pint (1 cup) lime sherbet in a mixing bowl or blender. Add ¼ cup (2 ounces) undiluted frozen concentrated limeade and 3 cups milk. Pour into five glasses, topping each with a scoop of lime sherbet. Garnish with fresh mint or a minted cherry.

SPINACH ITALIAN-STYLE

  2 (16-ounce) cans spinach, drained, or
  2 (10-ounce) packages frozen
     spinach, thawed and drained
  ½ cup commercial Italian dressing
  3 hard-cooked eggs, sliced

Marinate spinach in dressing for 30 minutes. Heat and serve. Garnish with egg slices. Yield: 6 servings.

TOMATO WEDGES WITH SOUR CREAM HERB DRESSING

  1 cup commercial sour cream
  2 tablespoons red wine vinegar
  1 teaspoon sugar
  ½ teaspoon salt
  ½ teaspoon celery seeds
     Dash of pepper
  ¼ teaspoon dried thyme
  4 tomatoes, cut into wedges
     Lettuce cups

Combine sour cream, vinegar, sugar, salt, celery seeds, pepper, and thyme; chill. Place tomato wedges in lettuce cups; top with dressing. Yield: 6 servings.

PEANUT BUTTER-FUDGE SAUCE

  1 (6-ounce) package semisweet
     chocolate morsels
  ⅓ cup milk
  ⅓ cup peanut butter
  ¼ cup corn syrup
  ½ teaspoon vanilla extract

Combine chocolate morsels, milk, peanut butter, and corn syrup in a saucepan; bring to a boil over medium heat, stirring constantly. Stir in vanilla. Serve warm over ice cream. Yield: 1½ cups sauce.
  Note: Add additional milk for thinner consistency, if desired.

Fourth of July Patio Supper

Outdoor Supper for Six

Chilled Vegetable Cocktail Juice
Glazed Ham Steaks
Sweet Potatoes and Applesauce
Broccoli Parmesan
Lettuce Wedges with Carlton Dressing
Bran Muffins (*see* Index)
Commercial Ice Cream Sandwiches
Iced Tea   Beer

 *Refrigerate vegetable juice several hours before serving. Prepare glaze for ham steaks. Prepare potato casserole and broccoli; then prepare dressing. Finally, bake bran muffins from prepared, mixed batter. While muffins are baking, grill steaks.*

GLAZED HAM STEAKS

- 1 **cup honey**
- 1 **tablespoon dry mustard**
- 1 **tablespoon prepared mustard**
- 1 **teaspoon lemon juice**
- 6 **medium ham steaks**

Combine honey, mustard, and lemon juice in mixing bowl; beat thoroughly. Grill ham steaks slowly over charcoal or cook under broiler. Brush frequently with honey sauce until brown and glazed on both sides. Yield: 6 servings.

SWEET POTATOES AND APPLESAUCE

- 1 **(25-ounce) can sweet potatoes, sliced**
- 1 **(16-ounce) can applesauce**
- 1 **tablespoon brown sugar**
- 2 **tablespoons butter or margarine**

Layer potatoes and applesauce alternately in a buttered 1½-quart casserole. Dot with brown sugar and butter. Bake at 350° for 30 minutes or until flavors are blended and top is brown. Yield: 6 servings.

Think through the menus before you begin to cook, or on the way home from the grocery. Plan tasks in order of time needed for preparation and cooking. Do the longest first so that other tasks can be done while cooking is going on. This will save time, and foods will be served at or near the peak of perfection.

BROCCOLI PARMESAN

- 2 **(10-ounce) packages frozen broccoli spears or chopped broccoli**
- 2 **egg whites**
- ½ **teaspoon salt**
- ⅓ **cup mayonnaise**
  Grated Parmesan cheese

Cook broccoli according to package directions; drain. Beat egg whites and salt until stiff; fold in mayonnaise. Spread over arranged spears or chopped broccoli. Sprinkle generously with cheese. Broil 3 to 5 minutes or until golden brown. Yield: 6 servings.

LETTUCE WEDGES WITH CARLTON DRESSING

- 1 **cup mayonnaise**
- 2 **teaspoons tarragon vinegar**
- 1 **teaspoon salt**
- ⅛ **teaspoon thyme**
- ¼ **teaspoon curry powder**
- 2 **tablespoons chili sauce or catsup**
- 1 **tablespoon chopped chives**
- 2 **tablespoons chopped onion**
  Dash of pepper
  Lettuce wedges

Combine first 9 ingredients; mix until blended. Serve over lettuce wedges. Yield: 1¼ cups.

Labor Day Gathering

Supper for Six

Southern Chicken Casserole
Spanish Rice
Greek Salad
Hot Biscuits (*see* Index)
Candied Bananas
Iced Tea   Coffee

 *Prepare the chicken casserole and Spanish rice. Prepare salad makings and store until ready to serve. Mix dressing, but do not toss with salad until ready to serve. Now prepare the sauce for the bananas. Prepare biscuits. Remove chicken from oven, turn up heat, and pop biscuits into the oven. Serve salad first and by the time you get to the main dish, the biscuits will be hot. Reset oven temperature, and bake bananas while guests enjoy dinner.*

SOUTHERN CHICKEN CASSEROLE

    2 (10-ounce) packages frozen broccoli
       spears
    3 cups cooked coarsely chopped
       chicken or turkey
    1 (10¾-ounce) can cream of chicken
       soup, undiluted
    ½ can water
    1 cup mayonnaise
    1 teaspoon lemon juice
    ½ teaspoon curry powder
       Buttered breadcrumbs

Cook broccoli according to package directions; drain and arrange in a greased 1½-quart casserole. Place chicken over broccoli. Combine soup, water, mayonnaise, lemon juice, and curry powder in a small bowl; mix well. Pour sauce over chicken. Top with breadcrumbs. Bake at 350° for 20 to 25 minutes or just until heated through. Yield: 4 to 6 servings.

SPANISH RICE

    1 cup uncooked rice
    2 tablespoons vegetable oil
    1 small onion, chopped
    1 small green pepper, chopped
    1 stalk celery, chopped
    1 (16-ounce) can tomatoes

Brown rice in oil in a medium skillet over low heat. Add onion, green pepper, celery, and tomatoes. Cover; cook gently about 25 minutes or until rice is tender. Yield: 6 servings.

Baked stuffed potatoes can be prepared ahead. Do not go through the final baking step. Simply bake the potatoes, unstuff, mix the filling, stuff, top with cheese, and wrap for freezing. Unwrap before cooking.

GREEK SALAD

- 1 head lettuce, torn into bite-size pieces
- 2 tomatoes, peeled and cut into wedges
- 6 pitted ripe olives, quartered
- 6 radishes, sliced
- 1 carrot, grated
- 1 cucumber, sliced
- ½ teaspoon whole oregano
  Garlic salt and pepper to taste
  Dressing (recipe follows)

Combine vegetables; sprinkle with oregano, garlic salt, and pepper. Add dressing and toss just before serving. Yield: 6 servings.

Dressing:

- ¼ cup olive oil
- ¼ cup wine vinegar
- 1 clove garlic, crushed

Combine all ingredients in a jar; shake well. Yield: about ½ cup.

CANDIED BANANAS

- 6 green-tipped bananas
- ¼ cup melted butter or margarine
- ½ cup molasses
- ¼ teaspoon salt
- 2 teaspoons grated lemon rind
- ¼ cup lemon juice
- ½ teaspoon ground cinnamon
- ½ cup flaked coconut

Peel bananas and cut in half lengthwise; place in shallow baking dish. Combine butter, molasses, salt, lemon rind, lemon juice, and cinnamon. Pour over bananas; sprinkle with coconut. Bake at 375° for 15 minutes, basting occasionally. Yield: 6 servings.

Halloween Treat

Supper for Six

Oriental Pork
Rice Pilaf (*see* Index)
Beets and Mandarin Orange Sections
White Salad
Commercial Hot Rolls
Banana Fritters
Hot Tea   Coffee

 *Assemble dessert and refrigerate until ready to serve. While chops marinate, prepare the salad and refrigerate. While you are broiling the chops, prepare the beet dish and then the pilaf.*

ORIENTAL PORK

⅓ cup soy sauce
¼ cup sugar
1 clove garlic, minced
½ teaspoon salt
1 teaspoon ground ginger
6 pork loin chops or blade steaks, cut ½ to ¾ inch thick

Combine soy sauce, sugar, garlic, salt, and ginger. Pour mixture over pork and marinate 15 minutes, turning occasionally. Drain pork chops. Place on rack in broiler pan and broil 5 to 7 inches from heat. Broil 10 to 15 minutes on one side; turn and broil 10 to 15 minutes on other side. Serve hot. Yield: 6 servings.

WHITE SALAD

1 small head cauliflower
1 medium onion
2 white or 8 red radishes
1 small cucumber
1 cup commercial sour cream
2 teaspoons lemon juice
2 tablespoons sugar
½ to 1 teaspoon salt
Coarsely ground pepper
Crisp salad greens

Break cauliflower into flowerets. Slice onion, radishes, and cucumber. Combine sour cream, lemon juice, sugar, salt, and pepper; pour over vegetables. Allow salad to marinate about 1 hour, if possible, before serving. Serve on crisp salad greens. Yield: 6 servings.

BEETS AND MANDARIN ORANGE SECTIONS

1 (11-ounce) can mandarin orange sections, undrained
Orange juice
¼ cup butter or margarine
¼ teaspoon ground ginger
¼ teaspoon ground nutmeg
Water
1½ tablespoons cornstarch
½ teaspoon salt
1 (16-ounce) can sliced beets, drained

Drain juice from orange sections and add enough orange juice to make 1½ cups. Heat orange juice, butter, ginger, and nutmeg in a large saucepan. Add enough water to cornstarch to dissolve. When juice mixture comes to a boil, add cornstarch and salt; cook, stirring constantly, until sauce thickens. Add orange sections and beets; heat to serve. Yield: 6 servings.

Sometimes it's a good idea to serve frozen fruits with some ice crystals still in them; the texture will be firmer, more like that of fresh fruits.

BANANA FRITTERS

2 cups cornflake crumbs
1 tablespoon sugar
4 to 6 ripe bananas, peeled
¼ cup orange juice
1 tablespoon butter or margarine

Combine crumbs and sugar. Cut bananas in half lengthwise and dip in orange juice. Roll banana in crumb mixture. Place on lightly greased cookie sheet; dot with butter. Bake at 400° for 15 minutes. Yield: 4 to 6 servings.

Section II

Recipes

Appetizers

*O*ne of the more persistent questions asked by even the most experienced cooks is what to serve in the way of party foods. The occasion could call for appetizers for a group of five or six or perhaps a hundred, but regardless, certain qualities become important. If the party is held during the dinner hour, you should have foods from all parts of a meal, for it is likely that this will be the only food the guests will have that evening. Therefore, in planning, choose items that span the basic foods spectrum—perhaps a meatball dish; a platter of fresh fruits or vegetable dippers; crackers, bread, or some other item in the cereal family; and, generally, a cheese ball or cheese dip to complete the nutrient requirements. It is nice to feel that you have furnished your guests with good company, good tasting food, and foods essential to their good health.

Recipes included here cover a wide variety of foods; all can be prepared in a limited time. With the appropriate garnish and table appointments, the guests will never suspect the little time spent in preparation.

One last rule: keep hot foods hot and cold foods cold for the sake of both taste and appearance.

BACON AND CHEESE APPETIZERS

3 slices uncooked bacon, finely chopped
1 teaspoon prepared mustard
¼ teaspoon paprika
1 cup (4 ounces) shredded sharp Cheddar cheese
16 very thin white or wheat bread slices

Combine bacon, mustard, paprika, and cheese. Toast bread on one side. Spread untoasted side of bread with 1 tablespoon of cheese mixture; cut into quarters and broil until cheese melts and bacon is crisp. Serve immediately. Yield: 64 squares.

HOT CRABMEAT CANAPÉS

½ cup mayonnaise
½ teaspoon prepared mustard
1 teaspoon Worcestershire sauce
2 teaspoons grated horseradish
1 (6½-ounce) can crabmeat, drained and flaked
½ cup grated Parmesan cheese
Assorted party crackers or party bread

Combine mayonnaise, mustard, Worcestershire sauce, horseradish, crabmeat, and Parmesan cheese; mix well. Spread on crackers. Bake at 300° about 3 to 4 minutes or until heated through. Yield: about 50 appetizers.

CHEESE TARTS

2 cups (8 ounces) shredded sharp Cheddar cheese
1 tablespoon half-and-half
½ teaspoon dry mustard
¼ teaspoon paprika
½ teaspoon Worcestershire sauce
¼ teaspoon hot sauce (optional)
24 (1-inch) baked commercial tart shells

Combine cheese, half-and-half, mustard, paprika, Worcestershire sauce, and hot sauce in top of double boiler; heat over hot water, stirring occasionally, until cheese melts. Spoon into tart shells; allow to stand 10 minutes before serving. Yield: 24 appetizers.

HAM AND CHEESE CANAPÉS

1 cup (4 ounces) shredded Cheddar cheese
½ cup finely chopped cooked ham
¼ cup sweet pickle relish
¼ cup commercial sour cream
1 (16-ounce) loaf unsliced sandwich bread
Softened butter or margarine

Combine cheese, ham, relish, and sour cream in a medium bowl. Cut crusts from bread. Slice bread lengthwise into four 3- x 7-inch strips. Place on foil-lined baking sheet. Butter each strip; then spread about ⅓ cup cheese mixture on each. Broil 3 inches from heat until cheese melts. Cut into 1½- x 1-inch pieces for serving. Yield: about 5 dozen canapés.

Don't "boil" eggs, "hard cook" them. For hard-cooked eggs, just bring the water to simmering and simmer 20 to 25 minutes. Do not let the water boil. Plunge the eggs at once into cold running water and leave until cold.

Sweet pickles start out as sour pickles from which the vinegar has been drained. They are finished in sweet, spicy liquors which are added from time to time until the desired sweetness is attained.

HAM AND EGG CANAPÉS

- 1 (4½-ounce) can deviled ham
- 2 hard-cooked eggs, finely chopped
- 2 teaspoons prepared horseradish
  Toast rounds or crackers
  Pimiento-stuffed olives, sliced

Combine ham, eggs, and horseradish; spread on toast rounds. Broil quickly. Garnish with olive slices. Yield: about 1 cup canapé spread.

SPICY HAM CANAPÉS

- ½ pound cooked ham, finely ground or chopped
- ½ cup commercial sour cream
- 1 tablespoon mayonnaise
- 1 teaspoon curry powder
- ¼ teaspoon garlic salt
- ¼ teaspoon onion powder
  Party bread rounds, toasted and buttered
  Fresh parsley (optional)
  Pimiento strips (optional)

Combine first 6 ingredients. Spread ham mixture on bread rounds. Heat under broiler until puffy and brown. Garnish with parsley and pimiento, if desired. Yield: 2 to 3 dozen canapés.

INDIAN CANAPÉS

- 1 cup smooth peanut butter
- 1 (9-ounce) jar chutney, finely chopped
- 10 slices bacon, cooked and crumbled
  Melba toast rounds

Combine peanut butter, chutney, and bacon. Place about 1 teaspoon of mixture on each toast round. Broil until heated through. Serve immediately. Yield: about 50 appetizers.

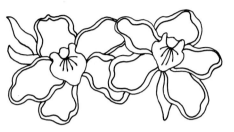

HERBED RYE APPETIZERS

- ¼ cup butter or margarine, softened
- ½ teaspoon dried sweet basil
- ¼ teaspoon dried marjoram
- ¼ teaspoon dried savory
- ¼ teaspoon seasoned salt
- 20 slices party rye bread

Combine all ingredients except bread. On each bread slice, spread butter mixture very thinly. Place bread on cookie sheet; broil without turning until butter melts, about 1 to 3 minutes. Serve immediately. Yield: 20 appetizers.

TOMATO AND ONION CANAPÉS

- 1 (10-ounce) package refrigerator buttermilk biscuits
- 2 to 3 small onions, thinly sliced
- 3 to 4 small tomatoes, thinly sliced
- 3 to 4 slices process American cheese
- 3 slices bacon, cut into 20 pieces

Separate each biscuit into 2 rounds and place on cookie sheet. Layer onion, tomato, cheese, and a piece of bacon on each biscuit round. Bake at 375° for 12 minutes. Serve hot. Yield: 20 canapés.

CHEDDAR BALLS

2 cups (8 ounces) shredded sharp
   Cheddar cheese
½ cup butter or margarine, softened
1 cup all-purpose flour
¼ teaspoon cayenne pepper
½ (1⅜-ounce) envelope dry onion soup
   mix (optional)

Blend cheese and butter. Work in flour, cayenne, and soup mix, if desired. Shape into small balls. Bake at 350° for 15 minutes. Yield: about 3 dozen.

CHEESE BALL

2 cups (8 ounces) shredded sharp
   Cheddar cheese
2 cups (8 ounces) shredded mild
   Cheddar cheese
¼ cup (1 ounce) crumbled blue cheese
1 (3-ounce) package cream cheese,
   softened
1 clove garlic, minced
¼ teaspoon chili powder
¼ teaspoon salt
   Dash of cayenne pepper
2 to 3 tablespoons sherry or wine
   Chopped fresh parsley or chopped
   nuts (optional)

Blend cheese together well. Add garlic, chili powder, salt, and cayenne pepper. Add sherry and blend until creamy. Shape into a ball; roll in parsley or nuts, if desired. Yield: about 2½ cups.

CHEESY PARTY LOG

1 (8-ounce) package cream cheese
⅓ cup soy sauce
   Sesame seeds

Marinate cream cheese in soy sauce. Roll in sesame seeds. Serve with assorted crackers. Yield: 1 cup.

CRISPIE CHEESE BALLS

½ cup butter or margarine, softened
1 cup all-purpose flour
1 cup (4 ounces) shredded Cheddar
   cheese
¼ teaspoon cayenne pepper
1 cup crisp rice cereal
½ teaspoon garlic or seasoned salt
½ teaspoon Worcestershire sauce

Combine all ingredients. Shape into 1-inch balls. Bake at 375° for 10 to 12 minutes. (Balls become firm and crisp on standing.) Yield: about 3 dozen appetizers.

Note: Combining of ingredients is easier if done by hand.

HOLIDAY CHEESE BALL

1 (8-ounce) package cream cheese,
   softened
1 (8½-ounce) can crushed pineapple,
   drained
2 cups chopped pecans, divided
¼ cup chopped green pepper
3 tablespoons chopped onion
1 teaspoon seasoned salt
2 tablespoons chopped chutney
   Maraschino cherries (optional)
   Fresh parsley (optional)

Beat cream cheese slightly; gradually stir in pineapple, 1 cup pecans, green pepper, onion, seasoned salt, and chutney. Chill well. Shape into a ball and roll in remaining pecans. Chill until serving time. Garnish with maraschino cherries and parsley, if desired. Serve with assorted crackers. Yield: 4½ cups.

OAHU APPETIZER

    2 (3-ounce) packages cream cheese,
        softened
    1 (4½-ounce) can deviled ham
    1 teaspoon prepared mustard
    2 cups (8 ounces) shredded Cheddar
        cheese
    2 tablespoons chopped chives
    ½ cup chopped macadamia nuts
        Paprika

Combine cream cheese, ham, and mustard in a medium mixing bowl; beat until smooth. Stir in cheese and chives. If necessary, chill for ease in handling. Shape into a ball; roll in nuts. Sprinkle with paprika. Serve with assorted crackers. Yield: about 2 cups.

Note: Cheese ball may be prepared ahead of time and stored in refrigerator.

BROCCOLI DIP

    2 (10½-ounce) packages frozen
        chopped broccoli
    ¼ cup butter, margarine, or bacon
        drippings
    2 large onions, chopped
    2 cups chopped celery
    2 cloves garlic, crushed
    1 (4-ounce) can mushroom stems and
        pieces, drained
    1 (3-ounce) package cream cheese
    1 (10½-ounce) can cream of
        mushroom soup, undiluted
    2 teaspoons garlic salt
    ¼ teaspoon cayenne pepper

Cook broccoli according to package directions but only until completely thawed; drain thoroughly. Melt butter in large skillet; add onion, celery, and broccoli; cook until onion is tender. Add remaining ingredients and cook over low heat until smooth and thick, stirring frequently. Serve hot in chafing dish with king-size corn chips. Yield: about 2 quarts.

HOT BEEF DIP

    1 (8-ounce) package cream cheese,
        softened
    ⅓ cup commercial sour cream
    1 (2½-ounce) jar sliced dried beef,
        finely chopped
    2 tablespoons dried minced onion
    1 small green pepper, finely chopped
        Hot sauce to taste
    ½ cup chopped pecans or walnuts

Blend cream cheese and sour cream until smooth; add beef, onion, green pepper, hot sauce, and nuts. Heat over low heat, stirring frequently, about 15 minutes. Serve in chafing dish with assorted crackers. Yield: about 2½ cups.

HOT CLAM DIP

    4 cups (1 pound) shredded Cheddar
        cheese
    ¼ cup all-purpose flour
    2 (10¾-ounce) cans condensed New
        England clam chowder, undiluted
    1 (8-ounce) can minced clams, drained
    2 tablespoons chopped onion
    4 or 5 drops of hot sauce

Toss together cheese and flour. Heat soup in a 3-quart saucepan. Reduce heat; add cheese mixture and stir until melted. Stir in clams, onion, and hot sauce. Serve hot with vegetable dippers, cubes of French bread, or king-size corn chips. Yield: 4½ cups.

Most hard cheeses can be kept for several weeks in the coldest part of your refrigerator. Keep cheese in the original wrapper until you are ready to use it. Wrap cut cheese in foil, waxed paper, or plastic to prevent drying. Soft cheese can be kept in the refrigerator from 3 to 5 days.

HOT CRAB DIP

3 tablespoons butter or margarine
2 small onions, chopped
1 cup finely chopped celery
3 tablespoons all-purpose flour
½ teaspoon paprika
1 teaspoon dry mustard
1 teaspoon salt
½ teaspoon pepper
1½ cups milk
¼ cup chopped pimiento
2 (6½-ounce) cans crabmeat, drained
2 tablespoons chopped parsley
1 tablespoon Worcestershire sauce
  Hot sauce to taste
¾ cup diced almonds
2 tablespoons chili sauce

Melt butter in medium skillet; add onion and celery and cook until soft. Add flour, paprika, mustard, salt, and pepper, stirring until smooth. Add milk slowly, stirring until smooth. Add remaining ingredients. If sauce is too thick, add more milk. Serve warm in chafing dish with melba toast, crackers, or tart shells. Yield: about 6 cups.

CUCUMBER DIP

2 medium cucumbers, peeled and grated
1 (8-ounce) package cream cheese, softened
½ teaspoon garlic salt
½ cup finely chopped green pepper
  Hot sauce to taste

Drain cucumber and squeeze liquid out by hand, reserving liquid. Beat cream cheese with small amounts of cucumber juice until it reaches a smooth dipping consistency. Add garlic salt, green pepper, and hot sauce. Stir in cucumber; chill. Serve with assorted crackers or king-size corn chips. Yield: about 2½ cups.

DUNKING SAUCE

1 cup currant jelly
⅔ cup prepared mustard
¼ cup grated onion

Combine all ingredients in top of double boiler; place over hot water and cook until jelly is melted and sauce is smooth. Use to dip cubes of cooked ham, sausage, or frankfurters. Yield: 2 cups sauce.

SMOKED EGG DIP

½ cup mayonnaise
¾ teaspoon liquid smoke seasoning
½ teaspoon salt
1 tablespoon butter, softened
1 tablespoon lemon juice or vinegar
1 teaspoon prepared mustard
¼ teaspoon pepper
1 teaspoon Worcestershire sauce
  Few drops of hot sauce
6 hard-cooked eggs, quartered

Combine all ingredients except eggs in container of electric blender; blend until smooth. Add eggs and blend until smooth. Serve with chips. Yield: about 2 cups.

HOT MUSTARD SAUCE

½ cup sugar
¼ cup plus 1 tablespoon dry mustard
½ teaspoon salt
2 tablespoons all-purpose flour
1 cup milk
1 egg yolk, beaten
½ cup vinegar

Combine sugar, mustard, salt, and flour in saucepan; set aside. Combine milk, egg yolk, and vinegar. Gradually stir liquid mixture into dry mixture. Cook over low heat, stirring constantly, about 10 minutes or until thickened. Serve over sliced ham or corned beef or use to dip ham cubes or frankfurters. Yield: about 1 cup.

HOT PARMESAN AND CHEDDAR DIP

4 cups (1 pound) shredded Cheddar
cheese
¼ cup grated Parmesan cheese
2 tablespoons all-purpose flour
1 (10¾-ounce) can condensed tomato
soup, undiluted
1 tablespoon instant minced onion
¼ cup dry sherry
1 teaspoon Worcestershire sauce
¼ teaspoon hot sauce

Toss together cheese and flour. Heat soup
and onion in a 2-quart saucepan. Reduce
heat; add cheese mixture and stir until
melted. Add sherry, Worcestershire
sauce, and hot sauce. Serve hot with vegetable dippers or cubes of French bread.
Yield: 3 cups.

PARMESAN CHILI DIP

1 (6-ounce) can chili without beans
½ cup grated Parmesan cheese
2 tablespoons instant minced onion

Combine all ingredients and heat through.
Serve with king-size corn chips. Yield: 2
cups.

HOT SHRIMP CHEESE DIP

1 (10¾-ounce) can condensed cream of
shrimp soup, undiluted
2 teaspoons instant minced onion
2 cups (8 ounces) shredded Swiss
cheese
1 (4½-ounce) can shrimp, drained and
diced
¼ cup dry sherry

Heat soup and onion in a 1½-quart saucepan. Reduce heat; add cheese and stir
until cheese is melted. Add shrimp and
sherry. Serve hot with vegetable dippers or
toasted breadsticks. Yield: 2¾ cups.

HASTY PARTY SPINACH DIP

1 (10-ounce) package frozen chopped
spinach
½ cup chopped green onions with tops
½ cup chopped fresh parsley
1 cup mayonnaise

Cook spinach according to package directions; drain well. Add remaining ingredients. Serve at room temperature with
king-size corn chips. Yield: about 3½
cups.

FRESH TOMATO AND ONION DIP

1 medium tomato, finely chopped
½ cup lemon juice
½ teaspoon salt
¼ teaspoon pepper
¼ cup finely chopped green onion
2 cups commercial sour cream
¼ teaspoon Worcestershire sauce
½ teaspoon sugar

Combine tomato, lemon juice, salt, and
pepper; add remaining ingredients and stir
well. Serve as dip for vegetables or potato
chips. Yield: about 3 cups.
Note: Dip may be used to stuff cherry
tomatoes by reducing lemon juice to 1
tablespoon.

VEGETABLE SAUCE

1 cup mayonnaise
2 teaspoons tarragon vinegar
1 teaspoon salt
⅛ teaspoon thyme
¼ teaspoon curry powder
2 tablespoons chili sauce or catsup
1 tablespoon dried minced onion
Dash of pepper

Combine all ingredients and mix well.
Chill until ready to serve. Serve with raw
vegetables. Yield: 1¼ cups.

FONDUE FOR TEENAGERS

> 2 tablespoons butter or margarine
> ¼ cup all-purpose flour
> 4 cups milk
> 4 cups (1 pound) shredded Swiss
>   cheese
> Dash of salt
> Dash of ground nutmeg (optional)

Melt butter in top of double boiler or over very low heat. Add flour, stirring until smooth. Cook 1 minute, stirring constantly. Gradually stir in milk; cook over medium heat, stirring constantly, until thickened and bubbly. Stir in cheese, blending until melted. Season with salt and nutmeg, if desired. Serve with cubes of garlic bread or toasted English muffins. Yield: 10 to 12 servings.

PIZZA FONDUE

> 1 medium onion, chopped
> ½ pound ground beef
> 2 tablespoons vegetable oil
> 2 (10½-ounce) cans pizza sauce
> 1 tablespoon cornstarch
> 1½ teaspoons fennel seeds
> 1½ teaspoons ground oregano
> ¼ teaspoon garlic powder
> 2½ cups (10 ounces) shredded Cheddar
>   cheese, divided
> 1 cup (4 ounces) shredded mozzarella
>   cheese

Brown onion and ground beef in oil; set aside. Combine pizza sauce, cornstarch, fennel, oregano, and garlic powder in blender container; blend until smooth. Add half of Cheddar cheese; blend until smooth. Gradually add remaining Cheddar cheese and mozzarella cheese; blend until smooth. Add to beef mixture and heat until cheese is melted. Serve in chafing dish or fondue pot with cubes of garlic bread or toasted English muffins. Yield: 10 to 12 servings.

SWISS FONDUE

> 4 cups (1 pound) shredded aged Swiss
>   cheese
> ¼ cup all-purpose flour
> 1 clove garlic, crushed
> 2 cups Sauterne
> ½ teaspoon salt
> ½ teaspoon Worcestershire sauce
> Dash of ground nutmeg

Toss together cheese, flour, and garlic. Heat Sauterne in large saucepan until bubbles rise. Reduce heat to low; add cheese, ½ cup at a time, stirring until cheese is melted after each addition. Add salt, Worcestershire sauce, and nutmeg. Serve hot with cubes of French bread, vegetable dippers, cooked ham cubes, or cooked shrimp. Yield: about 6 cups.

Variations:

Tomato-Swiss Fondue: Substitute tomato juice for Sauterne. Substitute 1 teaspoon crushed basil leaves for nutmeg.

Mock Fondue: Substitute white grape juice for Sauterne.

HEALTHY CEREAL SNACKS

> 2 cups quick-cooking oats, uncooked
> 1 cup wheat germ
> 2½ tablespoons sesame seeds
> 1 cup flaked coconut
> ½ cup slivered almonds
> ¾ cup raisins
> ½ cup chopped dates
> ¼ teaspoon ground cinnamon
> ⅛ teaspoon ground cloves
> ⅛ teaspoon ground ginger
> ½ teaspoon salt
> ¾ cup molasses
> ⅓ cup vegetable oil
> ½ teaspoon vanilla extract

Combine first 11 ingredients in a large bowl. Add molasses, oil, and vanilla; mix well. Spread mixture on baking sheets; bake at 300° for 30 minutes, stirring frequently. Cool and store in air-tight containers. Serve as a snack or as a cold cereal with milk. Yield: 5 cups.

CHEDDAR BOLOGNA WEDGES

½ cup (2 ounces) shredded Cheddar
  cheese
2 tablespoons cream cheese, softened
6 slices bologna sausage
12 pimiento-stuffed olives

Blend cheeses together in a small bowl. Spread about 2 tablespoons cheese mixture on each of 5 bologna slices; stack and top with additional slice. Chill. At serving time, cut into 12 wedges; garnish each with pimiento-stuffed olive secured with wooden pick. Yield: 12 appetizers.

MINTED PINEAPPLE HORS D'OEUVRES

1 (20-ounce) can pineapple chunks,
  drained
  White crème de menthe
  Fresh mint leaves (optional)

Cover pineapple with crème de menthe. Do not drain. Serve in watermelon shell or compote garnished with mint leaves. Chill thoroughly before serving. Serve with wooden picks. Yield: 12 to 15 servings.
  Note: This can be prepared a day or two ahead.

If there is no time to butter crumbs, simply shake crushed wheat germ right from the jar on to the food to be baked.

BACON AND YAM HORS D'OEUVRES

½ cup orange marmalade
1 tablespoon water
½ to 1 pound hickory smoked bacon
1 (29-ounce) can yams, drained and
  cut into 1-inch cubes

Combine marmalade and water; heat over low heat until melted. Cut each slice of bacon into 4 pieces. Dip cubes of potato in melted marmalade and wrap in piece of bacon. Secure with wooden pick. Bake at 350° for 5 minutes or until bacon is crisp. Serve hot. Yield: about 30 appetizers.

BLUE CHEESE SQUARES

1 to 1¼ cups (4 to 5 ounces) blue
  cheese
¼ cup butter or margarine, softened
  Garlic salt to taste (optional)
  Thinly sliced day-old bread

Cream cheese and butter thoroughly; season lightly with garlic salt, if desired. Cut crusts from bread; spread with cheese mixture. Cut each slice into 4 squares or 3 strips. Toast 20 to 30 minutes or until bread is very brown and crisp. Store in covered tin in refrigerator. Serve at room temperature. Yield: about 30 strips.

Observe these basic tips for food safety when shopping:
  Shop at clean, well-kept grocery stores.
  Run errands first, then shop for groceries—don't give frozen food a chance to defrost.
  Select refrigerated and frozen foods last before checking out.
  Make sure frozen foods are hard frozen.
  Make sure refrigerated foods are cold.
  Don't buy torn or damaged packages—even at so-called savings.

CHEDDAR CHEESE PUFFS

  1 **egg, separated**
  1 **cup (4 ounces) shredded Cheddar**
     cheese
  ½ **teaspoon baking powder**
     Melba toast rounds

Beat egg yolk and egg white separately. Combine egg yolk, cheese, and baking powder. Fold in egg white. Spread on toast rounds; broil until golden brown and puffy. Yield: 2 dozen appetizers.

CHEESE WAFERS

  1 **cup butter or margarine, softened**
  2 **cups (8 ounces) shredded Cheddar**
     cheese
  1 **cup all-purpose flour**
  1 **cup finely chopped nuts**
  ¼ **teaspoon cayenne pepper**

Combine all ingredients. Shape into a roll 1½ inches in diameter. Wrap in waxed paper; chill. Slice and place on a cookie sheet. Bake at 350° for 10 to 15 minutes. Yield: about 4 dozen.

HERBED CORNBREAD APPETIZERS

  2 **cups self-rising cornmeal**
  ½ **cup self-rising flour**
  2 **tablespoons sugar**
  ¼ **teaspoon ground nutmeg**
  ¼ **teaspoon ground oregano**
  ¼ **teaspoon thyme**
  ¼ **teaspoon sweet basil**
  1 **egg, beaten**
  1¼ **cups milk**
  ⅓ **cup melted shortening or**
     vegetable oil

Combine cornmeal, flour, sugar, nutmeg, oregano, thyme, and basil. Combine egg, milk, and shortening. Add liquid mixture to dry mixture, stirring well. Spoon into a well-greased 13- x 9- x 2-inch pan. Bake at 425° for 20 to 25 minutes or until golden brown. Cut into 3- x 1-inch pieces. Yield: 3 dozen appetizers.

FRIED EGGPLANT STICKS

  1 **large eggplant**
     All-purpose flour
     Salt and pepper to taste

Peel eggplant and cut into 2- x ½-inch sticks. Season flour with salt and pepper. Dredge eggplant in flour. Fry in hot oil until golden brown; drain well. Serve warm. Yield: 6 servings.

DEVILED HAM SQUARES

  2 **tablespoons butter or margarine,**
     softened
  1 **(4½-ounce) can deviled ham**
  2 **teaspoons minced onion**
  ½ **teaspoon prepared mustard**
  8 **slices white bread, toasted**
     Chopped fresh parsley
  8 **slices Cheddar cheese**

Combine butter, ham, onion, and mustard in small bowl; spread on bread. Place bread on baking sheet; sprinkle with parsley and top with cheese. Broil 2 to 3 minutes or until cheese starts to melt. Cut into quarters and serve. Yield: 32 appetizers.

The light or greenish yellow lemons are more tart than deep yellow ones.

CHEDDAR MUSHROOM CAPS

1 pound fresh mushrooms
Salt
1 pound Cheddar cheese, cubed
Paprika

Rinse mushrooms and remove stems. Sprinkle cavities with salt. Place a cheese cube in each mushroom cavity. Sprinkle with paprika. Place mushrooms on baking sheet; broil 2 to 3 minutes or until cheese bubbles. Yield: about 36 appetizers.

NACHOS

Shredded sharp Cheddar cheese
Large taco-flavored chips
Chopped green chili peppers

Place small amount of cheese on each chip. Top with piece of chili pepper. Bake at 350° or only until cheese melts. Serve immediately.

ONION PUFFS

½ cup mayonnaise
3 green onions, finely chopped
Melba toast rounds
Paprika

Combine mayonnaise and onion. Place teaspoonful of mayonnaise mixture on each toast round; spread to edge. Sprinkle with paprika. Broil about 1 to 3 minutes or until hot and bubbly. Yield: 1 dozen puffs.

Whole leaf herbs generally lose their freshness in a year or two and their color soon fades. Buy a little and use it fast.

COCKTAIL OYSTERS

½ cup finely chopped onion
2 tablespoons butter or margarine, melted
1 cup catsup
2 tablespoons Worcestershire sauce
1 teaspoon garlic salt
¼ teaspoon hot sauce
½ teaspoon monosodium glutamate (optional)
1 pint oysters, well drained

Sauté onion in butter. Add catsup, Worcestershire sauce, garlic salt, hot sauce, and monosodium glutamate, if desired; heat to boiling. Add oysters; heat only until edges of oysters curl. Serve hot in chafing dish with tiny pastry shells or small melba toast. Yield: 3¾ cups.

BABY PIZZAS

2 pounds ground beef
2 medium onions, chopped
2 cloves garlic, crushed
1 medium-size green pepper, chopped
2 (6-ounce) cans tomato paste
2 cans water
2 (8-ounce) cans tomato sauce
1 tablespoon ground oregano
2 teaspoons fennel seeds
1 teaspoon thyme
2 teaspoons garlic salt
1 (16-ounce) loaf party rye
Grated Parmesan cheese

Brown beef, onion, garlic, and green pepper in large skillet. Add next 7 ingredients and cook slowly until thick. Correct seasoning, if needed. Spread cooked sauce on party rye bread; sprinkle with Parmesan cheese. Bake at 350° just until heated through. Serve hot. Yield: about 4 dozen.

SAUSAGE IN APPLESAUCE

Cocktail sausage
Warm applesauce

Place sausage in baking dish; cover tightly. Steam in oven until hot. Serve from chafing dish with warm applesauce in compote. Spear with wooden picks and dip in applesauce.

Note: Bulk sausage may be used. Make tiny balls from highly seasoned sausage. Bake at 350° for 20 to 30 minutes or until well done. Drain thoroughly.

Smoked sausage may be used. Cut into ½-inch pieces and bake at 350° for 15 to 20 minutes.

COCKTAIL NUTTY MEATBALLS

- ½ cup peanut butter
- ½ pound ground beef
- ¼ cup finely chopped onion
- 2 tablespoons chili sauce
- 1 teaspoon salt
- 1 teaspoon ground sage
- ⅛ teaspoon pepper
- ½ cup quick-cooking oats, uncooked
- 1 egg, beaten
- ⅓ cup evaporated milk
- 2 (8-ounce) cans tomato sauce
- 1 teaspoon garlic salt
- ½ teaspoon ground oregano
- ¼ teaspoon pepper
- ¼ cup water

Combine first 10 ingredients. Shape into 30 balls. Bake at 350° for 20 to 25 minutes. Pour off drippings. Combine remaining ingredients and pour over meatballs; cover and simmer about 15 minutes. Serve with wooden picks from chafing dish. Yield: about 2½ dozen.

DEVILED MEATBALLS

- 1 cup (4 ounces) blue cheese
- ¼ cup mayonnaise
- 2 tablespoons Worcestershire sauce
- 1 teaspoon prepared mustard
- 2 cups crushed cornflakes
- ½ cup milk
- 1 egg, slightly beaten
- 1 pound ground beef
- 1½ teaspoons salt
- ⅛ teaspoon pepper

Combine all ingredients. Shape into 1-inch balls. Bake at 350° for 20 to 25 minutes. Yield: 2½ dozen.

Note: Balls may be made smaller to yield 40 to 50 appetizers. Bake at 350° for 15 minutes.

GERMAN MEATBALLS

- 1 pound ground beef
- ¾ cup catsup
- ½ cup water
- 3 bay leaves
- 2 tablespoons Worcestershire sauce
- ¼ cup vinegar
- 1 tablespoon lemon juice
- ¼ cup firmly packed brown sugar
- ¼ teaspoon dry mustard
- 2 gingersnaps, crushed

Shape meat into 1-inch balls. Bake at 350° for 20 minutes; drain. Combine remaining ingredients in saucepan; cook over medium heat for 5 minutes to dissolve sugar and gingersnaps. Add meatballs and simmer for 15 minutes. Serve with wooden picks. Yield: 30 meatballs.

Combine first 3 ingredients; shape into 1-inch balls. Bake at 350° for 15 minutes. Pour off drippings. Combine remaining ingredients in saucepan; add sausage balls. Simmer 20 minutes. Yield: 60 meatballs.

SAUSAGE BALLS IN CRANBERRY SAUCE

  1 **pound seasoned bulk pork sausage**
  2 **eggs, beaten**
  1 **cup fresh breadcrumbs**
  1 **teaspoon salt**
  ½ **teaspoon poultry seasoning**
  1 **(16-ounce) can jellied cranberry sauce**
  1 **tablespoon prepared mustard**

Combine sausage, eggs, breadcrumbs, salt, and poultry seasoning. Shape into 1-inch balls. Bake at 350° for 30 minutes. Combine cranberry sauce and mustard in medium saucepan; heat until melted. Add sausage balls. Cover and simmer 15 minutes. Yield: about 30 meatballs.

SWEET AND SOUR SAUSAGE BALLS

  2 **pounds bulk sausage**
  2 **eggs, beaten**
1½ **cups soft breadcrumbs**
1½ **cups catsup**
  ¼ **cup plus 2 tablespoons brown sugar**
  ¼ **cup wine vinegar**
  ¼ **cup soy sauce**

SPENCER-STYLE CATFISH MOLD

  ½ **pound catfish fillet (or any fish fillet), cooked and flaked**
1½ **cups (6 ounces) shredded Cheddar cheese**
  ½ **cup commercial sour cream**
  ¼ **cup chopped stuffed olives**
  2 **tablespoons lemon juice**
    Salt and pepper to taste

Combine all ingredients; chill. Shape into a mold and serve with crackers. Yield: about 3 cups.

CHEESE AND SHRIMP PÂTÉ

  2 **(8-ounce) packages cream cheese, softened**
  2 **(6½-ounce) cans shrimp, drained**
  3 **tablespoons lemon juice**
  2 **tablespoons grated onion**
  2 **tablespoons chopped parsley**
  1 **tablespoon prepared horseradish**
  2 **drops of hot sauce**
  ½ **cup crushed potato chips**
  ½ **cup chopped parsley**

Mix cream cheese until smooth. Mash shrimp. Combine first 7 ingredients; shape into a mound on a serving plate. Combine potato chips and parsley and sprinkle liberally over shrimp mold. Chill. Serve with party breads, crackers, or raw vegetables. Yield: about 3 cups.

LIVERWURST PÂTÉ

½ cup half-and-half
½ pound liver sausage
1 (3-ounce) package cream cheese, softened
1 tablespoon Worcestershire sauce
¾ to 1 teaspoon curry powder
2 tablespoons sherry
¼ teaspoon salt
¼ teaspoon coarse black pepper
¼ teaspoon thyme
¼ teaspoon marjoram
¼ cup chopped onion
2 hard-cooked eggs, chopped

Combine all ingredients; blend until smooth. Chill. Serve with assorted crackers. Yield: about 1½ cups.

STRAWBERRY CHEESE MOLD

4 cups (1 pound) shredded sharp Cheddar cheese
1 small onion, grated
2 tablespoons milk
   Cayenne pepper to taste
½ cup mayonnaise
1½ cups coarsely chopped pecans
   About ¾ cup strawberry preserves

Combine cheese, onion, milk, pepper, and mayonnaise. Stir in pecans until well blended. Pat mixture into a round container or serving plate, forming a slight rim around the top edge. Refrigerate until well chilled. Just before serving, fill center with strawberry preserves. Serve with assorted crackers. Yield: about 7½ cups.

SHRIMP MOLD

5 (4½-ounce) cans shrimp, drained
¼ cup lemon juice
½ cup butter or margarine, melted
1 tablespoon prepared horseradish
1 medium onion, grated
1 cup mayonnaise
½ teaspoon seasoned salt
¼ teaspoon seasoned pepper (optional)

Wash shrimp in cold water and mash thoroughly. Combine with remaining ingredients. Place mixture in a 4-cup mold. Chill until ready to serve. Unmold and serve with assorted crackers. Yield: about 3½ cups.

TUNA MOLD

2 (7-ounce) cans tuna, drained and flaked
2 (3-ounce) packages cream cheese, softened
2 tablespoons capers
2 tablespoons mayonnaise
½ teaspoon Worcestershire sauce
2 teaspoons prepared horseradish
¼ cup finely minced onion
2 cloves garlic, crushed
½ teaspoon celery salt

Combine all ingredients. Pack into a 3-cup mold; chill until ready to serve. Remove from mold and serve with sesame crackers. Yield: about 2½ cups.

Hard cook eggs the day before, store in refrigerator, shell, and chop or sieve at the last minute.

ARTICHOKE COCKTAIL SPREAD

1 (14-ounce) can artichoke hearts, drained and finely chopped
1 cup mayonnaise
1 cup grated Parmesan cheese
Dash of garlic salt (optional)
Dash of hot sauce (optional)
Curry powder

Combine artichoke hearts, mayonnaise, cheese, and garlic salt and hot sauce, if desired. Pour into shallow baking dish. Sprinkle top with curry powder. Bake at 350° for 30 to 40 minutes. Serve warm with assorted crackers. Yield: about 4 cups.

BEER CHEESE SPREAD

¼ cup beer
2 cups (8 ounces) crumbled blue cheese
1 (3-ounce) package cream cheese, softened
1 teaspoon Worcestershire sauce
¼ teaspoon salt
1 clove garlic, crushed
Dash of hot sauce

Place all ingredients in electric blender; blend until smooth, using rubber spatula as necessary. Serve with sesame crackers. Yield: about 2½ cups.
Note: Wine or brandy may be substituted for beer.

COCKTAIL CHEESE SPREAD

1 (16-ounce) package process cheese spread
½ cup mayonnaise
1 (5-ounce) jar prepared horseradish
5 drops of hot sauce
½ pound bacon, cooked and crumbled

Cut cheese into cubes and place in top of double boiler; cook over hot water until cheese melts. Add mayonnaise, horseradish, hot sauce, and bacon. Pour into a 3-cup serving container. Chill. Serve with assorted crackers. Yield: 4 cups.
Note: This will keep several weeks in the refrigerator.

CORNED BEEF SPREAD

1 (12-ounce) can corned beef
1 tablespoon prepared horseradish
1 tablespoon Dijon-style mustard
¼ cup sweet pickle relish
¼ to ⅓ cup mayonnaise

Mash corned beef; add horseradish, mustard, and pickle relish. Add mayonnaise to make spreading consistency. Serve with assorted crackers. Yield: about 2 cups.

QUICK AND EASY CRAB SPREAD

2 (6½-ounce) cans crabmeat, drained and flaked
2 (8-ounce) packages cream cheese
1 medium onion, grated
2 tablespoons prepared horseradish
¼ teaspoon garlic salt

Combine all ingredients in large saucepan. Cook over low heat just until cheese is melted and mixture is heated through. Serve with assorted crackers. Yield: about 3¾ cups.

CRAZY SPREAD

1 cup pecans
2 hard-cooked eggs
1 medium onion
1 (4½-ounce) jar pimiento-stuffed olives
1 cup mayonnaise
½ teaspoon garlic salt
½ teaspoon monosodium glutamate (optional)
¼ teaspoon cayenne pepper

Grind pecans, eggs, onion, and olives in food grinder; add remaining ingredients. Use as spread for cocktail sandwiches. Yield: about 3 cups.

SMOKED FISH SPREAD

1½ pounds smoked fish
2 teaspoons minced onion
2 teaspoons finely chopped celery
1 clove garlic, crushed
2 tablespoons finely chopped sweet pickle
1¼ cups mayonnaise
1 tablespoon prepared mustard
Dash of Worcestershire sauce
2 tablespoons chopped fresh parsley

Remove skin and bones from fish. Flake fish well. Combine with remaining ingredients and chill. Serve with assorted crackers or party breads. Yield: 3½ cups.

OLIVE COCKTAIL SPREAD

3 cups (12 ounces) shredded Cheddar cheese
1 cup mayonnaise
2 (4½-ounce) cans black olives, drained and chopped
¼ cup grated onion
Salt to taste
¼ teaspoon curry powder
1 (16-ounce) loaf thinly sliced bread

Combine first 6 ingredients. Spread mixture on bread; cut bread into quarters. Bake at 350° until cheese melts. Yield: about 80 appetizers.

SPINACH SPREAD

1 (10-ounce) package frozen chopped spinach
1 (8-ounce) package cream cheese
2 to 3 tablespoons milk
2 tablespoons butter or margarine
Dash of ground nutmeg
6 to 8 slices bacon, cooked and crumbled
1 to 1¼ tablespoons lemon juice
Salt and pepper to taste
¼ teaspoon monosodium glutamate (optional)

Cook spinach according to package directions; drain well. Combine cream cheese, milk, and butter in top of double boiler; cook over low heat stirring constantly until cheese is melted and mixture is smooth. Stir in spinach and remaining ingredients. Chill. Serve with assorted crackers. Yield: about 2½ cups.

CURRIED TUNA SPREAD

1 (6½-ounce) can tuna, drained and flaked
3 hard-cooked eggs, finely chopped
1 teaspoon curry powder
¼ teaspoon garlic salt
⅛ to ¼ teaspoon hot sauce
Mayonnaise

Combine first 5 ingredients. Add only enough mayonnaise to hold mixture together. Pack into a 2-cup mold and chill until ready to serve. Serve with butter-flavored crackers. Yield: 1½ cups.

Note: More or less curry can be added, if desired.

Entrees

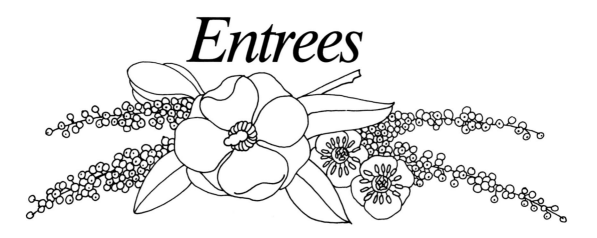

So you want to entertain, but you say you cannot find the time. The solution to the problem is to have a selection of quick and easy entree recipes readily available. Once the entree is selected, the remainder of the meal seems to fall in place.

An entree is usually a high protein main dish, but it can also be a vegetable or a meatless pasta. The secret is to have it well seasoned and served at the peak of perfection. Entrees usually will be your largest investment so they deserve careful consideration. Here is a collection of entrees that fit all categories: hearty, filling, satisfying, and tasty. And remember to plan for plenty, just in case the guests ask for seconds.

The popular meats are included here because it is hard to beat traditional Sunday chicken dinner, a quick meat loaf during the week, or the luscious steak on Saturday night. And what can be more elegant, but quick, than a colorful fish fillet or the highly respected liver served as a stroganoff? Quick and easy steps are paralleled with good flavor and good looks in these entrees.

Thus, even if you are busy, the following entree ideas will allow you to entertain easily or quickly prepare a surprise family meal.

BEEF FONDUE

1 pound boneless sirloin tip, cut into ¾-inch cubes
Brown Mushroom Sauce or Sour Cream Curry Sauce
1 cup butter or margarine
2 cups vegetable oil

Carefully trim off all fat and connective tissue from meat. Place meat in bowl and refrigerate. Prepare Brown Mushroom Sauce or Sour Cream Curry Sauce for dipping. About 20 minutes before serving, heat butter and vegetable oil in a saucepan. When mixture bubbles and begins to brown, pour it into a 2-quart fondue pot. The hot oil should not be more than 2 inches deep.

Place fondue pot on stand and light canned heat or use electric fondue pot. When oil begins to bubble, pierce a cube of beef with fondue fork and lower into hot oil. Cook 2 to 3 minutes. Push meat off fork onto individual plate. Dip into Brown Mushroom Sauce or Sour Cream Curry Sauce. Yield: 2 to 3 servings.

Brown Mushroom Sauce:

2 tablespoons butter or margarine
2 tablespoons all-purpose flour
⅔ cup consommé
1 teaspoon Worcestershire sauce
½ cup finely chopped mushrooms
½ cup commercial sour cream

Melt butter in a saucepan; stir in flour. Remove from heat and gradually stir in consommé. Return to heat and cook, stirring until thickened. Blend in Worcestershire sauce, mushrooms, and sour cream. Serve hot. Yield: 1⅓ cups.

Sour Cream Curry Sauce:

1 cup commercial sour cream
½ to 1 teaspoon curry powder
1 teaspoon prepared horseradish
¼ teaspoon sugar
⅛ teaspoon salt
Paprika

Combine all ingredients except paprika. Place in small serving bowl and sprinkle lightly with paprika. Yield: 1 cup.

BROILED FLANK STEAK

1 (1½-pound) flank steak
Salt
Pepper

Have meat at refrigerator temperature. With a sharp knife, remove tough membrane from surface of meat. Broil about 5 minutes on each side, and season to taste with salt and pepper. To serve, hold a sharp knife at an angle almost flat to the top of the meat and slice diagonally into very thin slices. Yield: 3 to 4 servings.

Note: Meat may be covered with prepared mustard on second side before broiling.

PANBROILED STEAKS

2 cloves garlic, sliced
Vegetable oil
4 slices of sirloin roast, cut ¼ to ½ inch thick

Sauté garlic in a small amount of oil in a medium skillet; remove garlic. Add meat, browning for 1½ to 2 minutes on each side. Meat slices are at their tender best when still slightly pink inside. Serve with juices from pan. Yield: 4 servings.

BROILED FROZEN PORTERHOUSE STEAK

Frozen Porterhouse steaks, cut 1¼ inch thick
Salt and pepper to taste

Set oven to broil. Place steak on rack in broiler pan. Broil steak 4½ to 5 inches from heat until browned on one side, about 22 minutes; season steak; turn and broil on other side. Allow 40 to 45 minutes total cooking time for broiling 1¼-inch thick steak to rare; 45 to 55 minutes to medium.

TERIYAKI STEAK

½ cup soy sauce
¼ cup dry white wine
1 clove garlic, crushed
2 tablespoons sugar
½ teaspoon ground ginger
2 pounds sirloin steak or rib steak, cut ½ inch thick

Combine first 5 ingredients and stir to dissolve sugar. Place steak in heavy-duty plastic bag; pour marinade over steak. Secure plastic bag making sure marinade surrounds the meat and place on tray in refrigerator for 15 minutes. Remove steak from sauce and place meat in heatproof dish. Broil 2½ minutes on each side for medium rare—3 minutes each side for medium well. Yield: 4 servings.

Note: To grill steak, remove meat from dish, and cook as above.

QUICK STROGANOFF

2 pounds round steak
Salt
Pepper
5 tablespoons butter or margarine, divided
3 tablespoons chopped onion
2½ tablespoons all-purpose flour
4 beef bouillon cubes
2 cups hot water
½ cup commercial sour cream
2 tablespoons tomato paste

Cut steak into thin strips, about 1 inch wide. Sprinkle with salt and pepper. Melt 3 tablespoons butter or margarine in medium skillet. Add meat and onion, cooking until meat is browned. Remove meat and onion from skillet and melt remaining butter over low heat. Add flour, stirring until smooth. Cook 1 minute, stirring constantly.

Dissolve bouillon cubes in 2 cups hot water; gradually add to skillet mixture and cook over medium heat, stirring constantly, until thickened and bubbly. Alternately add sour cream and tomato paste, stirring constantly. Simmer gently, without boiling, for 1 minute. Add meat and onion to sauce and simmer for 15 minutes. Yield: 6 servings.

EASY BEEF STROGANOFF

1 (1⅜-ounce) envelope dry onion soup mix
2 tablespoons all-purpose flour
½ cup water
1 (4-ounce) can mushroom pieces, undrained
3 cups cooked, diced beef
1 cup commercial sour cream
Hot cooked rice

Combine soup mix, flour, and water in large saucepan; heat until smooth and thick, stirring constantly. Add mushrooms and beef; heat. Add sour cream before serving. Serve beef mixture over rice. Yield: 6 servings.

When freezing meat patties, steaks, or chops, separate them with two thicknesses of wrapping material between them so that the pieces can be separated without thawing more than needed.

BEEF STROGANOFF AND NOODLES

1 pound cubed steak, cut in strips
  Vegetable oil
1 medium onion, sliced
1 clove garlic, crushed
1 (10-ounce) can cream of mushroom
  soup, undiluted
1 cup commercial sour cream
2 tablespoons catsup
2 teaspoons Worcestershire sauce
1 (3-ounce) can sliced mushrooms,
  undrained
3 cups cooked noodles
1 tablespoon melted butter or
  margarine

Brown meat strips in small amount of hot oil in large skillet. Add onion and garlic; cook just until tender. Combine soup, sour cream, catsup, Worcestershire sauce, and mushrooms; pour over meat and heat through. Toss noodles with butter. Serve sauce over noodles. Yield: 4 servings.

CHEESY CORNED BEEF BARBECUE

1 (12-ounce) can corned beef
6 slices bread, toasted
½ cup catsup
2 teaspoons prepared horseradish
2 teaspoons prepared mustard
2 teaspoons vinegar
2 teaspoons finely chopped onion
6 slices Swiss cheese

Cut corned beef into 6 slices. Place each slice of corned beef on a slice of toast in a shallow baking dish. Combine catsup, horseradish, mustard, vinegar, and onion; spread half of sauce over corned beef. Top with cheese. Spread remaining sauce over cheese. Bake at 350° for 10 to 15 minutes or until bubbly. Yield: 6 servings.

POACHED EGGS IN HASH

1 (7½-ounce) can corned beef hash
2 tablespoons chili sauce
4 eggs
  Mustard Sauce

Combine hash and chili sauce. Press mixture into two 1½-cup shallow baking dishes or ramekins. Make 2 depressions in mixture in each dish with back of spoon. Break and slip an egg into each depression. Bake at 350° for 30 to 35 minutes or until eggs are cooked to desired doneness. Top each serving with 1 to 2 tablespoons Mustard Sauce. Yield: 2 servings.

Mustard Sauce:

1 egg
¼ cup water
¼ cup vinegar
2 tablespoons sugar
1½ tablespoons dry mustard
1 tablespoon butter or margarine
¼ teaspoon salt
  Dash of ground nutmeg

Measure all ingredients into container of electric blender or small mixing bowl. Blend at medium speed. Pour into small saucepan. Cook over medium heat, stirring constantly, just until mixture comes to a boil. Remove from heat. Yield: 1 cup.

BARBECUED MEAT CAKES

1 pound ground beef
1 egg, beaten
1 cup puffed rice cereal, divided
1 teaspoon salt
¼ teaspoon pepper
¼ cup finely chopped onion
3 tablespoons brown sugar
¼ cup catsup
⅛ teaspoon ground nutmeg
1 teaspoon dry mustard

Combine meat, egg, ¾ cup cereal, salt, pepper, and onion; mix well. Combine sugar, catsup, nutmeg, and mustard; add half of sauce to meat mixture and mix well. Shape into 8 to 10 balls and place in 2-inch muffin pans. Top each with remaining sauce. Sprinkle with remaining ¼ cup cereal. Bake at 400° for 20 minutes. Yield: 4 to 5 servings.

BEEF BALLS ORIENTAL

 1 **pound ground beef**
 1 **egg**
 ¼ **cup cornstarch, divided**
 1 **teaspoon salt**
 2 **tablespoons chopped onion**
   Dash of pepper
 2 **tablespoons vegetable oil**
 1 **(16-ounce) can pineapple chunks**
 3 **tablespoons soy sauce**
 3 **tablespoons vinegar**
 ¼ **cup plus 2 tablespoons water**
 ½ **cup sugar**
 2 **small green peppers, chopped**

Combine beef, egg, 1 tablespoon cornstarch, salt, onion, and pepper; shape into 1-inch balls. Brown in 2 tablespoons hot oil in medium skillet; drain. Drain pineapple; add additional water, if necessary, to make 1 cup. Combine 3 tablespoons cornstarch, soy sauce, vinegar, water, and sugar; add to pineapple juice and cook until mixture thickens, stirring constantly. Add meatballs, pineapple, and green peppers. Heat thoroughly. Yield: 6 servings.

Note: May be served over hot rice or as an hors d'oeuvre.

Baste a roast with wine or wine vinegar for a distinctive flavor.

TOP-OF-STOVE CASSEROLE

 1 **pound ground beef**
 1 **small onion, chopped**
 1 **(16-ounce) can tomatoes**
 ½ **cup uncooked regular rice**
 ½ **cup water**
 1 **tablespoon sugar**
 1 **(16-ounce) can green peas**
   Salt and pepper to taste

Brown meat and onion in a large skillet; drain. Add tomatoes, rice, water, and sugar. Cover and cook over low heat about 25 minutes or until rice is tender. Add peas and season. Heat slowly until hot. Yield: 6 servings.

ONE-DISH DINNER

 1 **pound ground beef**
 1 **tablespoon vegetable oil**
 1 **small green pepper, finely chopped**
 1 **small onion, chopped**
 1 **teaspoon ground oregano**
 1 **teaspoon fennel seeds (optional)**
 1 **(8-ounce) package noodles, uncooked**
 1 **(17-ounce) can cream-style corn**
 ½ **teaspoon garlic salt**
 ⅛ **teaspoon pepper**
 1 **(10½-ounce) can tomato soup, undiluted**
 ½ **cup Burgundy wine (optional)**
   Grated Romano or Parmesan cheese (optional)

Brown beef in oil in skillet; add green pepper, onion, oregano, and fennel, if desired. Cook noodles in boiling salted water for 5 or 6 minutes; drain. Layer half of noodles, meat, and corn in a greased 2-quart casserole; season with garlic salt and pepper. Repeat layers. Combine tomato soup and wine, if desired; pour over casserole. Bake at 350° for 30 minutes. Top with cheese, if desired. Yield: 6 servings.

HAMBURGER SURPRISE

1 (8-ounce) package egg noodles, uncooked
2 beef bouillon cubes
2 pounds ground beef
1 large onion, chopped
1 (6-ounce) can tomato paste
¼ cup water
1 teaspoon garlic salt
¼ teaspoon pepper
1 (3-ounce) package cream cheese, softened
1 (10¾-ounce) can cream of mushroom soup, undiluted
1 cup commercial sour cream
1 cup (4 ounces) shredded Cheddar cheese

Cook noodles according to package directions, adding beef bouillon cubes to boiling water; drain. Place noodles in a greased 2-quart casserole. Combine beef and onion in large skillet; cook until meat is browned and onions are tender. Add tomato paste and water; mix well. Cook about 3 minutes. Add garlic salt and pepper; spoon over noodles. Beat cream cheese until smooth; add soup and sour cream; stir until blended. Pour over meat mixture. Bake at 350° for 15 minutes or until heated through. Top with Cheddar cheese. Bake 5 additional minutes or until cheese is melted. Yield: 8 servings.

QUICK CHOP SUEY ON RICE

2 pounds ground beef
2 medium onions, thinly sliced
1 medium-size green pepper, finely chopped
1 (16-ounce) can bean sprouts, drained
1 (8-ounce) can sliced water chestnuts, drained
2 tablespoons chopped pimiento
¼ cup soy sauce
Salt and pepper to taste
3 cups hot cooked rice

Brown meat quickly over medium heat in large skillet. Add onion and green pepper. Continue cooking until vegetables are tender, about 5 minutes. Add sprouts, water chestnuts, pimiento, and soy sauce. Season with salt and pepper. Cook until heated thoroughly. Serve on rice. Yield: 6 servings.

GROUND BEEF CURRY

1 large onion, chopped
1 clove garlic, crushed
3 tablespoons melted butter or margarine
1 pound ground beef
1 tablespoon curry powder
1½ teaspoons salt
⅛ teaspoon pepper
2 large tomatoes, peeled and diced
2 medium potatoes, peeled and diced
1 (10-ounce) package frozen green peas, partially thawed
Coconut (optional)
Hot cooked rice

Sauté onion and garlic in butter in large skillet. Add ground beef and cook until browned. Stir in curry, salt, pepper, tomatoes, potatoes, and peas. Cover and simmer for 25 minutes. Sprinkle with coconut, if desired. Serve over hot rice. Yield: 6 servings.

DEEP DISH MEAT LOAF PIE

1 egg, slightly beaten
¼ cup water
3 tablespoons Worcestershire sauce
½ teaspoon salt
1 pound ground beef
1 cup soft breadcrumbs
Pastry for single-crust 9-inch pie
2 slices American cheese

Combine egg, water, Worcestershire sauce, and salt in large mixing bowl. Add ground beef and breadcrumbs; mix lightly. Pat into an ungreased 9-inch piepan. Roll out pastry to 10-inch circle; cut slits to let steam escape. Arrange pastry over meat, fold edges under, and crimp. Bake at 400° for 30 to 35 minutes. Cut cheese into wedges; arrange on top of hot pie. Return to oven and bake 5 minutes longer. Yield: 6 servings.

SPAGHETTI IN ONE POT

 1 pound ground beef
 1 medium onion, sliced
 1 clove garlic, crushed
 2 teaspoons salt
¼ teaspoon pepper
 1 teaspoon whole oregano
 1 teaspoon sweet basil
 1 tablespoon prepared mustard
 1 (8-ounce) package spaghetti, broken into fourths
 3 cups tomato juice or cocktail vegetable juice
 1 (8-ounce) can tomato sauce
 1 (8-ounce) can mushrooms (optional)
 1 cup (4 ounces) cubed Cheddar cheese
   Grated Parmesan cheese (optional)

Combine ground beef, onion, and garlic in a 2-quart saucepan; cook until meat is browned and onion is tender. Drain. Add salt, pepper, oregano, basil, and mustard; stir. Add spaghetti, tomato juice, and tomato sauce. Cook 15 minutes or until spaghetti is tender, stirring occasionally. Add mushrooms, if desired, and Cheddar cheese; stir. Serve topped with Parmesan cheese, if desired. Yield: 5 to 6 servings.

For a delicious aroma, add some red wine to the skillet while frying hamburgers.

GOULASH SOUP

 2 cups chopped onion
 3 tablespoons melted butter or margarine
½ pound ground beef
 1 quart tomato juice
 2 beef bouillon cubes
½ cup uncooked regular rice
 1 teaspoon salt
½ teaspoon paprika
 1 bay leaf
⅛ teaspoon pepper

Sauté onion in butter in large saucepan until tender; add meat and cook until browned. Add remaining ingredients. Cover and simmer for 20 minutes. Yield: 6 servings.

PITA BREAD PIZZA

 1 (7- to 8-inch) pita bread round
 3 tablespoons tomato sauce or tomato soup
¼ pound cooked ground beef or bulk pork sausage, sliced pepperoni, or any desired cooked meat
½ small onion, chopped and partially cooked
 2 tablespoons chopped green pepper
 2 tablespoons chopped ripe olives
 2 tablespoons chopped mushrooms
¼ teaspoon ground oregano
   Garlic salt to taste
   Pepper to taste
¼ cup shredded mozzarella cheese

Cut pita bread crosswise to yield 2 round crusts. Place pita bread on baking sheet; spread cut side with tomato sauce, meat, and any or all of the remaining ingredients. Top with cheese. Bake at 400° for 20 minutes. Yield: 1 serving.

Note: Additional toppings: chopped and partially cooked green pepper, chopped anchovies, cooked shrimp, chopped green olives, and grated Parmesan cheese.

FRIED CATFISH FILLETS

2 pounds skinned catfish fillets, fresh
    or frozen
2 teaspoons salt
¼ teaspoon pepper
2 eggs, beaten
2 tablespoons milk
1½ cups cornmeal
    Hot vegetable oil
    Lemon wedges

Thaw frozen fish. Cut fish into serving-size portions; season with salt and pepper. Combine eggs and milk. Dip fish in egg mixture, then in cornmeal. Place in single layer in hot oil in a 10-inch skillet; fry over medium heat for 7 to 8 minutes. Turn carefully and fry for 7 or 8 minutes longer or until fish is brown and flakes easily when tested with a fork. Drain on absorbent paper. Garnish with lemon wedges. Yield: 6 servings.

POACHED SALMON

1 quart water
1 cup dry white wine
1 tablespoon cider vinegar
1 large carrot, sliced
1 celery stalk, sliced
2 tablespoons chopped parsley
1 bay leaf
2 teaspoons salt
¼ teaspoon pepper
4 salmon steaks
    Mayonnaise Sauce

Combine first 9 ingredients in a Dutch oven; simmer 15 minutes. Remove bay leaf. Add salmon steaks to Dutch oven; cover. Cook over low heat for 15 minutes or until fish flakes easily. Serve hot topped with Mayonnaise Sauce. Yield: 4 servings.

Mayonnaise Sauce:

1 (10¾-ounce) can cream of celery
    soup, undiluted
1 to 2 tablespoons lemon juice
½ cup mayonnaise

Combine all ingredients. Heat, stirring to make a smooth sauce. Yield: about 1½ cups.

Note: Salmon may be wrapped in cheese cloth to prevent separating.

SNAPPER FILLETS, YUCATAN STYLE

2 pounds snapper fillets, fresh or
    frozen
2 tablespoons lemon juice
1 teaspoon salt
1 cup sliced onion
¼ cup vegetable oil
1 tablespoon all-purpose flour
½ cup sliced stuffed olives
¼ cup chopped pimiento
¾ cup orange juice
⅛ teaspoon saffron (optional)

Thaw frozen fish. Place fillets in a single layer, skin side down, in a well-greased 12- x 8- x 2-inch baking dish. Sprinkle lemon juice and salt over fish. Sauté onion in a 10-inch skillet in oil until soft but not brown. Blend in flour. Add olives, pimiento, orange juice, and saffron, if desired. Cook, stirring constantly, until sauce is thickened. Pour sauce over fish. Bake at 350° for 20 minutes or until fish flakes easily with a fork. Yield: 6 servings.

Fish is at its best when thawed in the refrigerator. Place it in the refrigerator the night before using or for last minute defrosting, soak in cold water until fillets are separated.

BROILED FISH SURPRISE

2 pounds fish fillets, fresh or frozen
2 tablespoons melted butter or
 margarine
2 teaspoons salt
1 (8-ounce) can tomato sauce
1 medium onion, chopped
1 cup (4 ounces) shredded sharp
 Cheddar cheese

Thaw frozen fish; cut into 6 portions. Arrange fish, skin side down, in a well-greased baking pan; brush with butter. Sprinkle with salt. Broil about 3 inches from heat about 8 minutes. Pour tomato sauce over fish; sprinkle with onion and cheese. Broil until cheese melts and fish flakes easily when tested with a fork, about 4 minutes. Yield: 6 servings.

JIFFY BROILED FILLETS

2 pounds fish fillets, fresh or frozen
2 tablespoons vegetable oil
2 tablespoons soy sauce
2 tablespoons Worcestershire sauce
½ teaspoon chili powder
1 teaspoon paprika
½ teaspoon garlic powder
 Dash of hot sauce
 Lemon wedges

Thaw frozen fillets. Place fillets in a single layer, skin side down, on a well-greased large broiler pan. Combine remaining ingredients except lemon. Pour sauce over fillets. Broil about 4 inches from heat for 10 to 15 minutes or until fillets flake easily when tested with a fork. Baste once during broiling with sauce in pan. Garnish with lemon. Yield: 6 servings.

Store fresh, raw poultry and ground meat in the refrigerator 3 to 5 days or in the freezer up to 12 months.

FISH AND CHEESE

1 pound fresh or frozen fish fillets
 (perch, haddock, or turbot)
⅔ cup cream of celery soup, undiluted
¾ cup commercial sour cream
1 cup (4 ounces) shredded Cheddar
 cheese, divided

Thaw and drain frozen fillets. Arrange fish, skin side down, in a single layer in a greased 2-quart shallow baking dish. Combine soup, sour cream, and ¾ cup cheese in a small saucepan; heat until cheese melts. Spread over fillets. Bake at 375° for 20 to 25 minutes or until fish flakes easily when tested with a fork. Sprinkle with remaining ¼ cup cheese. Return to oven for 5 more minutes. Yield: 4 servings.

RICE-RINGED FISH

1 pound frozen fish fillets, thawed
 Melted butter or margarine
 Salt and pepper to taste
1 (4-ounce) can mushrooms
1 cup uncooked regular rice
1 teaspoon salt
1 (10¾-ounce) can cream of shrimp
 soup, undiluted

Separate fillets and arrange, skin side down, in a greased baking pan. Brush with butter and season. Bake at 375° for 15 minutes. Spread soup over fillets and bake 15 additional minutes.

To prepare rice, drain mushrooms, adding enough water to liquid to make 2 cups. Combine liquid, rice, mushrooms, and salt in a saucepan; heat to boiling and stir. Cover and simmer 14 minutes or until all liquid is absorbed. Serve rice ringed around fish and sauce. Yield: 4 servings.

STOVE-TOP FISH DINNER

1 large onion, chopped
3 tablespoons vegetable oil
2 tablespoons chopped parsley
1 (8-ounce) can tomato sauce
½ cup water
½ teaspoon salt
⅛ teaspoon pepper
1 pound frozen fish fillets, partially
    thawed

Sauté onion in vegetable oil in large skillet until tender. Add parsley, tomato sauce, water, and seasonings. Cook 5 minutes longer. Add fish; cover and simmer about 10 minutes or until fish flakes easily. Baste twice during cooking. Yield: 4 servings.

SKILLET-STYLE TUNA CASSEROLE

½ cup butter or margarine
1 (8-ounce) package elbow macaroni,
    uncooked
1 large onion, chopped
1 medium-size green pepper, chopped
1½ teaspoons salt
½ teaspoon pepper
1½ cups water
3 chicken bouillon cubes
1 tablespoon all-purpose flour
1 (13-ounce) can evaporated milk
2 tablespoons chopped pimiento
1 teaspoon poultry seasoning
2 cups (8 ounces) shredded sharp
    Cheddar cheese
1 (6½-ounce) can tuna, drained and
    flaked

Melt butter in large skillet over low heat; add macaroni, onion, green pepper, salt, and pepper. Cook, stirring occasionally, over medium heat 7 to 8 minutes or until onion becomes transparent. Add water and bouillon cubes; bring to a boil. Cover and cook 20 minutes or until macaroni is tender. Sprinkle flour over mixture and blend well. Stir in evaporated milk, pimiento, poultry seasoning, cheese, and tuna. Cook 5 minutes at low temperature until cheese is completely melted, stirring occasionally. Serve hot. Yield: 6 to 8 servings.

QUICK SEAFOOD CHOWDER

1½ cups milk
1 (10-ounce) can cream of shrimp
    soup, undiluted
1 (10-ounce) package frozen green
    peas and carrots
1 tablespoon instant minced onion
1 pound frozen fish fillets, thawed
1 cup (4 ounces) shredded Cheddar
    cheese (optional)

Combine milk, soup, frozen vegetables, and onion in a 2-quart saucepan. Cut fish fillets into small pieces; add to milk mixture. Cook 10 to 15 minutes or until vegetables are tender and fish is cooked. Stir occasionally. Stir in cheese, if desired, until melted. Yield: 6 servings.

SEAFOOD CASSEROLE

2 cups peeled and cooked shrimp
1 cup crabmeat, flaked
3 tablespoons grated onion
3 tablespoons chopped green pepper
1 cup cooked brown rice
1 cup cooked green peas
½ teaspoon salt
⅛ teaspoon pepper
1 teaspoon Worcestershire sauce
1 cup mayonnaise
½ cup buttered breadcrumbs

Combine all ingredients except breadcrumbs. Place in a greased 2-quart baking dish; sprinkle with breadcrumbs. Bake at 350° for 30 minutes. Yield: 6 servings.

CLAM CHOWDER

2 medium potatoes, pared and diced,
    or 1 (16-ounce) can potatoes,
    drained and diced
1 large onion, thinly sliced
¼ cup chopped celery, stalk and leaves
2 teaspoons chopped parsley
1½ cups water
½ teaspoon salt
1 (7½-ounce) can minced clams
3 cups milk
3 tablespoons all-purpose flour
    Salt and pepper to taste

Combine potatoes, onion, celery, parsley, water, and salt in a saucepan; cook gently until vegetables are tender. Mash some of the potatoes with a fork. Drain clams, reserving juice. Add clams and milk to vegetable mixture; heat just to boiling. Combine clam juice and flour; stir to make a smooth paste. Stir into chowder, stirring constantly until slightly thickened. Adjust seasonings. Do not boil. Serve hot. Yield: 6 to 8 servings.

BAKED RICE CRAB SALAD

1 cup cooked rice
1½ cups mayonnaise
1 cup crabmeat, flaked
1 cup half-and-half or milk
6 hard-cooked eggs, chopped
1 tablespoon chopped fresh parsley
1 teaspoon minced onion
½ teaspoon salt
¼ teaspoon cayenne pepper
⅛ teaspoon pepper
½ cup shredded process American
    cheese

Combine all ingredients except cheese; place in a 1½-quart baking dish. Sprinkle with cheese. Bake at 350° for 20 minutes. Yield: 6 servings.

ELEGANT CRAB LUNCH

1 tomato
½ pound crabmeat
2 English muffins, split, toasted, and
    buttered
½ cup mayonnaise
¼ cup chili sauce
1 tablespoon lemon juice
1 tablespoon Worcestershire sauce
4 slices bacon, cooked and crumbled
1 hard-cooked egg, sieved

Place 1 slice of tomato and one-fourth of crabmeat on each half of English muffin. Combine mayonnaise, chili sauce, lemon juice, and Worcestershire sauce; pour over crabmeat; top with bacon and egg. Yield: 2 to 4 servings.

HERITAGE OYSTER SCALLOP

1 pint oysters
2 cups cracker crumbs
½ teaspoon salt
⅛ teaspoon pepper
½ cup melted butter or margarine
¼ teaspoon Worcestershire sauce
½ cup milk

Drain oysters. Combine cracker crumbs, salt, pepper, and butter. Sprinkle one-third of crumb mixture in a greased 1½-quart casserole; cover with half of oysters. Repeat layers. Add Worcestershire sauce to milk; pour over casserole. Sprinkle remaining crumb mixture over top. Bake at 350° for 30 minutes or until brown. Yield: 4 servings.

HOLIDAY OYSTER STEW

2 (12-ounce) cans oysters
2 slices bacon, chopped
1 medium onion, chopped
1 (10¾-ounce) can cream of potato
   soup, undiluted
1 pint half-and-half
1½ teaspoons salt
   Dash of white pepper
   Chopped parsley

Drain oysters, reserving liquid. Fry bacon until crisp in large skillet. Remove from skillet, and drain on paper towels. Crumble bacon and set aside. Cook onion in bacon drippings until tender. Add soup, oyster liquid, half-and-half, and seasonings; heat, stirring occasionally. Add bacon and oysters; heat for 3 to 5 minutes longer or until edges of oysters begin to curl. Adjust seasoning. Sprinkle with parsley. Yield: 6 servings.

SHRIMP-OYSTER CREOLE

6 slices bacon, diced
1 small onion, sliced
1 cup sliced celery
1 small green pepper, sliced into
   strips
2 chicken bouillon cubes
1 cup boiling water
1 bay leaf, crushed
1 teaspoon chili powder
¼ teaspoon pepper
1 teaspoon sugar
2 teaspoons garlic salt
1 (16-ounce) can tomatoes
1 tablespoon vinegar
1 (8-ounce) package frozen cooked
   shrimp
1 pint oysters, drained
1 (8-ounce) can green peas, drained
1½ cups cooked rice
   Chopped fresh parsley

Cook bacon in Dutch oven until crisp. Add onion, celery, and green pepper;

cook until vegetables are tender. Dissolve bouillon cubes in boiling water. Add bay leaf, chili powder, pepper, sugar, garlic salt, tomatoes, vinegar, chicken bouillon, shrimp, and oysters to Dutch oven. Simmer for 5 minutes; add peas. Serve over rice. Garnish with chopped parsley. Yield: 6 servings.

CREAMED SHRIMP ON ASPARAGUS

3 cups milk
4 slices white bread
1 (12-ounce) package frozen cooked
   shrimp
½ teaspoon salt
¼ teaspoon pepper
1 (15-ounce) can asparagus spears
1 hard-cooked egg, sieved

Put milk and bread in container of electric blender; blend for 1 minute. Pour into top of double boiler and cook, stirring constantly, until consistency of white sauce. Add shrimp and seasonings. Heat asparagus and drain. Put asparagus on serving dish and cover with sauce. Garnish with egg. Yield: 4 servings.

SHRIMP AND CHEESE BAKE

3 cups cooked rice
2 (4½-ounce) cans shrimp, drained
1 cup commercial sour cream
4 ounces blue cheese, crumbled
1 teaspoon Worcestershire sauce

Spoon rice into 6 lightly greased individual casseroles. Arrange shrimp over rice. Combine sour cream, blue cheese, and Worcestershire sauce. Spoon over shrimp. Cover and bake at 350° for 15 to 20 minutes. Yield: 6 servings.
Note: 1 or 2 cups cooked fresh shrimp can be substituted for canned shrimp.

ELEGANT SHRIMP AND EGG CASSEROLE

1 (10½-ounce) can cream of shrimp soup, undiluted
1 cup milk
½ cup shredded Cheddar cheese
¾ cup mayonnaise
¼ cup dry white wine
1 (8-ounce) package uncooked vermicelli, broken into small pieces
1 (6½-ounce) can small shrimp, cut in half and undrained
6 hard-cooked eggs, sieved
1 (8-ounce) can sliced water chestnuts, undrained
½ teaspoon salt
¼ teaspoon pepper
1 (3-ounce) can French-fried onions

Combine soup, milk, cheese, mayonnaise, and wine; add vermicelli. Add shrimp, eggs, water chestnuts, salt, and pepper. Spoon into a greased 3-quart casserole. Cover and bake at 325° for 20 minutes. Sprinkle onions on top and bake 20 additional minutes. Serve hot. Yield: 6 to 8 servings.

Note: One-half pound cooked, peeled, and halved shrimp can be substituted for canned shrimp.

SHRIMP IN WINE

3 tablespoons olive or vegetable oil
3 dozen raw shrimp, peeled and deveined
1 large onion, finely chopped
1½ cups dry white wine
¼ teaspoon pepper
1½ teaspoons salt
¼ teaspoon ground thyme
3 tablespoons chopped parsley

Heat oil in large skillet over medium heat; add shrimp and cook until pink. Add onion, wine, seasonings, and parsley. Cover and cook over low heat 5 minutes. Do not overcook. Yield: 4 servings.

SHRIMP TARRAGON

2 tablespoons melted butter or margarine
3 tablespoons all-purpose flour
1 chicken bouillon cube
½ cup boiling water
1 (10½-ounce) can cream of shrimp soup, undiluted
¼ cup Sauterne
1 tablespoon plus 1 teaspoon lemon juice
½ teaspoon pepper
½ teaspoon seasoned salt
½ teaspoon onion powder
¼ teaspoon dried tarragon
1 pound shrimp, peeled and deveined Pimiento Rice

Combine butter and flour; cook over medium heat until smooth. Dissolve bouillon cube in boiling water. Slowly add soup, bouillon, Sauterne, lemon juice, and seasonings. Cook, stirring constantly, until thickened. Add shrimp and cook 5 to 10 minutes longer or until shrimp are pink. Serve over Pimiento Rice. Yield: 4 to 6 servings.

Pimiento Rice:

1½ cups uncooked instant rice
3 tablespoons butter or margarine
1 (4-ounce) jar chopped pimiento

Cook rice according to package directions. Add butter and chopped pimiento. Yield: 3 cups.

Remember that sour cream reacts as milk does to high temperature, and it may curdle when it becomes overly warm.

BAKED LAMB RISOTTO

½ lemon
4 (¾ inch thick) lamb chops
¾ cup uncooked brown rice
1 (10½-ounce) can consommé,
    undiluted
2 carrots, cut in julienne strips
10 small pearl onions or 1 (16-ounce)
    can onions, drained
1 cup Sauterne or any dry white wine
¼ teaspoon marjoram
⅛ teaspoon ground oregano
½ teaspoon salt
⅛ teaspoon pepper

Squeeze lemon over chops; let stand for 10 minutes. Combine rice, consommé, carrots, onions, and wine in casserole; top with lamb chops. Cover and bake at 350° for 30 minutes. Remove from oven; stir rice and add seasonings. Cover and continue baking 30 additional minutes. Yield: 4 servings.

LAMB MEDALLIONS

2 tablespoons vegetable oil
1 clove garlic, crushed
4 (1-inch thick) slices cooked lamb
  Salt
  Pepper
¼ cup red wine

Heat oil in medium skillet; add garlic and cook about 30 seconds. Season lamb with salt and pepper; add to skillet. Cook lamb for 1 to 2 minutes on each side. Add wine slowly while cooking. Yield: 4 servings.

LAMB PATTIES WITH MINT CREAM

1 pound ground lamb
1 small onion, chopped
¾ teaspoon celery salt
¼ teaspoon pepper
  Mint Cream

Combine lamb, onion, celery salt, and pepper; mix well. Shape into 4 patties. Broil 3 to 4 inches from heat for 5 to 7 minutes. Turn and broil 5 minutes on other side or until lamb is desired degree of doneness, but not overcooked. Serve with Mint Cream. Yield: 4 servings.

Mint Cream:

½ cup commercial sour cream
½ cup mint-flavored apple jelly

Combine sour cream and jelly; mix to a smooth consistency. Chill until ready to serve with lamb roast, chops, or patties. Yield: 1 cup.

PORK CHOPS PARMESAN

12 very thin center-cut pork chops
   Salt and pepper
⅓ cup all-purpose flour
½ cup butter or margarine
1 (10¾-ounce) can cream of
   mushroom soup, undiluted
½ cup grated Parmesan cheese
   Paprika

Season pork chops with salt and pepper. Dredge pork chops in flour in plastic bag. Shake off excess flour. Melt butter in large skillet; brown chops. Place chops overlapping in a shallow 13- x 9- x 2-inch baking dish. Spoon drippings over chops; cover with soup. Sprinkle with cheese and paprika. Cover and bake at 350° for 20 minutes. Yield: 6 servings.

Skillet Method:

After browning chops, pour off excess fat. Add mushroom soup to skillet. Sprinkle with cheese and paprika. Cover and cook over low heat for 20 minutes. Yield: 6 servings.

Marbling is flecks of fat within the lean of meat. Marbling enhances both flavor and juiciness.

VERMOUTH-BRAISED PORK CHOPS

- 4 (¾ inch thick) loin pork chops
  Salt
  All-purpose flour
  Paprika
  Melted butter or margarine
- ¼ cup plus 1 tablespoon dry
     vermouth, divided
- 1 teaspoon all-purpose flour
- 2 tablespoons commercial sour cream
     (at room temperature)

Trim fat from chops; salt lightly and coat well with flour. Sprinkle with paprika. Brown chops in butter over medium heat in large skillet. Reduce heat to simmer; add ¼ cup vermouth to chops. Cover and continue cooking 30 minutes or until tender, basting occasionally. Transfer chops to warm platter. Combine 1 tablespoon vermouth and 1 teaspoon flour; add to pan drippings and boil 1 minute. Remove from heat; stir in sour cream. Pour gravy over chops. Yield: 4 servings.

JIFFY SWEET-SOUR PORK

- 2 pounds fresh pork, cut into 3- x
     1-inch strips
  Hot vegetable oil
- 3 cups cooked instant rice
  Sweet-Sour Sauce
- ½ cup sliced toasted almonds (optional)

Cook pork in small amount of oil in 10-inch skillet until thoroughly cooked and browned. Arrange on rice in a warm serving dish. Spoon on Sweet-Sour Sauce. Top with almonds, if desired. Yield: 6 servings.

Sweet-Sour Sauce:

- 1 (15½-ounce) can pineapple chunks
- ¼ cup sugar
- ¼ cup vinegar
- 1 tablespoon soy sauce
- 2 tablespoons cornstarch
- 1 tablespoon water
- 1 cup sliced celery
- ½ cup sliced green onion
- 1 small green pepper, cut into ¼-inch
     strips

Drain juice from pineapple into a 2-quart saucepan; add sugar, vinegar, and soy sauce. Blend cornstarch and water; add to pineapple juice mixture. Cook over medium heat, stirring constantly, until clear and thick. Stir in pineapple, celery, onion, and green pepper. Continue cooking over low heat until vegetables are heated through and crisp-tender. Yield: 4 cups.

HAM AND ASPARAGUS ROLL-UPS IN CHEESE SAUCE

- 2 (14½-ounce) cans asparagus spears,
     drained
- 8 (6- x 4-inch) slices boiled ham
- 1 (10¾-ounce) can Cheddar cheese
     soup, undiluted
- ¼ teaspoon paprika
- 2 teaspoons prepared mustard
- ⅓ cup half-and-half

Divide asparagus spears evenly among ham slices. Place spears at the end of a slice of ham. Roll up and place in shallow casserole. Combine soup, paprika, mustard, and half-and-half; pour over ham roll-ups. Bake at 350° for 30 minutes. Yield: 4 servings.

Boned hams are boned, rolled, and fully cooked.

APRICOT-GLAZED HAM AND YAMS

½ cup apricot preserves
2 tablespoons raisins
2 tablespoons lemon juice
1 (½ inch thick) center-cut ham steak
2 (16-ounce) cans yams, drained

Combine preserves, raisins, and lemon juice; mix well. Arrange ham and yams in shallow baking dish; pour apricot mixture over all. Bake at 350° for 30 minutes. Yield: 4 to 6 servings.

HAM AND NOODLE SUPPER

1 cup diced cooked ham
1 (4-ounce) can sliced mushrooms, drained
¼ cup butter or margarine
2½ cups uncooked fine egg noodles
1 (17-ounce) can green peas
¾ cup grated Parmesan cheese

Sauté ham and mushrooms in butter in medium skillet. Cook noodles according to package directions; drain. Heat peas and drain. Combine noodles, peas, ham, mushrooms, and cheese. Serve immediately in heated serving dish with additional cheese, if desired. Yield: 4 to 6 servings.

HAM FONDUE CUBES AND DIPPING SAUCE

½ cup orange juice
1½ tablespoons cornstarch
1 (16-ounce) can whole cranberry sauce
1 tablespoon brown sugar
¼ teaspoon ground cinnamon
Fully cooked ham, cut into cubes

Combine orange juice and cornstarch in saucepan; add cranberry sauce, brown sugar, and cinnamon. Cook, stirring constantly, until mixture thickens and bubbles. Keep sauce warm in fondue pot. Dip ham cubes into sauce. Yield: 2 cups sauce.

QUICK HAM QUICHE

2 cups diced ham
1 cup (4 ounces) shredded Swiss cheese
1 medium onion, chopped
2 cups milk
½ cup Biscuit Mix (see Index)
4 eggs
½ teaspoon salt
¼ teaspoon pepper

Sprinkle ham, cheese, and onion in a greased 9-inch piepan. Blend remaining ingredients in blender on high speed 1 minute. Pour into piepan. Bake at 350° for 55 minutes. Let stand 5 minutes before serving. Yield: 6 servings.

Note: 12 slices bacon, cooked and crumbled, may be substituted for ham.

HAM SKILLET SUPPER

2 tablespoons butter or margarine
1 (17-ounce) can whole kernel corn, drained
1 (16-ounce) can cut green beans, drained
1 (10½-ounce) can cream of chicken soup, undiluted
½ cup commercial sour cream
1½ cups (¾-pound) cooked ham, cut into julienne strips
1 cup (4 ounces) diced Cheddar cheese

Melt butter in large skillet; add corn and beans. Combine soup, sour cream, and ham; stir into vegetable mixture. Heat thoroughly, stirring occasionally. Top with cheese and heat until cheese melts. Yield: 6 servings.

SPICY HAM BALLS

3 cups ground cooked ham
¼ cup melted butter or margarine
1 cup dry breadcrumbs
2 eggs, well beaten
½ cup milk
½ cup firmly packed brown sugar
½ teaspoon dry mustard
¼ cup vinegar
¼ cup water
1 tablespoon cornstarch
1 tablespoon water

Combine ham, butter, breadcrumbs, eggs, and milk. Shape into 12 balls. Place balls in a lightly greased baking dish. Combine brown sugar, mustard, vinegar, and water in a saucepan. Cook over low heat stirring constantly until sugar dissolves. Pour spicy mixture over ham balls. Bake at 350° for 30 minutes, basting several times with sauce. Remove balls from pan. Dissolve cornstarch in 1 tablespoon water; stir into pan drippings. Stir until sauce thickens. Serve sauce over ham balls. Yield: 6 servings.

Note: Ham mixture may be made into walnut-size balls and served as hors d'oeuvres.

QUICK SAUSAGE CURRY

1 (12-ounce) package smoked sausage links, cut into thirds
2 tablespoons melted butter or margarine
1 (10-ounce) can pineapple chunks
1 medium-size green pepper, thinly sliced
3 cups hot cooked rice
2 tablespoons cornstarch
½ teaspoon curry powder
½ teaspoon salt

Lighly brown sausage in butter. Drain pineapple, reserving syrup. Add pineapple and green pepper to sausage and continue cooking until browned; drain excess drippings. Arrange on bed of hot rice and keep warm. Add water to syrup to make 1¾ cups; blend with remaining ingredients and add to pan drippings. Cook, stirring constantly, until thickened. Pour over rice and serve immediately. Yield: 4 servings.

OVEN BAKED PANCAKES WITH SAUSAGE

2 eggs
1 cup milk
1¼ cups all-purpose flour
1 tablespoon baking powder
1 tablespoon sugar
½ teaspoon salt
2 tablespoons melted shortening
2 (8-ounce) packages precooked sausage links

Beat eggs until light and fluffy; add milk. Combine flour, baking powder, sugar, and salt; add dry ingredients and shortening to egg mixture. Beat until batter is smooth. Pour into two greased 8-inch round cake pans. Arrange sausage links on batter, spoke fashion. Bake at 450° for 15 minutes. Cut each pancake into 5 wedges; serve hot with butter and syrup. Yield: 8 servings.

BARBECUED FRANKFURTERS

1½ tablespoons meat drippings
½ cup minced onion
1 small green pepper, chopped
1 cup chili sauce or catsup
¾ teaspoon chili powder
  Few drops of Worcestershire sauce
¼ cup plus 2 tablespoons vinegar
3 tablespoons brown sugar
¾ teaspoon salt
1 pound frankfurters
10 to 12 frankfurter buns

Melt drippings in large skillet over low heat; add onion and green pepper. Cook until onion is transparent, but not brown. Add next 6 ingredients, and simmer slowly for 10 minutes. Score frankfurters and add to sauce. Simmer until frankfurters are hot and slightly puffed. Serve on hot buns. Yield: 10 to 12 servings.

BATTER PUPS

½ cup self-rising cornmeal
½ cup self-rising flour
1 teaspoon caraway seeds
¼ teaspoon onion salt
1 egg, beaten
¼ to ½ cup milk
1 tablespoon melted shortening or oil
8 frankfurters (at room temperature)
  Oil for deep frying

Combine cornmeal, flour, and seasonings. Combine egg, ¼ cup milk, and shortening. Add all at once to cornmeal mixture and mix lightly. If necessary, add more milk to make medium thick batter. Dip frankfurters into batter and coat carefully; drop into hot oil using tongs or skewers. (A wire basket will facilitate removal of frankfurters.) Fry for 4 to 5 minutes, turning once, or until golden brown. Drain on absorbent paper and serve hot. Serve with mustard, catsup, relish, or other sauce. Yield: 8 servings.
Note: If an electric skillet is used, fry at 375°.

GERMAN FRANK AND POTATO SALAD

1 (16-ounce) can potatoes
4 frankfurters
2 tablespoons vegetable oil
3 tablespoons white vinegar
1 teaspoon salt
¼ teaspoon pepper
¼ teaspoon dillseeds
1 medium onion, sliced

Drain liquid from potatoes into medium saucepan. Slice potatoes and frankfurters and add to saucepan. Bring to a boil and cook 5 minutes; drain. Combine oil, vinegar, salt, pepper, and dillseeds in mixing bowl; add to potatoes and frankfurters. Add onion. Serve hot. Yield: 4 servings.

POTATO ONION SOUP

3 large potatoes, peeled and diced
3 medium onions, sliced
2 teaspoons salt
3 cups water
1 (13½-ounce) can evaporated milk
2 frankfurters, sliced

Place potatoes, onion, and salt in a 2½-quart saucepan; add water. Bring to a boil; cover and cook until potatoes are tender. Stir in milk and frankfurters. Heat to serving temperature. Do not boil. Yield: 4 to 6 servings.

Jiffy Sweet-Sour Pork, page 141, combines great Oriental flavor, interesting color, and no-fuss preparations. An excellent entree for a busy day company meal.

Overleaf: *Chicken Cacciatore Modified, a traditional Latin dish, is truly quick and flavorful when prepared by the recipe on page 149.*

COMPANY CHICKEN

3 whole chicken breasts, split
Salt and pepper
Paprika
½ cup butter or margarine
¼ teaspoon sweet basil
¼ teaspoon rosemary
½ cup chopped onion
1 (4-ounce) can sliced mushrooms,
    drained
½ cup slivered almonds
¼ cup cooking sherry
Juice of ½ lemon
1 (10¾-ounce) can cream of
    mushroom soup, undiluted
3 cups hot cooked rice

Place chicken, skin side up, in a greased shallow baking dish; sprinkle with salt, pepper, and paprika. Melt butter in saucepan; add remaining ingredients except rice. Stir until blended; pour over chicken. Bake at 350° for 1 hour and 15 minutes. When ready to serve, remove chicken from baking dish. Serve gravy over rice and place chicken breast on mound of rice. Yield: 6 servings.

POACHED CHICKEN BREASTS WITH MUSHROOM WINE SAUCE

3 whole chicken breasts, split and
    boned
1 (8-ounce) can sliced mushrooms
2 chicken bouillon cubes
2 to 3 tablespoons lemon juice
¼ cup dry white wine
½ cup chopped celery
Salt and pepper to taste
Mushroom Wine Sauce
¼ cup grated Parmesan cheese

Place chicken in a greased 2-quart baking dish suitable for top-of-range cooking. Drain mushrooms, reserving liquid; add enough water to liquid to equal ½ cup. Bring liquid to a boil in a saucepan; add bouillon cubes, stirring until bouillon is dissolved. Add lemon juice, wine, and celery. Pour over chicken; sprinkle with salt and pepper. Cover and bake at 400° for 15 to 20 minutes; do not overcook. Remove poached chicken from baking dish; keep warm. Prepare Mushroom Wine Sauce in baking dish. Return chicken to dish; heat thoroughly. Sprinkle with Parmesan cheese; cover and keep warm until served. Yield: 6 servings.

Mushroom Wine Sauce:

½ cup milk
2 tablespoons soy sauce
½ teaspoon poultry seasoning
½ teaspoon monosodium glutamate
    (optional)
¼ cup plus 1 tablespoon all-purpose
    flour
¼ cup plus 3 tablespoons water
1 (8-ounce) can mushroom pieces,
    drained
Salt and pepper to taste

Heat liquid remaining in baking dish over low heat on top of range. Add milk, soy sauce, poultry seasoning, and monosodium glutamate, if desired. Combine flour and water; add gradually, stirring constantly to the desired thickness. Add mushrooms and seasoning. Yield: about 1 cup sauce.

PARTY CHICKEN BREASTS

3 whole chicken breasts, split
1 (1⅜-ounce) package dry onion soup
    mix
1 (8-ounce) bottle Russian dressing
1 (8-ounce) jar apricot preserves

Place chicken, skin side up, in a 10-inch casserole. Combine soup mix, dressing, and preserves; pour over chicken. Bake, uncovered, at 350° for 30 minutes. Cover and bake 30 additional minutes. Yield: 6 servings.

CHINESE CHICKEN

    2 tablespoons all-purpose flour
    ¼ teaspoon ground ginger
    1½ teaspoons garlic salt
    ¼ cup soy sauce
    1 tablespoon lemon juice
    2 whole chicken breasts, halved,
        boned, and cut into thin strips
    1 medium-size green pepper, cut into
        thin strips
    1 (8-ounce) can sliced water chestnuts,
        drained
    2 tablespoons chopped pimiento
    ¼ cup sliced almonds
      Chinese noodles or rice

Place an 18-inch square of aluminum foil
into bottom of piepan. Combine flour,
ginger, garlic salt, soy sauce, and lemon
juice in large bowl; add chicken, green
pepper, water chestnuts, and pimiento.
Toss lightly to coat all ingredients. Pour
mixture into center of piepan. Bring four
corners of foil together into pyramid
shape. Squeeze foil ends together; fold
over ends to seal. Bake at 450° for 20
minutes. Carefully open package; sprinkle
almonds on top. Bake 5 minutes longer.
Serve with Chinese noodles or rice. Yield:
4 servings.
Note: Can be baked in a bake-and-serve
casserole covered tightly with aluminum
foil.

SPANISH CHICKEN WITH RICE

    2 tablespoons all-purpose flour
    1 large green pepper, sliced
    ½ cup chopped onion
    1 (4-ounce) jar chopped pimiento,
        drained
    3 whole chicken breasts, split
    2 tablespoons vegetable oil
    1 teaspoon salt
      Dash of pepper
    1 (8-ounce) can tomato sauce
    ¼ cup sherry or chicken broth
      Hot cooked rice

Shake flour in regular size (16- x 10-inch)
baking bag; place in a 2-inch deep baking
pan. Place green pepper, onion, and pimiento in bag, mixing slightly. Brush
chicken with oil; sprinkle with salt and
pepper. Arrange chicken on top of vegetables in bag. Combine tomato sauce and
sherry. Pour over chicken in bag. Close
bag with twist tie. Make six (½-inch) slits
in top. Bake at 350° for 40 minutes or until
tender. Serve over rice. Yield: 6 servings.

EASY BAKED CHICKEN

    1 (2½- to 3-pound) broiler-fryer
        chicken, cut up
    1 (10¾-ounce) can cream of
        mushroom soup, undiluted
    1 (1⅜-ounce) envelope dry onion soup
        mix

Place chicken pieces in shallow greased
baking dish. Cover with soup. Sprinkle
with onion soup mix. Cover tightly with
foil. Bake at 400° for 50 minutes. Uncover,
pour off gravy, and brown chicken quickly
under broiler, if desired. Serve gravy with
hot noodles or rice. Yield: 6 servings.

SKILLET BARBECUE CHICKEN

    1 (2½- to 3-pound) broiler-fryer
        chicken, cut into serving pieces
      Salt and pepper
    ¾ cup or 1 (6-ounce) bottle cola drink
    1 cup hot catsup

Season chicken with salt and pepper; place
in ungreased large skillet. Combine cola
and catsup; pour over chicken. Cover and
cook over medium heat 40 to 45 minutes
or until chicken is tender. Yield: 4 to 6
servings.
Note: To oven barbecue, use 1 (14-
ounce) bottle catsup and cook at 350° for 1
hour.

CHICKEN CACCIATORE MODIFIED

2 pounds chicken pieces or 1 (2- to 2½-pound) broiler-fryer, cut up
3 medium onions, thinly sliced
1 medium-size green pepper, cut into strips
1 (4-ounce) can sliced mushrooms, drained
2 cloves garlic, crushed
1 (10½-ounce) can tomato soup, undiluted
¼ cup water
2 tablespoons lemon juice or vinegar
1 tablespoon Worcestershire sauce
½ teaspoon leaf thyme
1 teaspoon whole oregano

Place chicken in large heavy skillet. Add onion, green pepper, mushrooms, and garlic. Combine soup, water, lemon juice, Worcestershire sauce, thyme, and oregano; pour over chicken. Cover skillet; bring to a boil. Reduce heat immediately. Simmer for 35 to 40 minutes, stirring frequently. Yield: 4 to 6 servings.

Note: Chicken can be served over cooked and drained spaghetti.

BAKED SWEET-SOUR CHICKEN

1 (2- to 2½-pound) broiler-fryer chicken, cut into serving pieces
Salt and pepper
¼ cup vegetable oil
¼ cup honey
¼ cup lemon juice
¼ teaspoon paprika
½ teaspoon dry mustard

Sprinkle chicken with salt and pepper. Arrange skin side down in greased shallow baking pan. Combine oil, honey, lemon juice, paprika, and mustard in small bowl; baste chicken with sauce. Cover and bake at 375° for 30 minutes. Turn chicken and brush with sauce. Bake, uncovered, at 400° for 15 to 20 minutes or until tender. Yield: 4 servings.

Note: An additional ⅓ cup lemon juice can be added for a tangier flavor.

CHICKEN AND ARTICHOKE CASSEROLE

4 cups cooked chopped chicken
2 (8½-ounce) cans artichoke hearts, drained and quartered
1 cup butter or margarine
½ cup all-purpose flour
¼ teaspoon cayenne pepper
1 teaspoon salt
1 clove garlic, crushed
1 teaspoon monosodium glutamate (optional)
3½ cups milk
1 cup (4 ounces) shredded sharp Cheddar cheese
1 cup (4 ounces) shredded Gruyère cheese
1 (8-ounce) can mushroom buttons, drained
1 cup crisp cereal crumbs
2 tablespoons butter, melted

Spread chicken in a greased 3-quart baking dish; top with artichokes. Melt 1 cup butter in a 2-quart saucepan; add flour, cayenne, salt, garlic, and monosodium glutamate, if desired, stirring until smooth. Cook 1 minute, stirring constantly. Gradually stir in milk; cook over medium heat until thick and smooth. Add cheeses and stir until cheese is melted. Add mushrooms. Pour over chicken and artichokes. Combine cereal crumbs and 2 tablespoons melted butter; sprinkle over cheese sauce. Bake at 350° for 30 minutes. Yield: 8 servings.

QUICK CHICKEN AND RICE

1 (10½-ounce) can chicken and rice
    soup, undiluted
¾ cup uncooked instant rice
1 (6-ounce) can boned chicken

Bring soup to a boil; add rice and stir.
Cover and remove from heat; let stand 5
minutes. Break chicken into chunks; heat.
Add to rice mixture and serve. Yield: 4 to
6 servings.

SKILLET CRANBERRY BARBECUE

½ cup chopped onion
2 tablespoons melted butter or
    margarine
1 cup catsup
½ cup canned whole cranberry sauce
¼ cup firmly packed brown sugar
3 tablespoons vinegar
1 tablespoon Worcestershire sauce
1 tablespoon prepared mustard
2 cups chicken or ham, cut into
    julienne strips
  Hot cooked rice

Sauté onion in butter until tender in large
skillet. Stir in catsup, cranberry sauce,
brown sugar, vinegar, Worcestershire
sauce, mustard, and meat. Simmer, uncovered, for 15 minutes. Serve over hot
cooked rice. Yield: 6 servings.

Note: Any favorite meat can be substituted for chicken or ham.

HOT CHICKEN CASSEROLE

2 cups cooked chopped chicken
2 cups chopped celery
½ cup chopped almonds
⅓ cup chopped green pepper
2 tablespoons chopped pimiento
1 teaspoon salt
¼ teaspoon pepper
½ teaspoon monosodium glutamate
    (optional)
2 tablespoons lemon juice
½ cup mayonnaise
1 cup (4 ounces) shredded Swiss or
    Cheddar cheese
1 cup crushed potato chips

Combine all ingredients except potato
chips. Spoon into a greased 2-quart casserole. Top with potato chips. Bake at 350°
for 30 minutes. Yield: 6 servings.

CHICKEN CURRY

1 large onion, sliced
2 large stalks celery, diagonally sliced
1 small green pepper, coarsely
    chopped
1 cup chicken broth
1 cup chopped chicken
2 teaspoons curry powder
¼ teaspoon ground cinnamon
1 (4-ounce) can sliced mushrooms,
    drained
¾ cup milk
2 tablespoons all-purpose flour
  Hot cooked rice
¼ cup chutney (optional)

Combine onion, celery, green pepper,
broth, chicken, curry powder, and cinnamon in a 1½-quart saucepan. Cover and
bring to a boil. Lower heat and simmer
about 6 minutes or until vegetables are
crisp-tender. Stir in mushrooms; cook 1
minute. Combine milk and flour; stir into
chicken mixture. Cook and stir until thickened. Serve over hot rice. Top with chutney, if desired. Yield: 4 servings.

CHICKEN GUMBO

¼ cup chopped green pepper
¼ cup chopped onion
3 tablespoons melted butter or margarine
6 chicken bouillon cubes
4 cups boiling water
1 (20-ounce) can tomatoes
1 bay leaf
1 (10-ounce) package frozen cut okra
½ teaspoon salt
⅛ teaspoon pepper
½ teaspoon sweet basil
2 teaspoons sugar
1 tablespoon minced parsley
2 cups cooked chopped chicken
3 cups hot cooked rice

Sauté green pepper and onion in butter in large saucepan until soft. Dissolve bouillon cubes in boiling water; add to sautéed vegetables. Stir in tomatoes, bay leaf, and okra; simmer 15 minutes. Remove bay leaf. Add salt, pepper, basil, sugar, parsley, and chicken. Heat thoroughly. Serve with hot rice. Yield: 6 servings.

TETRAZZINI PRONTO

1 (10¾-ounce) can cream of chicken soup, undiluted
1 (5-ounce) can undiluted evaporated milk
¼ cup sherry
½ cup grated Parmesan cheese, divided
Salt
Pepper
3 (5-ounce) cans boned chicken
1 (4-ounce) can mushrooms, drained
1 (8-ounce) package spaghetti, uncooked

Combine soup and evaporated milk; heat to almost boiling. Add sherry, ¼ cup Parmesan cheese, salt, and pepper to taste; stir until cheese is melted. Add chicken and mushrooms; heat thoroughly. Cook spaghetti in boiling salted water until tender but not soft; drain well and pour into a greased 3-quart casserole. Pour sauce on top; sprinkle with remaining cheese. Bake at 375° for 20 minutes or until lightly browned. Yield: 6 servings.

TURKEY OR CHICKEN CASSEROLE

1½ cups cooked chopped chicken or turkey
1 cup quick-cooking oats, uncooked
1 cup (4 ounces) diced sharp Cheddar cheese
1 medium onion, chopped
¼ teaspoon pepper (optional)
½ teaspoon monosodium glutamate (optional)
1½ teaspoons salt
¾ cup nonfat dry milk powder
3 cups water
2 eggs, beaten

Combine all ingredients; spoon into a greased 13- x 9- x 2-inch baking dish. Bake at 400° for 30 minutes or until center is firm. Yield: 4 to 6 servings.

Gourmet cooking can be as simple as opening a jar. Herbs and spices add infinite variety to your favorite recipes. Sprinkle basil on lamb chops or simmer a bay leaf in meat stew. Oregano adds a touch of Italy to tomato dishes. Try tumeric in scrambled eggs and seafood salads. Tangy caraway seeds go with cabbage, so add some to cole slaw or sauerkraut. Sage adds a special touch to poultry stuffings and thyme to chicken stews and casseroles.

TURKEY-RICE CASSEROLE

2 cups cooked rice
1 cup cream of celery or mushroom
   soup, undiluted
1 tablespoon mayonnaise
1 (8-ounce) can green peas, drained
¼ cup chopped pimiento
1 teaspoon salt
¼ teaspoon pepper
4 cups cooked chopped turkey

Place rice in a greased 2-quart casserole. Combine soup, mayonnaise, peas, pimiento, salt, pepper, and turkey. Pour over rice. Bake at 350° about 20 minutes or until thoroughly heated. Yield: 6 servings.

TURKEY SLICES ON VEGETABLES

½ pound fresh small mushrooms
1 tablespoon melted butter or
   margarine
2 (10-ounce) packages frozen green
   peas, thawed
4 small tomatoes, peeled and halved
2 tablespoons chopped parsley
½ teaspoon salt
   Pepper to taste
2 tablespoons vegetable oil
4 thick slices cooked turkey breast

Sauté fresh mushrooms in butter in a medium saucepan. Add peas; cover and heat gently for 3 minutes. Add tomatoes and parsley; simmer another 3 minutes. Add salt and pepper. Heat oil in a large skillet over medium heat. Add turkey and cook 2 to 3 minutes on each side or until golden brown. Season to taste. Arrange vegetables on serving plate. Arrange turkey slices on top of vegetables. Yield: 4 servings.

Note: One (4-ounce) can sliced mushrooms can be substituted for fresh mushrooms.

ONION STRATA

8 slices white bread, cut in cubes
2 cups (8 ounces) shredded Cheddar
   cheese, divided
2 large sweet onions, thinly sliced
2 eggs
2 cups milk
1½ tablespoons prepared mustard
1 teaspoon salt
⅛ teaspoon pepper
   Paprika

Place half of bread cubes in a buttered 2-quart casserole. Sprinkle 1 cup cheese over bread and top with half of onion. Repeat layers of bread, cheese, and onion. Beat eggs, milk, mustard, salt, and pepper; pour over onion. Sprinkle with paprika. Bake at 325° for 1 hour. Yield: 6 servings.

TOMATO RAREBIT

1 (10¾-ounce) can tomato soup,
   undiluted
2 cups (8 ounces) shredded sharp
   Cheddar cheese
   Crackers or toast

Heat soup; add cheese. Simmer, stirring constantly, until cheese is melted. Serve over crackers or toast. Yield: 4 servings.

heat until smooth and thick. Place half of egg slices in a greased 1½-quart dish; top with half of peas and half of sauce. Repeat layers. Bake at 350° for 25 minutes. Top casserole with cheese. Bake about 5 minutes or until cheese melts. Serve hot. Yield: 4 servings.

WELSH RAREBIT

- 1 egg, beaten
- 1 teaspoon Worcestershire sauce
- ½ teaspoon salt
  Dash of cayenne pepper
- 1 teaspoon prepared mustard
- ¾ cup milk
- 2 cups (8 ounces) shredded sharp Cheddar cheese
- 4 English muffins, buttered and toasted

Combine egg, Worcestershire sauce, salt, cayenne, and mustard. Scald milk. Add cheese and stir until melted; add egg mixture and stir over low heat until slightly thickened. For thicker sauce, make paste of 1 tablespoon flour and 1 tablespoon milk. Stir into cheese mixture until thickened. Serve over English muffins. Yield: 4 servings.

EGG CASSEROLE

- ¼ cup butter or margarine
- ¼ cup all-purpose flour
- 1½ teaspoons salt
  Pepper
- 2 cups milk
- 4 hard-cooked eggs, sliced
- 1 (17-ounce) can green peas, drained
- 1 cup (4 ounces) diced Cheddar cheese

Melt butter in medium saucepan; add flour, salt, and pepper. Blend well. Add milk; stir until blended; cook over medium

COLORFUL EGG CASSEROLE

- 6 hard-cooked eggs, finely chopped
- 2 tablespoons chopped pimiento
- ¼ cup chopped celery
- 1 cup mayonnaise
- 1 teaspoon salt
- ¾ teaspoon garlic salt
- ¼ teaspoon pepper
- ¼ cup milk
- 1⅓ cups cracker crumbs, divided
- 2 tablespoons melted butter or margarine

Combine eggs, pimiento, celery, mayonnaise, salt, garlic salt, pepper, and milk in mixing bowl. Add 1 cup cracker crumbs. Spoon into a greased 1-quart casserole dish. Combine remaining crumbs and butter. Sprinkle over egg mixture. Bake at 400° for 25 minutes or until brown. Yield: 5 to 6 servings.

EGGS FLORENTINE

- ¼ cup melted butter or margarine
- ¼ cup all-purpose flour
- ½ teaspoon salt
- ¼ teaspoon pepper
- 2 cups milk
- 2 (10-ounce) packages frozen chopped spinach, cooked and drained
- 1 tablespoon lemon juice
- 12 poached eggs (recipe follows)
- ½ cup grated Parmesan cheese

Combine butter, flour, salt, and pepper in medium saucepan over low heat. Cook, stirring constantly, until smooth and bubbly. Add milk and cook, stirring constantly, until mixture thickens. Continue cooking and stirring for 1 minute. Remove from heat and set aside. Combine spinach and lemon juice; spread in a 2-quart baking dish. Arrange poached eggs on spinach. Pour white sauce over eggs. Sprinkle with cheese. Broil 6 inches from heat until lightly browned and bubbly about 3 to 5 minutes. Serve hot. Yield: 6 servings.

Poached Eggs:

- Vegetable oil
- Water
- Eggs

Lightly oil a saucepan. Add enough water to fill 2 inches deep; heat to boiling over medium high heat. Reduce heat to keep water at a simmer. Break eggs, one at a time, into dish; then slip each egg into water, holding dish close to water's surface. Simmer 3 to 5 minutes depending on desired doneness. When done, lift eggs with slotted pancake turner or spoon. Drain and serve.

For Individual Servings: Line six 8- to 10-ounce baking dishes or ramekins with ⅓ cup spinach. Place 2 poached eggs on spinach. Pour ⅓ cup sauce over each serving and sprinkle with 1 rounded tablespoon cheese. Broil as above.

Note: Two cups white sauce can be prepared from Basic White Sauce Mix (*see* Index).

NEVER-FAIL BAKED OMELET

- 6 slices bacon
- 1 medium onion, chopped
- 8 eggs, lightly beaten
- 1 cup milk
- 2 tablespoons chopped pimiento
- 1 tablespoon chopped parsley
- ½ teasoon salt
- ¼ teaspoon pepper
- 1 cup (4 ounces) shredded Cheddar cheese
- 1 cup (4 ounces) shredded Swiss cheese
- 1 tablespoon all-purpose flour

Fry bacon in medium skillet until crisp; remove from skillet, and drain on paper towels. Crumble bacon and set aside. Reserve 1 tablespoon bacon drippings; sauté onion in drippings until tender. Add bacon, eggs, milk, pimiento, parsley, salt, and pepper, mixing well. Combine cheese and flour; add to egg mixture. Pour into a 1½-quart casserole. Bake at 350° for 40 minutes. Serve immediately. Yield: 6 servings.

FRENCH OR PLAIN OMELET

- 2 eggs
- 2 tablespoons water
- ¼ teaspoon salt
- Dash of pepper
- 1 tablespoon butter or margarine

Beat eggs, water, salt, and pepper with a fork. Heat butter in an 8-inch omelet pan or skillet over medium heat until just hot enough to sizzle a drop of water. Pour egg mixture into skillet. As mixture starts to cook, gently lift edges of omelet with a spatula and tilt pan to allow uncooked egg mixture to run underneath. Cook over low heat for 5 minutes or until mixture is set on top and golden on bottom. Quickly run spatula around inside of skillet to loosen omelet. While top is still moist and creamy-looking, sprinkle filling on half of omelet. Fold omelet in half and place on a warm plate. Yield: 1 serving.

Variations: Omelets can be flavored with a variety of herbs and spices. Mix ⅛ to ¼ teaspoon herbs or spices per omelet.

Omelets can hold almost any leftover food. For each omelet fill with ⅓ to ½ cup of any of the following: shredded Cheddar, Swiss, mozzarella, Gouda, Muenster, or other firm cheese; cottage, ricotta, or cream cheese; cooked and crumbled bacon; sautéed sliced mushrooms; sautéed chopped onion or green pepper.

OMELET WITH SPANISH MUSHROOM FILLING

    4 eggs
    ¼ cup water
    ¾ teaspoon salt
    ⅛ teaspoon ground black pepper
    3 tablespoons butter or margarine
      Spanish Mushroom Filling

Beat eggs lightly; add water, salt, and pepper. Melt butter in a 10-inch skillet or omelet pan. Pour egg mixture into hot skillet. As mixture starts to cook, gently lift edges of omelet with a spatula and tilt pan to allow uncooked egg mixture to run underneath. Cook over low heat for 5 minutes or until mixture is set on top and golden on bottom. Quickly run spatula around inside of skillet to loosen omelet. Spoon 1 cup of Spanish Mushroom Filling over half of omelet; fold omelet in half and place on a warm plate. Spoon remaining filling over omelet. Yield: 2 to 3 servings.

Spanish Mushroom Filling:

    ½ cup chopped onion
    1 small green pepper, cut into thin strips
    ¼ cup melted butter or margarine
    1 (8-ounce) can sliced mushrooms, drained
    ½ teaspoon salt
    ⅛ teaspoon pepper
    1 (16-ounce) can tomatoes, chopped

Sauté onion and green pepper in butter in medium skillet. Add mushrooms, salt, and pepper; sauté 3 more minutes. Add tomatoes. Bring to boiling point; reduce heat and simmer, uncovered, for 5 minutes, stirring constantly. Yield: about 2 cups.

BIRD'S NEST

      Butter
    1 slice bread
    1 slice process American or sharp Cheddar cheese
    1 egg, separated
    2 slices bacon, partially cooked (optional)
    2 teaspoons shredded process American or Cheddar cheese

Butter one side of bread. Place buttered side down on baking sheet. Cover with cheese. Beat egg white until stiff; mound on top of cheese, covering entire surface. Wrap bacon, if desired, around edge of bread, forming a collar. Make a small dent in center of egg white; place egg yolk in dent. Cover yolk with cheese. Bake at 400° for 10 minutes. Yield: 1 serving.

BRUNCH FOR TWO

- 1 (10¾-ounce) can cream of mushroom soup, undiluted
- ½ cup shredded Swiss cheese
- 2 tablespoons milk
- 2 teaspoons instant minced onion
- ¼ teaspoon dried dillweed
- 4 eggs
- 2 English muffins, split, toasted, and buttered
  Pimiento strips (optional)

Combine soup, cheese, milk, onion, and dillweed in an 8-inch skillet. Cook and stir over medium heat just until sauce begins to bubble. Break an egg into a sauce dish. Slip egg into sauce, holding dish close to sauce surface. Repeat with remaining eggs. Spoon enough sauce over each egg to coat it lightly. Cover and cook over medium heat, basting with sauce once or twice, about 5 to 7 minutes or until eggs are cooked to desired degree of doneness. Serve eggs on English muffins. Spoon sauce over eggs. Garnish with pimiento, if desired. Yield: 2 servings.

EASY SOUFFLÉ

- Butter or margarine
- 3 tablespoons grated Parmesan cheese
- 4 eggs
- ¼ pound sharp Cheddar cheese, cubed
- 1 (3-ounce) package cream cheese, cubed
- ⅓ cup milk or half-and-half
- ¼ cup grated Parmesan cheese
- ½ teaspoon onion salt
- ½ teaspoon dry mustard

Butter bottom and sides of a 1-quart soufflé dish or casserole. Dust with 3 tablespoons Parmesan cheese and set aside. Combine remaining ingredients in container of electric blender. Blend at medium speed until smooth, about 30

seconds. Blend at high speed another 10 to 15 seconds. Carefully pour into prepared dish. Bake at 350° for 25 to 30 minutes or until puffy and delicately browned. Serve immediately. Yield: 2 to 4 servings.

MEXICAN BURGERS

- 2 tablespoons chopped onion
- 2 tablespoons melted butter or margarine
- 1 (15-ounce) can kidney beans, drained
- 1 pound ground beef
- 1 egg, beaten
- 2 teaspoons garlic salt
- 1 teaspoon chili powder
- 2 tablespoons catsup
- 1 teaspoon Worcestershire sauce
- 6 slices process American cheese
- 6 toasted hamburger buns (optional)

Sauté onion in butter in a large skillet. Combine onion, beans, beef, egg, garlic salt, chili powder, catsup, and Worcestershire sauce; mix well. Shape mixture into 6 patties. Place in heated skillet. Cook, turning once, until meat reaches desired doneness. Place a cheese slice on each patty, cover skillet, and cook until cheese melts. Serve on buns, if desired. Yield: 6 servings.

SLOPPY JOE SANDWICH

2 pounds ground beef
2 medium onions, thinly sliced
1 small green pepper, diced
2 teaspoons garlic salt
½ teaspoon pepper
2 teaspoons Worcestershire sauce
2 (10½-ounce) cans tomato soup,
    undiluted
¼ cup grated Parmesan cheese
    (optional)
    Butter or margarine, softened
    Sandwich buns

Combine beef, onion, green pepper, garlic salt, pepper, and Worcestershire sauce in large skillet. Cook until meat is browned and onion and green pepper are cooked. Add soup and cheese, if desired; simmer 15 to 20 minutes or until mixture is thick. Split, toast, and butter buns. Spoon on meat mixture. Yield: 6 to 8 servings.

HOT HAMWICHES

¼ cup butter or margarine, softened
2 tablespoons horseradish mustard
2 tablespoons chopped onion
2 tablespoons poppy seeds (optional)
8 slices rye bread
4 slices boiled or baked ham
4 slices Swiss cheese
    Butter or margarine, softened

Combine ¼ cup butter, mustard, onion, and poppy seeds, if desired; spread on 4 slices of bread. Top each with 1 slice ham, 1 slice cheese, and 1 slice rye bread. Butter top and bottom of each sandwich. Grill on both sides in a hot skillet or until heated through and the cheese is melted. Yield: 4 servings.

HAM AND EGG SANDWICH

2 tablespoons chopped onion
1 tablespoon chopped green pepper
1 tablespoon melted butter or
    margarine
6 eggs, beaten
1½ cups (6 ounces) shredded Cheddar
    cheese, divided
½ cup finely chopped cooked ham
1 tablespoon chopped pimiento
¼ teaspoon salt
    Dash of pepper
6 hamburger buns, toasted and
    buttered

Sauté onion and green pepper in butter in a 1-quart saucepan until tender. Combine sautéed vegetables, eggs, 1 cup Cheddar cheese, ham, pimiento, salt, and pepper. Shape into 6 patties and cook on buttered preheated griddle until eggs are set; turn and cook other side. Sprinkle remaining ½ cup cheese over tops. Serve on warm buns. Yield: 6 sandwiches.

Note: Mixture may be prepared in advance, stored in refrigerator, and cooked before serving on warm buns.

CREAMED CHICKEN SANDWICH

Creamed chicken can easily be varied for extra menu interest. Serve creamed chicken over golden toast or spoon over crisp melba toast. Add cooked peas, carrots, and mushrooms to the chicken for a colorful treat. For a crunchy texture, sprinkle toasted, sliced almonds over creamed chicken. Spark the cream sauce with sharp cheese. Garnish with hard-cooked egg slices or red pimiento strips.

OPEN-FACE TURKEY SALAD SANDWICH

Julienne strips of cooked turkey are easily fashioned into tasty sandwiches. Cut the long, thin strips from a boneless cooked turkey roast, either all white meat, all dark, or a combination of both. Place a layer of crisp shredded lettuce on a lightly toasted slice of bread, and cover with a medley of diced cheese, crumbled cooked bacon, and sliced hard-cooked eggs. Top with juilienne strips of turkey. French dressing is the crowning touch, or skip the dressing and use salt and lemon pepper. Serve as an open-faced sandwich.

HASTY TUNA CHEESEBURGER

1 (7-ounce) can tuna, drained
¼ cup chopped celery
¼ cup chopped green pepper
¼ to ½ cup Low Calorie Salad Dressing
½ cup diced Cheddar cheese
4 to 6 sandwich buns

Flake tuna with a fork; add celery and green pepper. Add enough Low Calorie Salad Dressing to moisten. Add cheese. Spoon into sandwich buns. Wrap in aluminum foil. Heat at 350° for 15 to 20 minutes. Serve hot. Yield: 4 to 6 servings.

Low Calorie Salad Dressing:

1 cup plain yogurt
½ teaspoon buttermilk salad dressing mix
2 tablespoons grated Parmesan cheese

Combine all ingredients. Dressing may also be used on salad greens. Yield: 1 cup.

Raw egg whites can be frozen. Place in plastic bag and tightly secure. Label so you will know how many egg whites are in each container. Defrost and use as fresh egg whites.

GRILLED PEANUT BUTTER AND JELLY SANDWICH

For each sandwich, spread 1 slice of bread with peanut butter, and another slice with favorite jam or jelly. Close sandwich. Spread softened butter over outside of top and bottom of sandwich. Grill until brown. Turn and grill other side.
Variations: Omit jelly and add a thin slice of boiled ham.
Add crumbled bacon to peanut butter and jelly sandwich.
Add crumbled bacon to peanut butter only, omitting jelly.

Everyone loves the all-American hamburger, so to a hot hamburger add a tasty topping that will give an entirely different flavor:

Give hamburgers a Spanish flair by combining 1 cup commercial sour cream, ½ cup shredded brick cheese, and ¼ cup chopped pimiento-stuffed olives.

For a mushroom-cheese topping, blend 1 can condensed cream of mushroom soup, 1 cup shredded Cheddar cheese, and ¼ cup chili sauce.

Try Blue Cheese Butter. Combine ½ cup (1 stick) softened butter with ½ cup crumbled Blue Cheese and 1 teaspoon Worcestershire sauce. Spread on hot juicy burgers.

Vegetables

*T*here was a time when vegetables were regarded as a minor part of a meal, perhaps because few could be purchased and the number produced in the home garden was limited. Today, because of improvements in production, processing, and shipping, you will find a great variety of vegetables available all year; and, therefore, this item has gained its rightful place of importance on every table.

Whether you use fresh or processed vegetables (canned, dried, or frozen), they add variety and a generous supply of nutrients to our diets. Although differences are not great, fresh vegetables and fruits are generally slightly superior to frozen, and frozen superior to canned. However, frozen and canned goods are a boon to any cook who is hurriedly preparing a meal, and often very little is sacrificed in the way of flavor or nutrients.

Since half of the vitamin C in canned vegetables is in the liquid, it is a good idea to use the liquid in soups or sauces. This is a bonus when using canned vegetables for a quick and easy meal. Another nutritive bonus can be obtained by cooking many of the thawed frozen vegetables just until they are hot. However, to hasten the use, place frozen vegetables in the refrigerator the night before or heat in a microwave oven. Overcooked vegetables lose not only nutritive value but also color and texture.

If properly cooked and served, vegetables have a lot going for them, including color, texture, flavor, and nutritive value.

ORIENTAL ASPARAGUS

    1 pound fresh asparagus spears
    3 tablespoons vegetable oil
      Salt
      Pepper
    ¼ teaspoon monosodium glutamate

Cut asparagus diagonally into 1½-inch
pieces. Heat oil in large skillet. Add asparagus and sprinkle with salt, pepper, and
monosodium glutamate. Shake skillet frequently. Cook until tender; do not overcook. Yield: 4 servings.

ASPARAGUS AND EGG CASSEROLE

    1 (11-ounce) can Cheddar cheese
      soup, undiluted
    ¼ cup milk
    1 (10-ounce) can asparagus spears,
      drained
    4 hard-cooked eggs, sliced
    ¼ cup toasted slivered almonds

Combine soup and milk; stir until blended.
Arrange alternate layers of asparagus,
soup mixture, eggs, and almonds in a
greased 1-quart casserole. Bake at 375° for
20 minutes. Yield: 4 servings.

GREEN BEAN CASSEROLE

    2 (16-ounce) cans French-style green
      beans, drained
    6 slices bacon, cut into 1-inch pieces
    ½ cup diced onion
    ¼ cup all-purpose flour
    ⅛ teaspoon pepper
    3 chicken bouillon cubes
    1½ cups boiling water
    ½ cup shredded Cheddar cheese

Place beans in a 1½-quart casserole. Cook
bacon and onion in medium skillet until
tender, stirring occasionally. Stir in flour

and pepper until blended. Dissolve
bouillon cubes in boiling water; gradually
add to skillet mixture. Cook, stirring constantly, until sauce thickens. Pour over
beans; sprinkle with cheese. Bake at 350°
for 30 minutes or until hot and bubbly.
Yield: 8 servings.

DOUBLE BEAN CASSEROLE

    1 (10¾-ounce) can cream of chicken
      soup, undiluted
    1 (10¾-ounce) can cream of
      mushroom soup, undiluted
    1 (16-ounce) can bean sprouts,
      drained
    1 (8-ounce) can sliced water chestnuts,
      drained
    1 (16-ounce) can French-style green
      beans, drained
    1 (3-ounce) can French-fried onion
      rings

Combine soups; pour half of soup into a
greased 2-quart casserole. Layer bean
sprouts, water chestnuts, and green beans
over soup. Add remaining soup. Bake at
350° for 20 minutes. Top with onion rings;
return to oven for 5 minutes. Yield: 6
servings.

GREEN BEANS IN HERB BUTTER

    1 (10-ounce) package frozen cut green
      beans or 1 (16-ounce) can cut
      green beans, drained
    3 tablespoons butter or margarine
    1 small onion, sliced
    1 stalk celery, sliced
    ½ clove garlic, crushed
      Fresh parsley
    ¼ teaspoon dried rosemary
    ¼ teaspoon dried sweet basil
    ¾ teaspoon salt
      Pepper

Cook beans according to package directions. Melt butter in medium skillet; add onion, celery, garlic, and parsley. Cook over low heat for 5 minutes. Add rosemary, basil, salt, and pepper. Cover and simmer for 10 minutes. Add sauce to green beans just before serving. Yield: 3 to 4 servings.

QUICK GREEN BEAN CASSEROLE

- 1 (10¾-ounce) can cream of mushroom soup, undiluted
- 1 cup commercial sour cream
- 5 cloves garlic, crushed, or ½ teaspoon garlic powder
- 3 (16-ounce) cans French-style green beans, drained
- 1 cup saltine cracker crumbs
- 2 cups (8 ounces) shredded sharp Cheddar cheese
- ¼ cup melted butter or margarine
- 1 (3-ounce) can French-fried onion rings or ⅓ cup toasted sliced almonds

Combine soup, sour cream, and garlic; add green beans and stir well. Put in a greased 1½-quart casserole. Combine cracker crumbs, cheese, and butter; sprinkle on casserole. Bake, uncovered, at 350° for 20 minutes. Top with French-fried onion rings or toasted sliced almonds. Bake 10 additional minutes. Yield: 10 to 12 servings.

Note: May substitute 3 (10-ounce) packages of frozen chopped broccoli, partially cooked and drained, for green beans.

To toast almonds, place in piepan and bake at 350° until lightly browned.

Cauliflower will keep nice and white when cooking if you add a teaspoon of lemon juice to the water. Cauliflower will discolor if overcooked.

GREEN BEANS AND SOUR CREAM

- ½ cup sliced onion
- 1 teaspoon minced parsley
- 2 tablespoons melted butter or margarine
- 2 tablespoons all-purpose flour
- 1 teaspoon salt
- ¼ teaspoon pepper
- ½ teaspoon grated lemon rind
- 1 cup commercial sour cream
- 2 (10-ounce) packages frozen cut green beans, thawed
- ½ cup shredded Cheddar cheese

Sauté onion and parsley in butter until tender. Add flour, salt, pepper, lemon rind, and sour cream; mix well. Stir in beans. Spoon into a greased 1½-quart casserole. Top with cheese. Bake at 350° for 30 minutes. Yield: 6 servings.

Note: Buttered breadcrumbs or chopped almonds may be used as a topping.

SWISS BEANS

- 2 (15½-ounce) cans French-style green beans, heated and drained
- 2 tablespoons butter or margarine
- 2 tablespoons all-purpose flour
- 1 teaspoon salt
- ¼ teaspoon pepper
- 1 teaspoon sugar
- ½ teaspoon grated onion
- 1 cup commercial sour cream
- 1 cup (4 ounces) shredded Swiss cheese

Melt butter in saucepan; stir in flour, salt, pepper, sugar, and onion. Add sour cream gradually and cook, stirring constantly, until thickened. Add green beans. Pour bean mixture into a greased 1½-quart casserole. Sprinkle with cheese. Place casserole under broiler for 5 minutes or until cheese is melted. Yield: 6 servings.

GREEN BEANS WITH SOUR CREAM AND SWISS CHEESE

2 (10-ounce) packages frozen cut beans or 2 (16-ounce) cans cut green beans, drained
3 tablespoons butter or margarine, divided
¼ cup fine, dry breadcrumbs
2 tablespoons all-purpose flour
1 teaspoon salt
¼ teaspoon white pepper
¼ teaspoon monosodium glutamate (optional)
1 teaspoon prepared mustard
1 cup commercial sour cream
½ cup finely shredded Swiss cheese
1½ teaspoons minced onion

Cook beans according to package directions; drain. Heat 1 tablespoon butter in large skillet; add breadcrumbs, stirring until toasted. Remove from skillet and set aside. Melt 2 remaining tablespoons butter in skillet; stir in flour, salt, pepper, and monosodium glutamate, if desired. Heat until mixture bubbles; gradually add mustard and sour cream and blend well. Heat thoroughly but do not boil. Add beans, cheese, and onion; toss gently until well mixed. Spoon into a greased 1½-quart casserole. Top with reserved breadcrumbs. Bake at 350° for 10 minutes. Yield: 6 servings.

GREEN BEANS AND TOMATO SAUCE

2 (10-ounce) packages frozen green beans or 2 (16-ounce) cans whole green beans, heated and drained
Tomato Sauce
Grated Parmesan cheese

Cook frozen green beans according to package directions; drain. Place beans in serving dish; cover with Tomato Sauce and top with cheese. Yield: 6 servings.

Tomato Sauce:

1 medium onion, chopped
¼ cup olive or vegetable oil
1 (16-ounce) can tomatoes or 2 cups chopped fresh tomatoes
1 tablespoon chopped fresh parsley
1 teaspoon sweet basil
¼ cup tomato paste

Sauté onion in olive oil; add remaining ingredients. Cook gently for 15 minutes, stirring occasionally. Yield: 2¼ cups.

SWEET AND SOUR BEETS

2 (16-ounce) cans sliced or cubed beets
1 cup sugar
¼ cup cornstarch
½ cup vinegar
¼ cup butter or margarine (optional)

Drain beets, reserving ½ cup liquid. Combine sugar and cornstarch in top of double boiler. Slowly add vinegar and reserved liquid; cook over medium heat, stirring constantly, until sauce thickens. Add beets and let stand over hot water until ready to serve. Just before serving, bring to a boil and add butter, if desired. Serve hot. Yield: 6 to 8 servings.

Delicious and unusual vegetable combinations will complement almost any entree. Try Green Beans and Broccoli with Water Chestnuts, page 175, or Mushroom Vegetable Medley, page 175, for your next company dinner.

Overleaf: Marmalade-Glazed Sweet Potatoes, page 170, is a colorful and tasty addition to any meal.

BROCCOLI CASSEROLE

2 (10-ounce) packages frozen chopped broccoli
1 (16-ounce) can small onions, drained
1 (4-ounce) can mushrooms, drained
1 (2-ounce) jar chopped pimientos, drained
¼ cup almonds, slivered and toasted
¼ teaspoon cayenne pepper
1 (10¾-ounce) can cream of celery soup, undiluted
1 cup (4 ounces) shredded sharp Cheddar cheese

Cook broccoli according to package directions; drain. Combine first 6 ingredients in a greased 1½-quart casserole. Cover with soup; top with cheese. Bake at 350° for 30 minutes. Yield: 6 to 8 servings.

BROCCOLI IN SOUR CREAM DRESSING

2 (10-ounce) packages frozen broccoli spears
½ cup commercial sour cream
¼ cup mayonnaise
½ teaspoon salt
½ teaspoon lemon juice
¼ teaspoon dry mustard
1 tablespoon grated onion

Cook broccoli according to package directions just until tender; drain. Combine remaining ingredients in top of double boiler; heat over hot water. Place broccoli on serving plate and top with sauce. Yield: 6 servings.

Remember that it is most important to cook vegetables to the just-done stage. Overcooked vegetables yield fewer servings than those cooked just to doneness.

CURRIED BROCCOLI OR ASPARAGUS

2 (10-ounce) packages frozen broccoli or asparagus spears
1 cup mayonnaise
½ teaspoon curry powder
1½ teaspoons lemon juice

Cook vegetable according to package directions; drain. Combine mayonnaise, curry powder, and lemon juice. Place vegetable in a serving dish, and top with dressing. Yield: 6 servings.

BRUSSELS SPROUTS CASSEROLE

3 stalks celery, chopped
½ cup chopped onion
2 (10-ounce) packages frozen Brussels sprouts, thawed
1 (10¾-ounce) can cream of celery soup, undiluted
1 beef bouillon cube
1 cup blanched slivered almonds, divided
Grated Parmesan cheese

Cook celery and onion in small amount of salted water until tender. Drain and reserve water. Cut Brussels sprouts in half lengthwise; cook according to package directions. Drain and reserve water. Heat soup in a small saucepan. Dissolve bouillon cube in soup. Add ¼ cup reserved water to soup to make thin sauce. Layer half of vegetables, soup mixture, and almonds in a greased 1½-quart casserole. Top with Parmesan cheese. Repeat layers. Bake at 350° for 30 to 45 minutes. Yield: 8 servings.

AUSTRIAN SHREDDED CABBAGE

1 medium onion, chopped
2 tablespoons bacon drippings
6 cups shredded cabbage (about 1
    pound)
½ cup commercial sour cream
1 teaspoon salt
½ teaspoon white pepper

Sauté onion in bacon drippings in large skillet until tender; add cabbage and sauté 10 minutes or until crisp-tender. Remove from heat. Stir in sour cream, salt, and white pepper. Heat only until hot. Yield: 4 servings.

CURRIED CARROTS

6 medium carrots, sliced
    Salt and pepper to taste
½ teaspoon curry powder (optional)
3 tablespoons water
    Butter or margarine (optional)

Rinse carrots but do not dry. Combine carrots, salt, pepper, and curry powder, if desired, in a medium saucepan. Add water. Cover and cook over low heat about 20 minutes or until tender. Shake covered pan a few times during cooking to prevent sticking. Add butter, if desired. Yield: 6 servings.

ELEGANT CAULIFLOWER

1 medium head cauliflower, broken
    into flowerets, or 2 (10-ounce)
    packages frozen cauliflower
1 cup commercial sour cream
1 cup (4 ounces) shredded sharp
    Cheddar cheese
    Salt
    Pepper

Cook cauliflower in small amount of boiling salted water; drain. Layer half of cauliflower, sour cream, cheese, salt, and pepper in a greased 1½-quart casserole. Repeat layers. Bake at 350° for 5 to 10 minutes or until cheese is melted. Yield: 4 to 6 servings.

CAULIFLOWER WITH CHEESE SAUCE

1 medium head cauliflower
    Salt
1 (10¾-ounce) can Cheddar cheese
    soup, undiluted

Wash cauliflower, and remove damaged leaves. Make a deep X in base of core. Place in a 2½-quart saucepan. Cover with cold water. Drain water. Add 2 tablespoons cold water and salt to season. Cover tightly and cook over medium heat until steam flows around rim of lid. Reduce heat to lowest temperature and cook 12 to 15 minutes. Do not uncover while cooking. Heat soup and pour over cauliflower. Yield: 4 servings.

CAULIFLOWER IN MUSTARD SAUCE

3 (10-ounce) packages frozen
    cauliflower
1 cup commercial sour cream
1 to 2 tablespoons lemon juice
2 tablespoons sugar
¾ teaspoon salt
1 tablespoon prepared mustard

Cook cauliflower according to package directions; drain well. Whip the sour cream and slowly add the other ingredients. Blend well. Yield: 6 to 8 servings.

CAULIFLOWER AND PEAS WITH CHEESE SAUCE

1 (10-ounce) package frozen peas
1 (10-ounce) package frozen cauliflower
Breadcrumb Cheese Sauce

Cook peas and cauliflower according to package directions; drain. Pour Breadcrumb Cheese Sauce over hot vegetables and serve. Yield: 6 servings.

Breadcrumb Cheese Sauce:

3 slices white bread (crusts trimmed off)
1 cup hot milk
½ teaspoon salt
¾ cup shredded Cheddar cheese

Combine bread, milk, and salt in container of electric blender; blend on high until smooth. Add cheese and blend until smooth. Yield: 1½ cups.

Note: Cheese may be omitted for a delicious white sauce.

CELERY CASSEROLE

3 cups diced celery
2½ cups water
¼ cup slivered almonds
1 (8-ounce) can sliced water chestnuts, drained
1 (4-ounce) can sliced mushrooms, drained
2 chicken bouillon cubes
1 cup Basic White Sauce Mix (*see* Index)
¼ teaspoon pepper
⅓ cup grated Parmesan cheese
2 tablespoons crushed wheat germ or buttered breadcrumbs

Place celery in 1½-quart saucepan. Cover with water. Bring water to a boil. Cook for 5 minutes; drain, reserving water. Place celery in a 1½-quart casserole; add almonds, water chestnuts, and mushrooms.

Heat reserved water; add bouillon cubes. When dissolved, gradually stir in Basic White Sauce Mix, stirring constantly over low heat until mixture is smooth. Add pepper to sauce; pour over celery. Sprinkle with cheese. Top with crushed wheat germ. Bake at 350° for 20 minutes. Yield: 6 servings.

Note: Green beans or lima beans may be substituted for celery.

BRAISED CUCUMBERS

3 medium cucumbers
2 tablespoons butter or margarine
½ teaspoon salt
¼ teaspoon pepper
Dill Sauce

Pare cucumbers and cut in half lengthwise; scoop out seeds. Cube in 1-inch pieces. Melt butter in a 2-quart saucepan over low heat. Add cucumbers; toss to coat with butter. Cover and simmer gently over low heat for 10 minutes. Remove from heat and add salt and pepper. Serve the cucumbers with Dill Sauce. Yield: 6 servings.

Dill Sauce:

2 tablespoons butter or margarine
1 tablespoon all-purpose flour
1 teaspoon celery salt
¼ teaspoon white pepper
2 chicken bouillon cubes
½ cup boiling water
1 cup commercial sour cream
1 teaspoon dillweed

Melt butter in a 1-quart saucepan over low heat. Blend in flour, celery salt, and pepper. Cook several minutes, stirring constantly. Dissolve bouillon cubes in boiling water. Add bouillon, stirring until mixture thickens; remove from heat. Stir in sour cream and dillweed. Heat over low heat but do not allow to boil. Yield: 1½ cups.

SKILLET-STYLE CREOLE EGGPLANT

½ cup chopped onion
2 tablespoons melted butter or margarine
½ cup chopped green pepper
1 cup canned tomatoes
1 small eggplant, peeled and cubed
1 teaspoon salt
¼ teaspoon pepper
Breadcrumbs (optional)

Sauté onion in butter in medium skillet. Add green pepper, tomatoes, eggplant, salt, and pepper; cover and cook over medium heat for 5 minutes. Uncover and cook until thick, stirring occasionally. If desired, add breadcrumbs to thicken at serving time. Yield: 4 servings.

HOMINY AND CHEESE CASSEROLE

3 tablespoons butter or margarine
3 tablespoons all-purpose flour
¼ cup minced onion
1 teaspoon salt
¾ teaspoon chili powder
Dash of pepper
1½ cups milk
2 (16-ounce) cans white hominy
1 cup (4 ounces) shredded Cheddar cheese

Melt butter in medium saucepan over medium heat; stir in flour until smooth. Add onion, salt, chili powder, and pepper; stir until well blended. Slowly stir in milk; cook, stirring contantly, until thickened. Wash and drain hominy well; stir into sauce. Spoon mixture into a greased 1½-quart casserole. Sprinkle with cheese. Bake at 325° for 10 minutes or until hot and bubbly. Yield: 6 servings.

OKRA CASSEROLE

¼ cup chopped onion
¼ cup chopped green pepper
⅓ cup melted butter or margarine
2 tablespoons all-purpose flour
½ teaspoon salt
¼ teaspoon pepper
¼ teaspoon sweet basil
1 (16-ounce) can tomatoes, undrained
½ pound process cheese spread, divided
1 (10-ounce) package frozen baby okra, thawed

Sauté onion and green pepper in butter in large skillet until tender. Blend in flour, salt, pepper, and basil. Add tomatoes and half of cheese; cook, stirring until thickened. Stir in okra. Spoon into a 1-quart casserole. Bake at 350° for 20 minutes. Slice remaining cheese and arrange on top. Bake until cheese melts. Yield: 4 to 6 servings.

FRESH BUTTERED OKRA

1 pound okra
1 teaspoon salt
2 tablespoons butter or margarine

Wash okra; cut off stem end. Keep okra whole if small; otherwise, cut in half. Place okra in a 1-quart saucepan; cover with water; drain water off completely. Add salt. Cover tightly and cook over medium heat until lid spins freely, about 2 to 3 minutes. Do not lift cover. Reduce heat to the lowest temperature; cook 6 minutes. Remove cover and add butter. Replace cover; turn off heat. Keep covered until butter melts or until ready to serve. Yield: 4 to 6 servings.

To hasten any meal preparation, assemble all ingredients before starting. This will eliminate trips to the pantry.

PAN-FRIED ONIONS

4 large onions
3 tablespoons butter, margarine, or
    bacon drippings
½ teaspoon salt

Peel, wash, and slice onions thinly. Heat butter to sizzling point in a skillet; add onion slices and salt; cover, reduce heat, and cook until delicately browned on underside, 4 to 5 minutes. Carefully turn onion slices over using a spatula; brown other side and cook until barely tender. Serve immediately. Yield: 6 servings.

Note: White or yellow onions may be used; however, the white onions will have a milder flavor.

CREOLE PEAS

4 slices bacon
¼ cup butter or margarine
2 medium onions, chopped
1 clove garlic, crushed
⅔ cup chopped celery
1 medium-size green pepper, chopped
1 (10-ounce) package frozen green
    peas, thawed
1 (10¾-ounce) can tomato soup,
    undiluted
3 hard-cooked eggs, chopped
    Salt and pepper to taste
    Buttered cracker crumbs

Fry bacon until crisp; remove from pan, and drain on paper towels. Crumble bacon. Add butter to bacon drippings; sauté onion, garlic, celery, and green pepper in butter mixture. Stir in peas and soup. Layer half of vegetable mixture, eggs, and bacon in a 1½-quart casserole. Season with salt and pepper. Repeat layers. Top with cracker crumbs. Bake at 350° for 30 minutes. Yield: 4 servings.

DEVILED PEAS

1 cup chopped celery
1 medium-size green pepper, chopped
1 (16-ounce) can green peas,
    undrained
1 (10¾-ounce) can cream of
    mushroom soup, undiluted
1 (2-ounce) jar chopped pimiento
1 cup (4 ounces) shredded Cheddar
    cheese
½ cup chili sauce
1 teaspoon Worcestershire sauce
6 hard-cooked eggs, sliced
    Cracker crumbs

Combine celery, green pepper, and peas in a medium saucepan; cook over medium heat until celery is tender. Drain. Combine remaining ingredients except cracker crumbs in large mixing bowl; add celery mixture. Spoon into a well-greased 2-quart baking dish. Sprinkle with cracker crumbs. Cover and bake at 350° for 10 minutes. Remove cover and bake 5 additional minutes or until crumbs have browned. Yield: 4 to 6 servings.

POTATO CASSEROLE

4 cups cooked cubed potatoes
1 cup plain yogurt
1 cup low-fat cottage cheese
¼ teaspoon salt
    Dash of garlic powder

Combine all ingredients. Pour into a greased 1½-quart baking dish. Bake at 350° for 30 minutes or until bubbly. Yield: 8 servings.

Potatoes retain nutrients better if cooked whole. However, they may be halved, sliced, or diced before cooking if shorter cooking time is desired.

POTATO PANCAKES

- 4 large potatoes, peeled and grated
- 1 medium onion, grated
- ½ cup milk
- 1 teaspoon salt
- 1 egg, beaten
- 2 tablespoons all-purpose flour
  Vegetable oil

Combine potato and onion. Add milk, salt, egg, and flour; mix well. Heat ¼ inch oil in a heavy skillet. Spoon ¼ cup batter into oil to form a medium-size pancake. Brown pancakes on both sides. Repeat until all batter is used. Serve hot with sour cream, catsup, syrup, or favorite topping. Yield: 6 servings.

SOUR CREAM POTATOES

- 6 medium potatoes or 2 (16-ounce) cans potatoes, drained and cubed
- ½ cup half-and-half
- ½ cup commercial sour cream
- 1 teaspoon Worcestershire sauce
- 1 teaspoon salt
- ¼ teaspoon pepper
  Parsley

Boil potatoes; remove skin and cube. Combine half-and-half and sour cream in a large saucepan. Add Worcestershire sauce, salt, pepper, and potatoes. Simmer until potatoes are heated through and some of the sauce is absorbed. Garnish with parsley. Yield: 6 servings.

CANDIED SWEET POTATOES

- 1 (29-ounce) can sweet potatoes, drained and quartered
- ½ cup firmly packed brown sugar
- ½ cup butter or margarine, melted
- ½ teaspoon salt
- ¼ cup water

Place potatoes in a buttered 1½-quart casserole. Combine brown sugar, butter, salt, and water; heat to dissolve sugar. Pour brown sugar syrup over sweet potatoes. Bake at 375°, basting frequently until bubbly. Yield: 4 to 6 servings.

HALF-BAKED SWEET POTATOES WITH LEMON BUTTER SAUCE

- 4 medium-size sweet potatoes
- ½ cup butter or margarine
- 3 tablespoons lemon juice
- 2 tablespoons finely chopped fresh parsley
- ¼ teaspoon salt

Wash and dry sweet potatoes. Cut in half lengthwise; prick each with fork. Place cut side down in greased shallow baking pan. Bake at 400° for 35 to 40 minutes or until soft. Melt butter in a small saucepan; stir in lemon juice, parsley, and salt. Serve butter-lemon mixture with potatoes. Yield: 4 servings.

MARMALADE-GLAZED SWEET POTATOES

- 6 sweet potatoes, boiled and peeled
- 1 (16-ounce) jar orange marmalade
- 2 tablespoons butter or margarine
- 3 tablespoons water
- ¼ teaspoon salt
  Orange slices

Cut sweet potatoes lengthwise into 3 slices. (If small potatoes are used, cut in half.) Combine marmalade, butter, and water in large skillet; bring mixture to a boil. Add potatoes and salt; cook over medium heat, turning frequently until thoroughly glazed. Garnish with orange slices. Yield: 6 servings.

SHERRIED SWEET POTATOES

1 (29-ounce) can sweet potatoes or
   yams, drained
½ cup maple syrup
¼ cup water
2 tablespoons sherry

Slice or quarter potatoes. Combine all ingredients in top of double boiler. Cover and heat through. Yield: 4 servings.

FRENCH-FRIED YAMS

4 medium yams (about 2¼ pounds)
Vegetable oil
Salt (optional)

Deep Fry Method:

Wash and dry yams. Pare and cut into lengthwise strips approximately ½ inch thick. Heat oil in deep fryer or kettle to 350°. Fry medium amounts of yams for 5 minutes or until yams are brown and tender. Repeat with remaining yams. Remove from hot oil and drain on paper towels. Sprinkle with salt, if desired. Yield: 4 servings.

Skillet Method:

Wash and dry yams. Pare and cut into lengthwise strips about ½ inch thick. Heat 1½-inch deep vegetable oil to 350° in large, deep skillet. Add yams to cover bottom of skillet; fry for 5 minutes or until brown and tender. Repeat with remaining yams. Remove from hot oil and drain on paper towels. Sprinkle with salt, if desired. Yield: 4 servings.

CHEESE-RICE MOLD

1½ cups uncooked regular rice
1½ cups (6 ounces) shredded Swiss
   cheese

Cook rice according to package directions. Remove from heat; add cheese and toss lightly. Pack into a buttered 4-cup mold. Invert immediately onto serving plate. Yield: 6 servings.

RICE VERDE

1 cup chopped onion
⅓ cup vegetable oil
3 eggs, beaten
2 cups milk
1 teaspoon Worcestershire sauce
¼ teaspoon garlic powder
1 cup chopped fresh parsley or ½ cup
   dried parsley flakes
2 cups regular cooked rice
1 cup (4 ounces) shredded Cheddar
   cheese
Salt and pepper to taste

Sauté onion in vegetable oil. Combine eggs, milk, Worcestershire sauce, garlic powder, parsley, rice, cheese, salt, and pepper. Pour into a greased 1½-quart casserole; bake at 350° for 40 minutes. Yield: 8 to 10 servings.

SPINACH AND CREAM CHEESE

1 (10-ounce) package frozen chopped
   spinach
¼ cup butter or margarine
1 (3-ounce) package cream cheese, cut
   into cubes
Salt and pepper to taste
Grated Parmesan cheese

Cook spinach according to package directions; drain. Combine butter and cream cheese in small saucepan; cook over low heat, stirring constantly. Add spinach, salt, and pepper. Spoon into a 1-quart casserole. Sprinkle with Parmesan cheese. Bake at 350° for 15 minutes. Yield: 3 to 4 servings.

SPINACH PARMESAN

- 3 (10-ounce) packages frozen chopped spinach
- ¼ cup plus 2 tablespoons grated Parmesan cheese
- ¼ cup plus 2 tablespoons finely minced onion
- ¼ cup plus 2 tablespoons whipping cream
- ¼ cup plus 1 tablespoon melted butter or margarine, divided
- ½ cup cracker crumbs

Cook spinach according to package directions; drain well. Add cheese, onion, cream, and ¼ cup butter. Spoon into a well-greased 4-cup ring mold. Combine cracker crumbs and remaining 1 tablespoon butter; sprinkle over spinach. Bake at 350° for 10 to 15 minutes. Yield: 8 servings.

SPINACH SOUFFLÉ

- 1 (10-ounce) package frozen chopped spinach, thawed
- ½ (1⅜-ounce) envelope dry onion soup mix
- 1 cup commercial sour cream

Combine all ingredients and mix thoroughly. Place in a 1-quart casserole; bake at 350° for 20 to 25 minutes or until brown on top. Yield: 3 to 4 servings.

SPINACH SUPREME

- 3 (10-ounce) packages frozen chopped spinach
- 1 (1⅜-ounce) envelope dry onion soup mix
- 1 cup commercial sour cream

Cook spinach according to package directions. Drain. Stir in soup mix and sour cream. Spoon into a greased 1½-quart casserole; bake at 350° for 15 minutes. Yield: 6 to 8 servings.

CREOLE SQUASH

- 2 pounds yellow squash, thinly sliced
- 2 medium onions, thinly sliced
- 1 teaspoon prepared mustard
- ½ teaspoon salt
- ⅛ teaspoon pepper
- 1 (16-ounce) can tomatoes, undrained
  About ¼ cup grated Parmesan cheese (optional)

Place squash and onion in large skillet. Add mustard, salt, pepper, and tomatoes. Simmer until tender. Add Parmesan cheese, if desired. Yield: 8 servings.

SQUASH CASSEROLE

- 6 medium-size yellow squash, sliced
- 1 medium onion, chopped
  Salt and pepper
- 1 medium carrot, grated
- 1 cup commercial sour cream
- 1 (10¾-ounce) can cream of celery soup, undiluted
- ½ cup melted butter or margarine
- ½ (8-ounce) package herb stuffing
- ½ (8-ounce) package cornbread stuffing

Cook squash and onion in small amount of boiling salted water 10 to 15 minutes or until tender; drain. Season to taste. Combine squash mixture, carrot, sour cream, and soup. Combine butter and stuffing. Line a 2-quart casserole with stuffing, reserving ½ cup for topping. Add squash mixture and top with remainder of stuffing. Bake at 350° for 30 to 45 minutes. Yield: 8 to 10 servings.

SQUASH WITH SOUR CREAM

1½ pounds yellow squash or 3
    (10-ounce) packages frozen sliced
    squash
1 small onion, chopped
2 tablespoons butter or margarine
  Salt and pepper
1 tablespoon all-purpose flour
1 cup commercial sour cream
  Paprika

Wash squash and slice. Cook with onion in small amount of salted water until tender; drain. If frozen, cook according to package directions. Add butter, and season to taste. Remove to serving dish. Combine flour and sour cream in saucepan; heat thoroughly. Pour over squash mixture. Top with paprika. Yield: 6 servings.

ITALIAN ZUCCHINI

1 medium onion, chopped
1 clove garlic, minced
1 cup chopped celery
⅓ cup olive or vegetable oil
2 pounds zucchini, sliced ½ inch thick
1 teaspoon salt
¼ teaspoon pepper
1 (2-ounce) jar chopped pimiento
1 cup buttered breadcrumbs
½ cup shredded Cheddar cheese

Sauté onion, garlic, and celery in heated oil until onion is tender. Add zucchini, salt, and pepper; cover and simmer about 10 minutes. Add pimiento. Spoon into a 1½-quart casserole; top with breadcrumbs and cheese. Bake at 350° for 20 minutes or until cheese is melted and breadcrumbs are brown. Yield: 8 servings.

STUFFED SUMMER SQUASH

4 medium-size yellow squash
¼ teaspoon paprika
½ teaspoon Worcestershire sauce
¼ teaspoon garlic salt
1 tablespoon butter or margarine
¼ cup shredded Cheddar cheese
⅛ teaspoon dry mustard or curry
    powder
  Buttered breadcrumbs or crushed
    wheat germ

Wash squash thoroughly; steam in small amount of water for 15 to 20 minutes or until tender. Slice squash lengthwise. Scoop out center leaving a shell at least ⅓ inch thick. Mash pulp. Combine remaining ingredients except breadcrumbs. Stuff mixture in shells and place in a baking dish; sprinkle with breadcrumbs. Bake at 400° for 10 minutes. Serve hot. Yield: 4 servings.

Note: One-half pound cooked and drained bulk pork sausage may be added to filling.

ZUCCHINI SQUASH PATTIES

3½ cups grated zucchini (about 1
    pound)
2 tablespoons grated onion
1 tablespoon parsley flakes
3 tablespoons grated Parmesan cheese
1 cup soft breadcrumbs
¾ teaspoon salt
¼ teaspoon pepper
2 eggs, well beaten
  Fine dry breadcrumbs
  Melted butter or margarine

Squeeze liquid out of zucchini with hands. Combine zucchini, onion, parsley, cheese, 1 cup breadcrumbs, salt, pepper, and eggs. Shape into patties and cover with dry breadcrumbs. Place on a greased cookie sheet; brush with melted butter. Bake at 350° for 30 to 40 minutes or until golden brown. (Patties can be browned in skillet in butter.) Yield: 10 patties.

STIR-FRIED ZUCCHINI

    3 tablespoons vegetable oil
    1 pound small zucchini, unpeeled and
        cut into 2- x ¼-inch strips
    1 medium onion, sliced
    2 tablespoons sesame seeds
    1 tablespoon soy sauce
    ½ teaspoon salt

Heat oil in large skillet. Add zucchini and onion; cook 5 to 10 minutes over medium heat, stirring frequently, until crisp-tender. Quickly stir in sesame seeds, soy sauce, and salt. Yield: 4 servings.

TOMATOES PROVENCALE

    4 medium tomatoes, halved
        Prepared mustard
        Seasoned salt and pepper
    1 cup soft breadcrumbs
    2 tablespoons finely chopped parsley
    1 tablespoon grated onion (optional)
    1 tablespoon olive oil, vegetable oil, or
        melted butter

Arrange tomatoes, cut side up, in greased shallow pan. Spread tomatoes lightly with mustard; sprinkle with salt and pepper. Combine breadcrumbs, parsley, onion, if desired, and olive oil; sprinkle over tomatoes. Bake at 450° for 10 to 15 minutes or until breadcrumb mixture is golden. Yield: 8 servings.

Note: Soft breadcrumbs can be made from day old bread torn into tiny pieces.

MASHED TURNIPS

    1½ pounds young white turnips
        Salt
        Freshly ground black pepper
    1 teaspoon sugar
        Butter or margarine

Peel turnips and cut into small pieces. Place in medium saucepan with boiling salted water to barely cover. Simmer, covered, until tender, about 20 minutes; drain. Mash turnips; add remaining ingredients. Yield: 6 servings.

COMPANY BEANS

    1 (10-ounce) package frozen
        French-style green beans
    1 (10-ounce) package frozen baby lima
        beans
    1 (10-ounce) package frozen green
        peas
        Mayonnaise Dressing

Cook vegetables according to package directions. Drain and place in a 1-quart casserole. Top with Mayonnaise Dressing. Serve warm. Yield: 8 servings.

Mayonnaise Dressing:

    1 cup mayonnaise
    1 tablespoon vegetable oil
    2 teaspoons Worcestershire sauce
        Dash of hot sauce
    1 small onion, minced
    2 hard-cooked eggs, sieved
        Salt and pepper to taste

Combine all ingredients, and serve at room temperature. Yield: about 2 cups.
Note: Refrigerate any leftover dressing.

BEAN AND CORN CASSEROLE

    1 (8¾-ounce) can whole kernel corn,
        drained
    1 (28-ounce) can baked beans
    ¼ cup imitation bacon
    ¼ cup chopped onion

Combine all ingredients in a 2½-quart saucepan. Cook, stirring often, over medium heat until hot. Yield: 6 servings.

GREEN BEANS AND BROCCOLI WITH WATER CHESTNUTS

- 1 (10-ounce) package frozen cut green beans
- 2 (10-ounce) packages frozen chopped broccoli
- 1 (8-ounce) can sliced water chestnuts, drained
- ¼ cup melted butter or margarine
  Sliced pimiento

Cook green beans according to package directions. Add broccoli when beans are partially cooked. Continue cooking until beans and broccoli are tender. Drain, if necessary. Sauté water chestnuts in butter over medium heat for 5 minutes. Pour over vegetables. Toss lightly. Garnish with pimiento. Serve immediately. Yield: 8 servings.

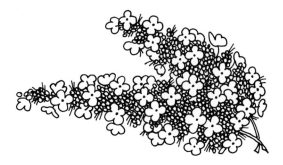

CORN-ASPARAGUS CASSEROLE

- 2 (16-ounce) cans whole kernel corn
- 1 (10½-ounce) can cut asparagus spears, drained
- ½ cup blanched sliced almonds, toasted
- ½ cup shredded Cheddar cheese
  Béchamel Sauce
- 1 cup cracker crumbs

Drain corn, reserving ½ cup liquid for Béchamel Sauce. Combine corn, asparagus, almonds, and cheese in large mixing bowl. Spoon into a greased 3-quart casserole. Pour Béchamel Sauce over mixture and top with cracker crumbs. Bake at 350° for 20 minutes. Yield: 6 servings.

Béchamel Sauce:

- 2 tablespoons butter or margarine
- 2 tablespoons all-purpose flour
- ½ cup milk
- ½ cup reserved liquid from corn
- 1 teaspoon salt
- ½ teaspoon pepper
- 1 teaspoon monosodium glutamate, (optional)
- 1 egg, beaten

Melt butter in heavy saucepan over low heat; add flour, stirring until smooth. Cook 1 minute, stirring constantly. Gradually stir in milk and reserved corn liquid. Cook over medium heat, stirring until thickened and bubbly. Stir in salt, pepper, and monosodium glutamate, if desired. Gradually stir in egg. Cook 1 minute longer. Yield: 1¼ cups.

MUSHROOM VEGETABLE MEDLEY

- 1 cup sliced celery
- ½ cup minced onion
- ¼ cup plus 2 tablespoons melted butter or margarine
- 1 pound fresh mushrooms, sliced, or 2 (8-ounce) cans sliced mushrooms, drained
- ¼ cup diced pimiento
- 1½ teaspoons salt
- ¼ teaspoon pepper
- 4 cups hot cooked rice
- ¼ to ½ cup chopped green chiles (optional)

Sauté celery and onion in butter in large skillet for 2 minutes. Stir in mushrooms; sauté 2 more minutes. Add pimiento, salt, and pepper; heat only until hot. Combine rice and green chiles, if desired; arrange around edge of heated platter. Spoon hot mushroom mixture in center of platter. Yield: 6 servings.

ORANGES, YAMS, AND COCONUT

1 (29-ounce) can yams
3 tablespoons butter or margarine
2 tablespoons sugar
½ cup fresh orange sections or
    mandarin orange sections
¼ cup flaked coconut
½ teaspoon grated lemon rind
2 tablespoons butter or margarine

Drain and mash yams; add remaining ingredients except 2 tablespoons butter. Spoon into a greased 1-quart casserole. Dot with remaining 2 tablespoons butter. Bake at 450° for 20 minutes or until top is lightly browned. Yield: 6 servings.

PEAS AND ONIONS

1 (16-ounce) can baby onions, drained
1 (16-ounce) can green peas,
    undrained
⅓ cup butter or margarine
    Salt and pepper to taste
2 tablespoons chopped fresh parsley

Combine onions and peas in a medium saucepan; heat thoroughly over medium heat; drain. Add butter and stir until melted. Season to taste. Sprinkle with parsley. Yield: 6 servings.

SQUASH AND TOMATOES

4 small zucchini or yellow squash,
    thinly sliced
1 small onion, chopped
1 (16-ounce) can tomatoes, undrained
½ teaspoon salt
¼ teaspoon pepper
2 slices bread

Combine all ingredients except bread in a medium skillet. Cover and simmer about 25 minutes or until squash is tender. Add water during cooking, if needed. Tear bread into pieces and add to squash. Yield: 4 servings.

FRESH TOMATO AND ZUCCHINI CASSEROLE

2 large tomatoes
4 small or 2 large zucchini
½ teaspoon sweet basil
1 to 2 teaspoons whole oregano
1 to 2 teaspoons salt
    Pepper
1 to 2 tablespoons olive or vegetable
    oil
¼ cup grated Parmesan cheese

Peel tomatoes; cut into ¼-inch slices. Cut zucchini into ¼-inch slices. Layer half of tomatoes and then half of zucchini in large saucepan. Top with half of seasonings, oil, and cheese. Add remaining zucchini; cover with remaining tomatoes, seasonings, oil, and cheese. Cover and cook over medium heat for 15 to 20 minutes or until zucchini is just tender. Yield: 4 servings.

VEGETABLE SUPREME

2 tablespoons butter or margarine
1 (16-ounce) can baby white onions
1 (10-ounce) package frozen whole
    kernel yellow corn
6 medium zucchini, unpeeled and cut
    into 2-inch slices
1 teaspoon salt
¼ cup water

Melt butter in large skillet. Drain onions, reserving ¼ cup liquid. Add onions and remaining ingredients to skillet. Cover and cook over medium heat 10 minutes or until zucchini is tender. Yield: 4 servings.

Salads

*I*n many homes a day's menu is really not complete unless at least one salad is included. It may accompany the main dish or be hearty enough to be the main dish for a luncheon or supper. Regardless of how it is treated, a salad will supply vivid colors, delicious flavors, and, best of all, valuable minerals, vitamins, and even protein. The final touch is the piquant flavor of a well-seasoned dressing.

A gorgeous salad can be as simple as a tray of crisp vegetables and fruits or a green salad with a prepared dressing. The bright colors inherent in salad fixings make it a natural showpiece; and salads offer you the opportunity to be highly creative because almost any food, cooked or uncooked, can be made into a salad, depending on the place the salad takes in the menu. However, when you combine chopped foods, cut the pieces large enough to retain the identity of the ingredients.

The dressing for the salad must be carefully seasoned and, most important, used sparingly. Its purpose is to enhance the flavor of the salad ingredients, not to overpower them. For a tossed salad, use just enough dressing to coat the greens, leaving them sparkling, shiny, and not dripping.

With few exceptions, salads fit well into a quick and easy meal because they should be mixed just before serving to retain their natural texture.

JIFFY PARTY CHICKEN SALAD

2 cups cooked coarsely chopped
   chicken
1 (8-ounce) can sliced water chestnuts,
   drained
1 cup mayonnaise
1 tablespoon soy sauce
Lettuce

Combine chicken and chestnuts. Combine
mayonnaise and soy sauce; mix with
chicken. Serve chilled on lettuce. Yield: 4
servings.

CRAB SALAD

1 tablespoon lemon juice
¼ cup commercial Italian dressing or
   mayonnaise
½ cup chopped celery
1 teaspoon grated onion
⅛ teaspoon salt
1 cup crabmeat, flaked
Lettuce cups

Combine first 5 ingredients; fold in crabmeat. Serve in lettuce cups. Yield: 2
servings.

BAKED CRAB SALAD

1 medium onion, chopped
1 cup chopped celery
¼ cup chopped green pepper
¼ cup chopped parsley
¼ cup melted butter or margarine
6 slices dry toast
2 tablespoons water
1 pound crabmeat
1 cup mayonnaise
Buttered breadcrumbs

Sauté onion, celery, green pepper, and
parsley in butter in large skillet until

tender. Break toast into small pieces, and
moisten with water; add to vegetables.
Add crabmeat and mayonnaise; mix well.
Spoon into 6 individual crab shells or 1-
quart casserole. Top with buttered breadcrumbs. Bake at 350° for 30 minutes.
Yield: 6 servings.

CHEF SALAD CHESAPEAKE

¾ pound fresh or frozen blue
   crabmeat
2 (10-ounce) packages frozen
   asparagus spears or 2 (14½-ounce)
   cans asparagus spears
6 lettuce cups
Lemon Caper Dressing
3 hard-cooked eggs, sliced
Paprika

Thaw frozen crabmeat; drain. Remove
any shell or cartilage from crabmeat;
flake. Cook asparagus spears according to
package directions; drain and chill. Divide
asparagus spears among lettuce cups.
Place about ⅓ cup crabmeat on asparagus.
Cover with approximately 2 tablespoons
Lemon Caper Dressing. Top with 3 slices
hard-cooked egg. Sprinkle with paprika.
Yield: 6 servings.

Lemon Caper Dressing:

½ cup mayonnaise
1 tablespoon drained capers
1 tablespoon lemon juice
½ teaspoon prepared mustard
½ teaspoon Worcestershire sauce
2 drops hot sauce

Combine all ingredients and mix well.
Chill. Yield: ⅔ cup.

CHILLED FISH SALAD

1½ pounds fish fillets, fresh or frozen
4 cups water
1 tablespoon salt
¼ cup mayonnaise
2 tablespoons chopped onion
2 tablespoons sweet pickle relish
1 tablespoon lemon or lime juice
1 teaspoon salt
1 cup shredded green cabbage
1 cup shredded red cabbage
Lemon or lime wedges

Thaw frozen fish. Bring water to a boil in a large skillet; add salt. Place fillets in skillet. Cover and simmer about 10 minutes or until fish flakes easily when tested with a fork. Drain and flake. Combine mayonnaise, onion, relish, lemon juice, salt, and fish. Chill to blend flavors. Add cabbage and toss lightly. Serve with lemon wedges. Yield: 6 servings.

MEXICAN SHRIMP-CORN SALAD

1 (8-ounce) package frozen cooked shrimp
1 (17-ounce) can whole kernel corn, chilled and drained
½ cup diced green pepper
2 tablespoons diced pimiento
1 tablespoon minced onion
1 teaspoon chili powder
½ teaspoon salt
½ cup commercial French dressing
Lettuce

Prepare shrimp according to package directions. Reserve 6 whole shrimp; dice remaining shrimp. Combine shrimp and next 7 ingredients in large bowl; toss gently. Serve on lettuce-lined platter; garnish with whole shrimp. Yield: 6 servings.

SHRIMP MACARONI SALAD

3 (4½-ounce) cans shrimp, drained
2 cups cooked shell macaroni
1 cup diced celery
¼ cup chopped parsley
¼ cup chopped sweet pickle
½ cup mayonnaise or salad dressing
3 tablespoons commercial garlic French dressing
1 tablespoon lemon juice
1 teaspoon grated onion
1 teaspoon celery seeds
½ teaspoon salt
¼ teaspoon pepper

Combine shrimp, macaroni, celery, parsley, and pickle. Combine mayonnaise, French dressing, lemon juice, onion, and seasonings; mix thoroughly. Adjust seasonings to suit taste. Just before serving, add mayonnaise mixture to shrimp and toss lightly. Yield: 6 servings.

CRISP FRESH FRUIT BOWL

1 cup sugar
1 cup water
¼ cup lemon juice
1 cup sliced fresh plums
1 cup seedless grapes
1 cup sliced fresh nectarines (if available)
1 cup fresh pear chunks
1 cup sliced fresh peaches
1 cup fresh strawberry halves
Whipped cream or sour cream
Chopped nuts or toasted coconut

Combine sugar and water in a 2-quart saucepan; bring to a boil, stirring to dissolve sugar. Boil rapidly 5 minutes. Cool completely; then stir in lemon juice. Add fruit to lemon syrup. Cover and refrigerate. Serve with whipped cream or sour cream; garnish with nuts or toasted coconut. Yield: 10 to 12 servings.

FANTASTIC FRUIT SALAD

1 (10-ounce) can fruit cocktail,
    drained
2 cups commercial sour cream
    Lettuce cups

Combine fruit cocktail and sour cream;
mix well. Chill until ready to serve. Fill
lettuce cups. Yield: 6 servings.

QUICK SWEET FRUIT SALAD

1 cup miniature marshmallows
1 (16-ounce) can pineapple chunks,
    drained
1 (11-ounce) can mandarin orange
    sections, drained
1 (4-ounce) can flaked coconut
1 cup commercial sour cream
    Lettuce cups

Combine marshmallows, pineapple, orange sections, and coconut. Add sour
cream and stir until blended. Serve on
lettuce cups. Yield: 6 to 8 servings.

*All fruits should be washed to remove
surface soil, sprays, and preservatives (such
as wax on apples) before they are served
raw or cooked.*

ELEGANT FRUIT-CHEESE SALAD

2 large heads lettuce, torn
4 ounces sliced sharp Cheddar cheese,
    cut into thin strips
½ cup sliced celery
⅔ cup vegetable oil
⅓ cup wine vinegar
½ cup sugar
2 teaspoons grated onion
1 teaspoon dry mustard
½ teaspoon salt
1 (11-ounce) can mandarin orange
    sections
1 (8-ounce) can jellied cranberry
    sauce, chilled and cubed
1 medium avocado, peeled and sliced

Combine lettuce, cheese, and celery in
large salad bowl. Combine oil, vinegar,
sugar, onion, mustard, and salt; pour
dressing over lettuce to coat lightly; toss.
Add orange sections, cranberry, and avocado; toss gently. Pass remaining dressing.
Yield: 12 servings.

ORANGE AND ONION SALAD

2 slices mild-flavored onion
2 tablespoons commercial French
    dressing or French Fruit Dressing
    (*see* Index)
6 orange slices (peel removed)
2 lettuce cups

Separate onion slices into rings; marinate
for 30 minutes in French dressing. Arrange
orange slices in lettuce cups; top with
onion rings. Yield: 2 servings.

*To peel tomatoes quickly, dip in boiling
water for 8 to 10 seconds. Loosened skin
will slip off easily.*

PEACH SALAD PLUS

Fresh peach and cottage cheese salad is a summertime favorite, but even its most loyal fans will admit that it can be a little bland. An easy way to perk it up is to add a little lemon juice, ground cinnamon, and coarsely chopped walnuts to the cottage cheese. Delicious!

Peach and cottage cheese combination is not your only option. Sour cream or yogurt with a sprinkling of brown sugar is excellent with peaches, too. And fresh peaches filled with tuna, shrimp, crab, or chicken salad make delicious one-course luncheon and summer supper fare.

ARTICHOKE AND AVOCADO SALAD

  1 medium avocado, cut into chunks or slices
  1 (14-ounce) can artichoke hearts, drained and quartered
  ½ teaspoon crushed fresh garlic
  ½ teaspoon salt
  ¼ cup lemon juice
  ¼ teaspoon dried dillweed
  ¼ cup vegetable oil

Place avocado and artichokes in small salad bowl. Combine garlic, salt, lemon juice, and dillweed; slowly beat in oil. Pour over vegetable mixture. Serve as an appetizer or salad. Yield: 4 servings.

GREEN BEANS AND SOUR CREAM DRESSING

  2 (16-ounce) cans green beans
  1 medium onion, thinly sliced
  1 tablespoon vegetable oil
  1 tablespoon vinegar
     Salt
     Coarsely ground pepper
  1 cup commercial sour cream
  ½ cup mayonnaise
  1 tablespoon chopped green onion
  1 tablespoon lemon juice
  ½ teaspoon dry mustard
  1 tablespoon prepared horseradish

Combine green beans, onion, oil, vinegar, salt, and pepper; chill. Combine sour cream, mayonnaise, green onion, lemon juice, mustard, and horseradish; pour over marinated beans. Mix well. Chill. Yield: 6 to 8 servings.

HOT BEAN SALAD

  1⅓ cups fine cracker crumbs, divided
  1 (16-ounce) can kidney beans, drained
  ⅓ cup chopped sweet pickle
  ¼ cup sliced green onion
  1 cup (4 ounces) shredded Cheddar cheese
  ½ cup mayonnaise

Combine all ingredients except ⅓ cup cracker crumbs. Toss lightly and spoon into a greased 1-quart casserole. Sprinkle reserved crumbs on top. Bake at 450° for 10 minutes. Yield: 4 servings.

Slicing, chopping, and marinating can often be done a day or two ahead of time, and the prepared foods can then be stored in the refrigerator.

HOT BROCCOLI SALAD

2 (10-ounce) packages frozen chopped broccoli
1 (10½-ounce) can cream of celery soup, undiluted
1 cup mayonnaise
3 hard-cooked eggs, quartered
1 cup (4 ounces) shredded sharp Cheddar cheese
½ cup wheat germ

Cook broccoli according to package directions; drain. Add soup, mayonnaise, and eggs to broccoli. Spoon into a greased 1½-quart casserole; sprinkle with cheese and wheat germ. Bake at 350° for 30 minutes. Yield: 6 servings.

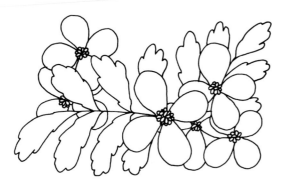

MEXICAN SALAD WITH PICANTE DRESSING

1 large head lettuce
1 cup chopped pecans
2 avocados, peeled and cut into half rings
4 hard-cooked eggs, sliced
   Picante Dressing

Tear lettuce into salad bowl; add pecans, avocado, and egg slices. Toss with Picante Dressing. Yield: 6 servings.

Picante Dressing:

⅓ cup vegetable oil
⅔ cup lemon juice
¼ cup powdered sugar
¼ cup vinegar
2 teaspoons salt
2 teaspoons paprika
½ teaspoon dry mustard
½ teaspoon onion salt
½ teaspoon pepper

Combine all ingredients and blend until smooth. Yield: 1½ cups.

CELERY REMOULADE

¾ cup mayonnaise
2 tablespoons chopped fresh parsley
2 tablespoons sweet pickle relish
2 teaspoons chopped capers
2 teaspoons prepared mustard
2 teaspoons anchovy paste
6 cups celery slices, diagonally sliced ½ inch thick
   Lettuce
   Tomato wedges (optional)

Combine mayonnaise, parsley, relish, capers, mustard, and anchovy paste in large bowl. Add celery and toss well. Serve on lettuce leaves; garnish with tomato wedges, if desired. Yield: 6 servings.

SWISS CHEESE SALAD

½ cup mayonnaise
2 tablespoons Dijon mustard
½ teaspoon pepper
½ teaspoon celery seeds
½ pound Swiss cheese, cut into strips
1 cup chopped celery
1 small onion, thinly sliced
4 lettuce cups

Combine mayonnaise, mustard, pepper, and celery seeds in a small bowl. Combine cheese, celery, and onion in a larger bowl. Add dressing to cheese mixture. Serve in lettuce cups or lettuce-lined bowl. Yield: 4 servings.

SAUTÉED MUSHROOM SALAD

1 pound fresh mushrooms, sliced
1 medium onion, sliced
1 green pepper, cut into strips
1 tablespoon melted butter or
    margarine
2 tablespoons soy sauce
    Lettuce cups
4 slices bacon, cooked and crumbled

Sauté mushrooms, onion, and green pepper in butter until tender. Stir in soy sauce. Spoon vegetable mixture into lettuce cups; sprinkle with bacon. Serve immediately. Yield: 4 to 5 servings.

Note: One (8-ounce) can mushroom stems and pieces, drained, can be substituted for 1 pound sautéed mushrooms.

RICE SALAD

3 cups cooked rice
¼ cup commercial French dressing
¼ cup minced onion
1 teaspoon salt
¼ teaspoon pepper
⅔ cup mayonnaise
½ cup minced celery
⅓ cup minced green pepper
⅓ cup sweet pickle relish
¼ cup minced sour pickles
2 tablespoons minced pimiento
2 hard-cooked eggs, chopped

Combine rice, French dressing, onion, salt, and pepper; let stand for 5 minutes. Add remaining ingredients; toss lightly. Chill thoroughly. Pack rice salad into a greased 6-cup mold. Let stand in warm water for 1 minute. Unmold on chilled serving plate. Yield: 6 servings.

RICE AND EGG SALAD

2 cups cooked rice
6 hard-cooked eggs, chopped
6 slices bacon, cooked and crumbled
3 tablespoons finely chopped green
    pepper
1 tablespoon minced onion
1 teaspoon salt
⅛ teaspoon pepper
½ teaspoon prepared mustard
¼ cup mayonnaise
½ cup diced Cheddar cheese

Combine rice, eggs, bacon, green pepper, onion, salt, pepper, and mustard. Add mayonnaise and mix well. Toss lightly with cheese. Chill. Yield: 4 servings.

7-CUP PARTY SALAD

1 (17-ounce) can shredded sauerkraut,
    drained
1 cup chopped green pepper
1 cup chopped celery
1 cup chopped onion
1 cup chopped pimiento
¾ cup sugar
¾ cup white vinegar

Squeeze all liquid out of sauerkraut; separate shreds. Add remaining vegetables to sauerkraut. Combine sugar and vinegar; add to vegetables and stir until sugar is dissolved. Chill before serving. Yield: 8 servings.

Potatoes should be stored in a cool dark place with good ventilation. The most desirable temperature is from 45° to 50°. Potatoes stored at 70° or 80° should be used within a week. The high temperature often causes sprouting and shriveling.

ALABAMA SLAW

    1 small head cabbage, thinly sliced
    1 medium onion, finely chopped
    1 medium-size green pepper, finely
        chopped
    2 teaspoons celery seeds
    1 teaspoon Seasoning Salt (*see* Index)
    1 teaspoon Salad Herbs (*see* Index)
    ¼ teaspoon pepper
    ½ cup tarragon vinegar
    ½ cup vegetable oil

Combine cabbage, onion, and green pepper. Combine remaining ingredients in jar; shake well. Combine dressing and vegetables. Serve chilled. Yield: 8 servings.

FLUFFY HARLEQUIN SLAW

    1 cup whipping cream
    ¼ cup apple cider
    1 tablespoon sugar
    ½ to 1 teaspoon prepared horseradish
    1 teaspoon salt
    3 cups shredded green cabbage
    1 medium-size green pepper, cut into
        strips

Combine cream, cider, sugar, and horseradish; beat until cream holds soft peaks. Add salt to cabbage. Fold dressing into cabbage just before serving. Garnish with green pepper. Yield: 4 to 6 servings.

FRESH SPINACH SALAD AND ZESTY DRESSING

    2 pounds fresh spinach
    ½ cup sliced green onion with tops
        Zesty Dressing
    4 hard-cooked eggs, sliced

Tear spinach into bite-size pieces; add onion. Top with ½ cup or less of Zesty Dressing. Garnish with egg slices. Yield: 6 servings.

    Zesty Dressing:

    1 teaspoon salt
    ½ teaspoon white pepper
    ¼ teaspoon cayenne pepper
    ½ teaspoon celery salt
    ¼ teaspoon dry mustard
    2 tablespoons vinegar
    2 tablespoons tomato juice or catsup
        Dash of hot sauce
    1 clove garlic, crushed
    1 cup vegetable oil

Mix all ingredients except oil. Slowly beat in oil until mixture is well blended. (Store leftover dressing at room temperature.) Yield: 1¼ cups.

SPRING SALAD

    1 medium head cauliflower, cut into
        flowerets
   10 radishes, thinly sliced
    5 green onions with tops, thinly sliced
    3 tablespoons sesame seeds
    1 cup commercial sour cream
    2 tablespoons mayonnaise
    1 (0.6-ounce) package Italian salad
        dressing mix
        Lettuce

Combine vegetables in large bowl; sprinkle with sesame seeds and mix well. Combine sour cream, mayonnaise, and salad dressing mix. Add to vegetables; mix well. Serve in lettuce-lined bowl. Yield: 6 to 8 servings.

CELERY SEED DRESSING

¼ cup sugar
½ teaspoon salt
½ teaspoon dry mustard
3 tablespoons vinegar or lemon juice
½ cup vegetable oil
1½ teaspoons celery seeds

Combine sugar, salt, mustard, and vinegar. Slowly beat in oil until mixture is thick and transparent. Add celery seeds and serve over fruit salad. Yield: 1 cup.

FLORIDA SALAD DRESSING

⅓ cup vegetable oil
½ cup grapefruit juice
2 tablespoons vinegar
1 teaspoon salt
1 teaspoon paprika
¼ teaspoon Worcestershire sauce
½ teaspoon dry mustard

Blend all ingredients together; chill. Serve over fruit salad. Yield: 1 cup.

FRENCH FRUIT DRESSING

⅓ cup sugar
1 teaspoon salt
½ teaspoon paprika
¼ cup orange juice
3 tablespoons lemon juice
1 tablespoon vinegar
¾ cup vegetable oil
2 teaspoons grated onion (optional)

Combine all ingredients in a jar; shake well. Serve on citrus fruits, avocado slices, or apples. Yield: 1⅓ cups.

Note: If dressing is made in a blender, add oil last, pouring in slowly. Emulsion will form and hold 24 hours.

HONEY DRESSING

¾ cup vegetable oil
¼ cup lemon juice
½ teaspoon paprika
½ teaspoon salt
¼ teaspoon dry mustard
Dash of cayenne pepper
¼ cup honey

Combine all ingredients in a covered jar; shake well and chill. Shake vigorously just before serving over assorted fresh fruits and lettuce. Yield: 1¼ cups.

Note: Drained, canned fruit may be used in salad.

SOUR CREAM DRESSING

1 cup commercial sour cream
¼ cup sugar
½ teaspoon salt
¼ cup vinegar
Dash of paprika

Combine all ingredients and beat until mixture is thick. Serve with fruit or chopped cabbage. Yield: 1½ cups.

To mold salads quickly:
Use ice water or partially frozen fruit or vegetable juices for the cold liquid in the recipe. Place the bowl of liquid gelatin mixture in a bowl of ice and water and chill until slightly thickened.

Place mixture in cold metal pans or molds.

Set the completed salad in a pan of ice and water; then place in the refrigerator. Salad should be firm in about 1 hour.

BACON DRESSING

    4 slices bacon
    ¼ cup water
    ½ cup vinegar
    ½ teaspoon salt
    1 tablespoon plus 1 teaspoon sugar
    1 tablespoon plus 1 teaspoon minced
        onion
        Dash of cayenne pepper

Fry bacon in medium skillet until crisp;
remove from skillet, and drain on paper
towels. Crumble bacon. Add remaining
ingredients to bacon drippings and heat to
boiling. Pour over salad ingredients and
garnish with crumbled bacon. Yield: about
1 cup.

SLAW DRESSING

    1 cup evaporated milk
    ½ cup sugar
    ½ teaspoon salt
        Dash of pepper
    ½ cup vinegar

Combine evaporated milk, sugar, salt, and
pepper in a small bowl; stir in vinegar, 1
tablespoon at a time. Mix with chopped
cabbage or slaw mix. Yield: 1½ cups.

THOUSAND ISLAND DRESSING

    2 cups mayonnaise
    ½ teaspoon dry mustard
    2 tablespoons Worcestershire sauce
    ½ cup chopped onion
    ½ cup chopped green pepper
    ½ cup chopped sweet pickle relish
    ¾ cup chili sauce
    ½ cup catsup

Mix all ingredients together. Chill. Yield:
1 quart.

TASTY VEGETABLE DRESSING

    1½ teaspoons paprika
    ½ teaspoon celery salt
    1 teaspoon salt
    2 tablespoons sugar
    ½ cup vegetable oil
    ¼ cup wine vinegar
    1 tablespoon chopped fresh parsley
    1 small onion, finely chopped
    1 clove garlic, crushed

Combine first 4 ingredients in mixing
bowl. Add one third of oil and beat 5 to 10
minutes. Add 1 tablespoon vinegar and
continue to beat. Repeat the process, al-
ternating oil and vinegar. Add parsley,
onion, and garlic; mix and let stand until
ready to serve. Serve over vegetable
salads. Yield: 1 cup.

*"Don't Buys" for Salad Fruits
and Vegetables:*

*Don't buy damaged fruits or vegetables.
By the time the rind is cut off there may not
be much left. Those that are punctured,
bruised, or decayed do not last very long.*

*Never buy carrots with green tops at-
tached. The greens absorb the nutritive
value.*

*If you must buy green tomatoes, put
them in a warm spot but never in direct
sunlight or the refrigerator to ripen.*

*Onions with green sprouts indicate that
the onions have been stored too long at
room temperature.*

*Do not buy leafy vegetables that look
wilted or are edged in brown. They are too
old.*

*Do not buy fresh fruits and vegetables
that you cannot store properly. If left at
room temperature, they lose nutritive value
and crispness.*

Breads

*N*o matter how limited your time is to prepare for dinner, the fragrance of hot bread is truly tantalizing. Even the simplest muffin, if freshly baked and served hot with butter and a favorite jam, gives a festive warm feeling to any meal.

The bread recipes included here are called quick breads, for they are leavened with baking powder, steam, or soda. But this does not mean that there is no variety. From this book, a different quick bread can be served each day of the week, using various cereal products in place of the standard flour or meal. Cornmeal, bran, rye flour, whole wheat flour, white flour, or oats can each produce a different, yet equally delicious, bread or muffin.

Hot quick breads have always been important in the diet of the Southerner. In The Chimes, *Charles Dickens said, "In the North man may not be able to live by bread alone; but in the South he comes mighty near to it, provided the bread is hot."*

SODA BISCUITS

2 cups all-purpose flour
2½ teaspoons baking powder
¼ teaspoon soda
1 teaspoon salt
¼ cup plus 2 tablespoons shortening
¾ to 1 cup sour milk

Combine flour, baking powder, soda, and salt; cut in shortening with pastry blender until mixture resembles coarse meal. Add milk, stirring until milk is blended. Turn dough out onto a lightly floured board and knead lightly about 20 seconds. Pat dough to ½-inch thickness; cut into rounds with a 2-inch biscuit cutter. Place on a greased baking sheet and bake at 450° for 10 to 12 minutes. Yield: 1 dozen.

Note: One tablespoon vinegar plus milk to equal 1 cup can be substituted for sour milk.

QUICK BISCUIT BRAID

1 (8- to 10-ounce) can refrigerator
    buttermilk biscuits
Milk
Dried dillweed or poppy seeds

Cut each biscuit into thirds. Roll each piece into a 6-inch rope. Make a braid using 3 ropes; seal ends. Place on a greased cookie sheet. Brush with milk; sprinkle with dillweed or poppy seeds. Place on lightly greased cookie sheet; bake at 350° for 8 to 10 minutes or until lightly browned. Yield: 10 braids.

ANGEL BISCUITS

1 package dry yeast
2 tablespoons warm water (105° to
    115°)
5 cups all-purpose flour
1 tablespoon plus 1 teaspoon baking
    powder
¼ cup sugar
1 teaspoon salt
1 teaspoon soda
1 cup shortening
2 cups buttermilk

Dissolve yeast in water. Sift together dry ingredients; cut in shortening with pastry blender. Add yeast mixture and buttermilk to dry ingredients. Turn dough out onto floured surface and knead lightly. Refrigerate dough until needed. Roll dough to ½-inch thickness; cut into rounds with a 2-inch biscuit cutter. Fold in half, as for pocketbook rolls, if desired. Bake on lightly greased cookie sheet at 400° for 20 minutes. Yield: about 3 dozen.

CHEESE-BACON BISCUITS

2 cups all-purpose flour
1 tablespoon baking powder
1 teaspoon salt
½ teaspoon dry mustard
¼ cup shortening
¾ cup milk
1 egg, beaten
½ cup (2 ounces) shredded sharp
    Cheddar cheese
4 slices bacon, partially cooked

Combine flour, baking powder, salt, and mustard; cut in shortening until mixture resembles coarse meal. Add milk and stir until well blended. Turn dough out onto a floured board; knead lightly until dough is no longer sticky. Roll or pat dough to ⅓-inch or ¼-inch thickness; cut into rounds with a 2-inch biscuit cutter. Brush with egg. Top half of biscuits with cheese and bacon. Cover with another biscuit round. Press edges together. Brush top with beaten egg. Bake at 400° for 15 minutes. Yield: 10 to 12 biscuits.

JIFFY ONION BISCUITS

    2 tablespoons melted butter or
        margarine
    2 tablespoons instant minced onion
    1 (8- to 10-ounce) can refrigerator
        biscuits

Combine butter and onion; let stand a few
minutes. Arrange biscuits on an ungreased
baking sheet. Make a depression in the
center of each biscuit with back of spoon
or bottom of small glass. (A rim will be
formed when baked.) Fill each depression
with 1 teaspoon onion-butter mixture.
Bake at 450° for 8 to 10 minutes or until
biscuits are done and onion is toasted.
Yield: 10 to 12 biscuits.

WHOLE WHEAT BISCUITS

    ½ cup whole wheat flour
    1 cup all-purpose flour
    1 teaspoon baking powder
    ¼ teaspoon soda
    ½ teaspoon salt
    ¼ cup shortening
    ½ to ⅔ cup buttermilk

Combine flour, baking powder, soda, and
salt; cut in shortening until mixture resembles coarse meal. Add buttermilk and stir
until well blended. Turn dough out onto a
lightly floured board; knead lightly about
20 seconds. Roll or pat dough to ½-inch
thickness; cut into rounds with a 2-inch
biscuit cutter. Place on a greased baking
sheet and bake at 450° for 10 to 12 minutes. Yield: 1 dozen.

*In preparing biscuits, do not overmix.
Knead lightly (20 seconds) to develop only
enough gluten so the biscuit will hold its
shape but not become tough.*

CINNAMON BISCUITS

    2 (8- to 10-ounce) cans flaky biscuits
    ½ cup sugar
    2 tablespoons ground cinnamon
        Melted butter or margarine
    1 cup powdered sugar
        Milk
    3 tablespoons orange juice or lemon
        juice
        Finely chopped pecans

Separate each biscuit into halves or thirds.
Combine sugar and cinnamon in small
bowl. Dip one side of biscuit in butter and
then in sugar mixture. Fold in half and
stand in pan. Repeat with remaining biscuits, lining them in pan so they touch.
Bake at 400° for 10 to 15 minutes. Mix
powdered sugar with enough milk to make
a pouring consistency. Stir in juice and
pecans. Pour over biscuits. Yield: 24 to 30
biscuits.

CINNAMON-NUT BISCUITS

    2 tablespoons melted butter or
        margarine
    3 tablespoons honey
    1 teaspoon ground cinnamon
    1 teaspoon grated orange rind
    ½ cup chopped pecans
    1 (8- to 10-ounce) can refrigerator
        biscuits

Combine butter, honey, cinnamon, orange
rind, and pecans in a saucepan; cook over
medium heat, stirring constantly, until
mixture is smooth and nuts are glazed,
about 3 minutes. Place biscuits on baking
sheet according to package directions; flatten slightly. Spoon cinnamon-nut mixture
over top of biscuits. Bake according to
package directions. Yield: 10 biscuits.

CORN FRITTERS

1 (17-ounce) can whole kernel corn
1 egg, beaten
2⅓ cups Biscuit Mix (*see* Index)
    Vegetable oil

Drain liquid from corn into medium bowl; add egg and Biscuit Mix and stir until smooth. Fold in corn. Drop by tablespoonfuls into oil heated to 375°. Fry until golden brown on both sides (3 to 5 minutes). Drain. Yield: about 2 dozen.

GERMAN BREAKFAST BREAD

1½ cups all-purpose flour
  2 teaspoons baking powder
  ½ teaspoon salt
  ½ cup water
  ¼ cup butter or margarine
  3 eggs
  1 cup sugar
  2 tablespoons grated lemon rind
  1 tablespoon fine breadcrumbs
    Powdered sugar

Combine flour, baking powder, and salt; set aside. Heat water to boiling in small saucepan; add butter and stir until melted. Beat eggs in large bowl; gradually add sugar and continue beating until mixture is light and thick. Stir in flour mixture, lemon rind, and water mixture. Grease a 9- x 5- x 3-inch loafpan; dust with breadcrumbs. Pour mixture into pan; bake at 350° for 1 hour or until cake tester comes out clean. Cool slightly before removing from pan. Sprinkle top with sifted powdered sugar. Yield: 1 loaf.
Note: This bread freezes well.

Do-ahead buttered crumbs: Add 3 tablespoons melted butter or margarine to 1 cup bread or cracker crumbs. Stir until crumbs are well coated. Store in covered container in refrigerator. Yield: 1 cup.

CHEESE LOAF

3 cups self-rising flour
2 tablespoons sugar
1 to 2 tablespoons minced onion
1 cup (4 ounces) shredded sharp
    Cheddar cheese
1 egg, beaten
1½ cups milk
¼ cup melted shortening or vegetable
    oil

Combine flour and sugar in mixing bowl; add onion and cheese. Combine egg, milk, and shortening; add to flour mixture, stirring only until flour is moistened. Spoon into a greased 9- x 5- x 3-inch loafpan. Bake at 350° about 1 hour and 10 minutes. Cool in pan on wire rack 10 minutes before removing. Serve warm. Yield: 1 loaf.

CHEESE-BACON BREAD

4 cups all-purpose flour
½ cup sugar
2 tablespoons baking powder
2 teaspoons salt
2 eggs, slightly beaten
2 cups milk
½ cup vegetable oil
2 cups (8 ounces) shredded Cheddar
    cheese
⅔ cup (5 to 6 slices) cooked, crumbled
    bacon
2 teaspoons caraway seeds

Line two 9- x 5- x 3-inch loafpans with aluminum foil, leaving a ½-inch collar around edges; grease bottom and sides of foil. Combine first 7 ingredients in a large mixing bowl; beat on medium speed of electric mixer for 30 seconds, scraping sides and bottom of bowl constantly. Stir in remaining ingredients. Spoon batter into prepared pans. Bake at 350° for 45 to 50 minutes or until toothpick inserted in center comes out clean. Cool in pans for 5 to 10 minutes; remove from pans and cool thoroughly. Yield: 2 loaves.

Note: To freeze, cover with a piece of foil the size of the top of loaf and collar. To seal, press air out from center towards sides; fold edges up and over and press together. Freeze.

QUICK CHEDDAR CHEESE BREAD

3½ cups Biscuit Mix (*see* Index)
2½ cups (10 ounces) shredded Cheddar
    cheese
 2 eggs, slightly beaten
1¼ cups milk

Combine Biscuit Mix and cheese. Combine eggs and milk. Add liquid to cheese mixture, mixing just enough to moisten cheese mixture. Pour into a greased and floured 9- x 5- x 3-inch loafpan. Bake at 350° for 55 minutes. Yield: 1 loaf.

SUMMERTIME FRUIT BREAD

 1 (8-ounce) package cream cheese,
    softened
 1 cup butter or margarine, softened
1½ cups sugar
1½ teaspoons vanilla extract
 4 eggs
2¼ cups all-purpose flour
1½ teaspoons baking powder
 1 (17-ounce) can fruit cocktail,
    drained
 ½ cup chopped nuts

Line two 9- x 5- x 3-inch loafpans with aluminum foil, leaving a ½-inch collar around edges; grease bottom and sides of foil. Combine cream cheese, butter, sugar, and vanilla; add eggs, one at a time, beating well after each addition. Gradually add flour and baking powder; fold in fruit and nuts. Spoon batter into prepared pans.

Bake at 325° for 1 hour or until tests done with a toothpick. Cool in pans for 5 to 10 minutes; remove from pans and cool thoroughly. Yield: 2 loaves.

Note: To freeze, cover with a piece of foil the size of the top of loaf and collar. To seal, press air out from center towards sides; fold edges up and over, press together. Freeze.

OATMEAL BREAD

 2 cups all-purpose flour
 2 teaspoons baking powder
 ¾ teaspoon soda
 1 teaspoon salt
 ⅓ cup firmly packed brown sugar
 1 cup quick-cooking oats, uncooked
 1 cup raisins
 2 tablespoons molasses
 2 tablespoons melted shortening
1¼ cups sour milk or buttermilk

Combine flour, baking powder, soda, salt, and sugar. Crush oats with rolling pin; stir oats and raisins into dry ingredients; mix well. Combine molasses, shortening, and buttermilk; add to flour mixture and stir just to moisten dry ingredients. Pour into greased 9- x 5- x 3-inch loafpan. Bake at 350° for 1 hour. Yield: 1 loaf.

Note: One tablespoon plus 2 teaspoons vinegar plus milk to equal 1¼ cups can be substituted for sour milk.

Hints for quick perfect baking:
  Read recipe carefully.
  Check ingredients and equipment before starting.
  Preheat the oven unless recipe specifies otherwise.
  Measure all ingredients before starting to mix.
  For easy clean up, measure ingredients on waxed paper until ready to use.

PEANUT BUTTER BREAD

4½ cups all-purpose flour
2 tablespoons baking powder
1¼ teaspoons salt
⅔ cup sugar
1 cup peanut butter
2 eggs, well beaten
2 cups milk
1 tablespoon grated orange rind
½ cup chopped salted peanuts

Combine flour, baking powder, salt, and sugar. Cut in peanut butter with two knives or pastry blender until mixture resembles coarse meal. Combine eggs, milk, orange rind, and chopped peanuts; stir into flour mixture until blended. Pour batter into a greased 9- x 5- x 3-inch loafpan. Bake at 350° for 1 hour or until bread tests done with a toothpick. Remove from pan; cool. Wrap in aluminum foil and store overnight before slicing. Yield: 1 loaf.

IRISH SODA BREAD

2 cups all-purpose flour
¾ teaspoon soda
½ teaspoon baking powder
¾ teaspoon salt
1 tablespoon sugar
¼ cup plus 2 tablespoons shortening, chilled
1 tablespoon caraway seeds (optional)
¾ cup buttermilk
Milk

Combine flour, soda, baking powder, salt, and sugar in a large bowl; cut in shortening until mixture resembles coarse meal. Add caraway seeds, if desired. Gradually add buttermilk. Turn dough out onto a floured surface and knead lightly. Shape into a ball. Place in a well-greased 9- x 5- x 3-inch

loafpan or 8-inch ovenproof skillet. Cut a cross in top of bread; brush with milk. Bake at 375° for 40 to 50 minutes. Yield: 1 loaf.

Note: One tablespoon vinegar plus milk to equal 1 cup can be substituted for the buttermilk.

QUICK BOSTON BROWN BREAD

1 cup cornmeal
2 cups whole wheat flour
2 teaspoons baking powder
1 teaspoon salt
¾ cup dark molasses
1¾ cups milk

Combine cornmeal, flour, baking powder, and salt in a medium bowl; mix well. Combine molasses and milk; add to dry ingredients, mixing well. Spoon into a greased 8-inch square pan. Bake at 350° for 50 minutes. Yield: 9 servings.

ONION-CHEESE BREAD

1 cup chopped onion
2 tablespoons melted butter or margarine
3 cups self-rising flour
½ cup shortening
2 eggs, beaten
1 cup milk
2 cups (8 ounces) shredded sharp Cheddar cheese, divided
¼ cup melted butter or margarine

Sauté onion in 2 tablespoons butter until tender. Place flour in large mixing bowl; cut in shortening until mixture resembles coarse meal. Combine eggs and milk; add to dry ingredients and stir only until moistened. Add onion and 1 cup cheese. Spread dough in greased 9-inch square baking dish. Sprinkle top with remaining cheese; drizzle with ¼ cup melted butter. Bake at 400° for 25 minutes. Cut into 3- x 1-inch strips and serve hot. Yield: 27 servings.

MEXICAN CORNBREAD

  3 eggs, slightly beaten
  1 cup milk
1½ cups self-rising cornmeal
  1 cup cream-style corn
1½ cups (6 ounces) shredded Cheddar
     cheese
  1 medium onion, chopped
  3 jalapeño peppers, chopped (optional)
 ½ cup vegetable oil

Combine eggs and milk; add to cornmeal. Stir in corn, cheese, onion, peppers, if desired, and oil. Pour into a greased 9-inch square baking pan. Bake at 375° for 25 to 30 minutes. Yield: 9 servings.

ONION SHORTCAKE

  1 large sweet onion or 2 medium
     onions, sliced
 ¼ cup melted butter or margarine
1½ cups Cornmeal Mix (see Index)
  1 egg, beaten
 ⅓ cup milk
  1 cup cream-style corn
  2 drops hot sauce
  1 cup commercial sour cream
 ½ teaspoon salt
  1 cup (4 ounces) shredded sharp
     Cheddar cheese, divided

Sauté onion in butter; set aside. Combine Cornmeal Mix, egg, milk, corn, and hot sauce. Spoon into a buttered 8-inch square pan. Add sour cream, salt, and ½ cup cheese to sautéed onion; spread over batter. Sprinkle with remaining cheese. Bake at 425° for 25 to 30 minutes. Serve warm. Yield: 9 servings.

CELEBRATION CORN MUFFINS

1¼ cups all-purpose flour
 ⅔ cup cornmeal
  3 tablespoons sugar
  1 tablespoon baking powder
 ¾ teaspoon salt
  1 egg
  1 cup milk
 ⅓ cup shortening, melted
  2 tablespoons strawberry or
     orange-flavored gelatin, divided

Combine flour, cornmeal, sugar, baking powder, and salt. Add egg, milk, and shortening. Stir until blended. (Do not overmix.) Spoon a small amount of batter into each of 12 greased muffin pans. Sprinkle 1 tablespoon gelatin evenly over spooned batter. Fill muffin pans with remaining batter; sprinkle with remaining gelatin. Bake at 425° for 20 to 25 minutes or until lightly browned. Yield: 1 dozen.

APPLE MUFFINS

1¾ cups all-purpose flour
  1 tablespoon baking powder
 ½ teaspoon salt
  2 tablespoons sugar
 ½ teaspoon ground cinnamon
  1 egg
  1 cup milk
  3 tablespoons melted shortening
  1 cup grated apple, unpeeled
 ⅓ cup firmly packed brown sugar
 ⅓ cup chopped nuts
 ½ teaspoon ground cinnamon

Combine flour, baking powder, salt, sugar, and ½ teaspoon cinnamon; make a well in center of dry ingredients. Beat egg until light; add milk, shortening, and apple. Pour liquid into well and stir until dry ingredients are moistened. Do not overbeat. Fill muffin pans one-half full. Combine brown sugar, nuts, and ½ teaspoon cinnamon; sprinkle over muffin batter. Bake at 425° for 20 to 25 minutes. Yield: 10 to 12 muffins.

BLUEBERRY MUFFINS

1¾ cups all-purpose flour
1 tablespoon baking powder
½ teaspoon salt
¼ cup sugar
1 egg
1 cup milk
3 tablespoons melted shortening
1 cup fresh blueberries or ¾ cup well-drained canned or frozen blueberries
2 tablespoons all-purpose flour

Combine 1¾ cups flour, baking powder, salt, and sugar. Make a well in center of dry ingredients. Beat egg until light; add milk and shortening. Pour liquid into well and stir until dry ingredients are moistened. Combine the blueberries and 2 tablespoons flour; add to muffin mixture. Fill muffin pans one-half full. Bake at 425° for 20 to 25 minutes. Yield: 10 to 12 muffins.

CRANBERRY MUFFINS

2 cups Biscuit Mix (see Index)
⅓ cup sugar
1 egg
¾ cup milk
2 tablespoons vegetable oil or melted butter or margarine
1 (16-ounce) can whole cranberry sauce

Combine Biscuit Mix, sugar, egg, milk, and oil; mix until dry ingredients are moistened. Break up cranberry sauce and fold in carefully. Fill greased muffin pans two-thirds full. Bake at 425° for 20 to 25 minutes. Yield: 1½ dozen.

Due to the tangy flavor of buttermilk, it cannot successfully replace other forms of milk in recipes.

JELLIED CRANBERRY MUFFINS

1¾ cups all-purpose flour
¼ cup sugar
2½ teaspoons baking powder
¾ teaspoon salt
1 egg, well beaten
¾ cup milk
⅓ cup vegetable oil
1 (8-ounce) can jellied cranberry sauce, chilled and cut into ½-inch cubes

Combine flour, sugar, baking powder, and salt; make a well in center of dry ingredients. Combine egg, milk, and oil; add all at once to dry ingredients, mixing just enough to moisten. Fill greased muffin pans one-third full. Sprinkle cranberry over batter in muffin pans. Top with remaining batter. Bake at 400° for 25 minutes. Yield: 1 dozen.

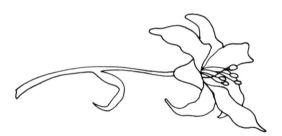

POLKA DOT MUFFINS

1 cup fresh cranberries, chopped
½ cup sugar
1 teaspoon grated orange rind
1 egg, beaten
¼ cup sugar
½ cup orange juice
2 tablespoons vegetable oil
2 cups Biscuit Mix (see Index)

Combine cranberries, ½ cup sugar, and orange rind; set aside. Combine egg, ¼ cup sugar, orange juice, and oil; add to Biscuit Mix. Stir just until moistened. Fold in cranberry mixture. Fill greased muffin pans two-thirds full. Bake at 400° for 20 to 25 minutes or until done. Yield: 1½ dozen.

JELLY MUFFINS

    2 cups all-purpose flour
    2 tablespoons sugar
    1 tablespoon baking powder
    ⅛ teaspoon salt
    1 egg, slightly beaten
    1 cup milk
    ¼ cup shortening, melted
      Jelly

Combine flour, sugar, baking powder, and salt; set aside. Combine egg, milk, and shortening. Pour egg mixture into dry ingredients; stir only until flour mixture is moistened. Batter will be lumpy. Do not overbeat. Fill greased muffin pans one-third full. Add 1 teaspoon of jelly. Top with remaining batter. Bake at 425° for 20 to 25 minutes. Yield: 10 to 12 muffins.

PEANUT BUTTER MUFFINS

    2 cups all-purpose flour
    1 tablespoon baking powder
    1 teaspoon salt
    ¼ cup sugar
    ½ cup peanut butter
    1 cup milk
    1 egg, slightly beaten
    ¼ cup melted butter

Combine dry ingredients; cut in peanut butter until mixture resembles coarse meal. Combine milk, egg, and butter; add to flour mixture, stirring just until moistened. Spoon batter into greased muffin pans. Bake at 400° for 20 to 25 minutes or until golden brown. Yield: 1 dozen.

If you use glass or glass ceramic dishes, you can lower oven heat by 25°. (If you're using a recipe that calls for 375° you can usually use 350°.) If you have an electric range, cut your time by 5 minutes, turn the oven off, and let the reserved heat continue to bake your food.

PINEAPPLE MUFFINS

    1 (8½-ounce) can crushed pineapple,
      drained
    ½ cup melted butter or margarine
    ½ cup firmly packed brown sugar
    1 teaspoon ground cinnamon
    ¼ teaspoon ground nutmeg
    ¼ cup chopped nuts
    2 cups Biscuit Mix (*see* Index)
    ¼ cup sugar
    ¼ cup milk
    ⅓ cup melted butter or margarine

Combine pineapple, ½ cup melted butter, brown sugar, cinnamon, nutmeg, and nuts; spoon into 12 muffin pans. Combine Biscuit Mix, sugar, milk, and ⅓ cup melted butter; stir until blended. Spoon over mixture in muffin pans. Bake at 425° for 15 to 20 minutes. Turn upside down immediately on tray to remove muffins. Yield: 1 dozen.

PRUNE MUFFINS

    2 cups all-purpose flour
    2 tablespoons sugar
    1 tablespoon baking powder
    ⅛ teaspoon salt
    1 egg, slightly beaten
    1 cup milk
    ¼ cup shortening, melted
    ¾ cup cooked prunes, well-drained
      and chopped

Combine flour, sugar, baking powder, and salt. Combine egg, milk, and shortening; add to dry ingredients and stir only until moistened. Fold in prunes. Batter will be lumpy. Do not overbeat. Fill greased muffin pans two-thirds full. Bake at 425° for 20 to 25 minutes. Yield: 10 to 12 muffins.

Keep white, ivory, or colored candles that match your china around for the last minute dinner party.

RAISIN OR DATE MUFFINS

1¾ cups all-purpose flour
1 tablespoon baking powder
½ teaspoon salt
2 tablespoons sugar
1 egg
1 cup milk
3 tablespoons melted shortening
1 cup raisins or 1 cup chopped dates
2 tablespoons all-purpose flour

Combine 1¾ cups flour, baking powder, salt, and sugar. Make a well in center of dry ingredients. Beat egg until light; add milk and shortening. Pour liquid into well and stir until dry ingredients are moistened. Combine raisins and 2 tablespoons flour; add to muffin mixture. Do not overbeat. Fill muffin pans about one-half full. Bake at 425° for 20 to 25 minutes. Yield: 10 to 12 muffins.

SWEET POTATO MUFFINS

1¾ cups all-purpose flour
¼ cup firmly packed brown sugar
1 tablespoon baking powder
1 teaspoon salt
2 tablespoons ground cinnamon
½ cup coarsely chopped nuts
2 eggs, beaten
¾ cup milk
1 (16-ounce) can sweet potatoes,
    drained and mashed
¼ cup melted butter or margarine
½ teaspoon ground cinnamon
2 tablespoons sugar

Combine flour, brown sugar, baking powder, salt, cinnamon, and nuts; set aside. Combine eggs, milk, sweet potatoes, and butter; add to dry ingredients. Mix just until moist. Fill greased muffin pans two-thirds full. Combine cinnamon and sugar; sprinkle over muffin batter. Bake at 425° for 35 minutes. Yield: 1½ dozen.

TWIN MOUNTAIN MUFFINS

2 cups all-purpose flour
¼ teaspoon salt
1 tablespoon baking powder
¼ cup butter or margarine, softened
¼ cup sugar
1 egg, separated
¾ cup milk

Lightly grease muffin pans. Combine flour, salt, and baking powder; set aside. Cream butter; add sugar slowly. Beat egg yolk and add to butter mixture; alternately add flour mixture and milk, beginning and ending with flour. Beat egg white until stiff; fold into batter. Fill muffin pans one-half full. Bake at 400° for 20 minutes. Serve hot. Yield: 10 to 12 muffins.

POPOVERS

2 eggs, beaten
1 cup milk
1 tablespoon melted shortening
1 cup all-purpose flour
½ teaspoon salt

Combine eggs, milk, and shortening in mixing bowl; add flour and salt and beat until mixture is smooth. Pour into hot greased custard cups or hot iron muffin pans. (Cups should not be more than one-half full.) Bake at 425° for 40 minutes. Yield: 8 to 12 popovers.

The tantalizing odor and variety of quick hot breads immediately capture the attention of folks who like good food: Cheese-Bacon Biscuits, page 188; Quick Cheddar Cheese Bread, page 191; and Blueberry Muffins, page 194.

Overleaf: One of these colorful, crisp salads add a special touch to any meal. Pictured from left to right: Easy Waldorf Salad with Cheese Dressing, page 87; 7-Cup Party Salad, page 183; and Mexican Shrimp-Corn Salad, page 179.

Mala Melua seu Citria.

Poma Aurantia nana dicta.

Poma Aurantia.

CRISP CORN TOAST

1 cup cornmeal
2 eggs
¼ teaspoon salt
1¼ cups evaporated milk
3 tablespoons butter or margarine
8 slices day-old white bread
 Butter
 Syrup or jelly (optional)

Place cornmeal in piepan. Beat eggs in medium bowl; stir in salt and milk. Melt butter in large skillet. Dip bread in egg mixture; turn once and let stand until bread is moist but not too soft to turn. Place in cornmeal, turning to coat both sides. Cook in hot butter until brown; turn and brown on other side. Add butter as needed to keep skillet well greased. Serve hot with additional butter and syrup or jelly, if desired. Yield: 8 servings.

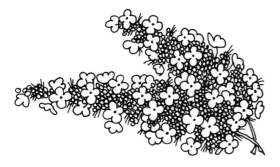

THIN GARLIC CHEESE TOAST

1 (1-pound) loaf French bread
 Butter or margarine, softened
 Garlic salt
 Shredded sharp Cheddar cheese or grated Parmesan cheese

Cut bread into ½-inch slices. Spread generously with butter; sprinkle with garlic salt. Top each slice with desired cheese. Bake at 425° for 10 minutes or until cheese is melted. Serve hot. Yield: 10 to 12 servings.

SEASONED BREADSTICKS

Bread slices
Butter or margarine, softened
Onion salt or garlic salt
Grated Parmesan cheese
Oregano

Toast bread under broiler on one side; butter other side and sprinkle with onion salt, Parmesan cheese, and oregano. Remove crusts and cut into ½-inch strips. Toast buttered side until lightly browned. Yield: 4 sticks per slice.

CRUNCH STICKS

1 (4- to 5-ounce) can refrigerator biscuits
¾ cup crisp rice cereal, coarsely crushed
1 tablespoon caraway seeds or celery seeds
1 teaspoon salt
 Milk

Cut biscuits in half; roll each piece to pencil thickness, about 4 inches long. Combine cereal, caraway seeds, and salt in a shallow pan. Roll sticks in milk and then in cereal mixture. Place on greased baking sheet. Bake at 450° for 10 minutes or until lightly browned. Yield: 10 to 12 sticks.

Muffins are a quick bread. To be sure your muffins have a tender texture, with a pebbly golden brown crust and a gently rounded shape, proper mixing is essential. The secret is not to overdo it. Stir together gently the dry and liquid ingredients, using only the minimum number of strokes needed to incorporate the flour mixture.

GARLIC BUTTER FINGERS

2 cups Biscuit Mix (*see* Index)
⅓ cup butter or margarine, melted
Garlic salt

Prepare Biscuit Mix according to directions. Roll dough into a 10- x 6-inch rectangle. Cut rectangle in half lengthwise and then cut each half crosswise into 12 strips. Pour melted butter into a 13- x 9- x 2-inch baking pan. Turn biscuit strips over in butter and sprinkle with garlic salt. Bake at 425° for 15 minutes or until golden brown. Yield: 24 strips.

CINNAMON PINWHEELS

2 cups all-purpose flour
¾ teaspoon salt
1 tablespoon baking powder
¼ cup shortening
¾ cup milk
Melted butter or margarine
½ cup sugar
1 tablespoon ground cinnamon
¼ cup raisins

Combine flour, salt, and baking powder in a mixing bowl; cut in shortening until mixture resembles coarse meal. Add milk, stirring quickly until milk is blended. Turn dough out onto a lightly floured board and knead lightly about 20 seconds. Roll dough in a rectangular shape to ½-inch thickness. Brush with butter. Combine sugar and cinnamon; sprinkle over dough. Sprinkle with raisins. Roll up jellyroll fashion, beginning at long side. Cut into 1-inch slices. Place on greased baking sheet with cut surface down. Bake at 400° for 15 to 20 minutes. Yield: 10 to 12 servings.

Don't take time to frost a good cake. Just sift powdered sugar over the top for that finished look.

EASY COFFEE CAKE

½ cup melted butter or margarine
½ cup firmly packed brown sugar
1 teaspoon ground cinnamon
2 (8- to 10-ounce) cans refrigerator biscuits
⅓ cup chopped pecans

Combine butter, brown sugar, and cinnamon; dip each biscuit into mixture. Overlap in an 8- or 9-inch round cake pan in a spiral fashion; fill center of pan with remaining biscuits. Combine remaining butter mixture with pecans; pour over biscuits. Bake at 350° for 10 minutes. Yield: 6 to 8 servings.

Note: To reheat coffee cake, cover with aluminum foil to retain moisture.

OLD-FASHIONED COFFEE CAKE

2 cups all-purpose flour
2 teaspoons baking powder
½ teaspoon salt
¼ teaspoon ground nutmeg
¼ cup sugar
1 cup milk
¼ cup vegetable oil
Topping (recipe follows)

Combine flour, baking powder, salt, nutmeg, and sugar in a medium bowl. Combine milk and oil; stir into dry ingredients. Pour into a greased 8-inch square pan. Sprinkle topping over batter. Bake at 425° for 30 minutes or until cake tester comes out clean. Yield: 9 servings.

Topping:

½ cup sugar
1 tablespoon brown sugar
1 tablespoon all-purpose flour
1 teaspoon ground cinnamon
½ teaspoon ground nutmeg
3 tablespoons melted butter or
    margarine

Combine sugar, flour, cinnamon, and nutmeg. Stir in melted butter. Yield: about ⅔ cup.

QUICK PRUNE COFFEE CAKE

½ cup chopped cooked prunes
2 tablespoons honey
1 tablespoon melted butter or
    margarine
1½ cups all-purpose flour
2 teaspoons baking powder
½ teaspoon salt
1 egg
½ cup honey
½ cup milk
3 tablespoons melted butter or
    margarine

Combine prunes, 2 tablespoons honey, and 1 tablespoon melted butter. Spread in a greased 8-inch square pan. Combine flour, baking powder, and salt; set aside. Beat egg; add ½ cup honey, milk, and 3 tablespoons butter. Blend thoroughly. Add to flour mixture, stirring only until moistened. Spoon over prunes in pan. Bake at 400° for 25 minutes. Invert on a serving plate. Yield: 9 servings.

Glasses of milk, when water also is served, are placed to the right and a little in front of the water glass, that is, a little closer to the table edge. This permits easy removal of empty milk glasses.

RAISIN CASSEROLE BREAD

4 cups all-purpose flour
1¼ teaspoons salt
1½ teaspoons soda
¾ cup firmly packed dark brown
    sugar
1¼ cups raisins
2 tablespoons melted butter or
    margarine
2 eggs, slightly beaten
1½ cups buttermilk

Combine flour, salt, soda, sugar, and raisins; add butter, eggs, and buttermilk. Mix only until dry ingredients are moistened. Spoon into two greased 1-quart casseroles. Bake at 350° for 45 minutes. Turn out onto rack to cool. Yield: 2 loaves.

CREAM SCONES

2 cups all-purpose flour
1 tablespoon plus 1 teaspoon baking
    powder
2 teaspoons sugar
½ teaspoon salt
¼ cup butter or margarine
2 eggs
⅓ cup half-and-half or whipping cream
Sugar
Jam or jelly

Combine flour, baking powder, 2 teaspoons sugar, and salt; cut in butter until mixture resembles coarse meal. Reserve 1 tablespoon egg white. Beat eggs, add half-and-half, and beat again; add to dry mixture. Toss dough onto a lightly floured board; roll into a ¾-inch thick rectangle. Cut dough into diamond shapes. Brush tops with reserved egg white and sprinkle with sugar. Place on greased baking sheet. Bake at 450° for 15 minutes. Serve hot with jam or jelly. Yield: 18 to 24 scones.

Note: Dough may be rolled or patted into a circle and cut into wedges.

FOUR O'CLOCK SCONES

- 2 cups all-purpose flour
- ½ teaspoon salt
- 1 tablespoon sugar
- 1 tablespoon plus 1 teaspoon baking powder
- ¼ cup shortening
- ½ to ⅔ cup milk
- 1 egg, well beaten
  Melted butter or margarine
  Sugar

Combine flour, salt, 1 tablespoon sugar, and baking powder; cut in shortening until mixture resembles coarse meal. Combine ½ cup milk and egg; gradually add to flour mixture. If mixture is dry, add remaining milk. Turn out onto a floured surface and knead lightly. Roll dough in circle to ½-inch thickness. Cut into 15 wedges. Place on greased baking sheet; brush with melted butter and dredge with sugar. Bake at 400° for 15 minutes. Yield: 15 scones.

TEA ROLLS

- 2 cups all-purpose flour
- ¼ cup sugar
- ¾ teaspoon soda
- ½ teaspoon salt
- ⅓ cup shortening
- ½ cup milk
- 3 tablespoons lemon juice
  Melted butter

Combine flour, sugar, soda, and salt in large bowl; cut in shortening until mixture resembles coarse meal. Combine milk and lemon juice; quickly stir into flour mixture to form a soft dough.

Turn dough out onto a lightly floured board; knead slightly. Shape into small balls about the size of marbles. Put three balls into each greased muffin pan (about 2¼-inch diameter). Bake at 450° for 15 minutes or until lightly browned. Brush with melted butter. Yield: 1 dozen.

To prevent contamination, thaw frozen foods in the refrigerator; don't allow them to thaw at room temperature.

Whenever you cut raw meat or poultry, wash the counter or cutting board with hot soapy water after each use.

Do not leave hot foods to cool at room temperature. Put them in shallow containers and into the refrigerator to be cooled quickly.

To prevent food spoilage, do not leave leftovers on the table. Put them in the refrigerator as soon as you've finished eating.

The transparent wrap on prepackaged meat, poultry, or fish is designed for refrigerator storage for one or two days.

Always store poultry stuffing, broth, or gravy away from the meat when you put it in the refrigerator; store in separate containers.

For freezer storage use moisture, vapor-resistant (air-tight) wrapping. (Improper wrapping or a puncture in the package may cause freezer burn, which means drying out of the surface tissues of the food.)

When storing commercial sour cream, turn the carton upside down in refrigerator to prevent air from entering the carton. Sour cream will last for four or five days when stored in this manner.

Do not eat mold on any food not intended to have mold. It isn't safe to scoop off mold and eat the remaining food. The whole item should be destroyed. If you subscribe to the theory that a little mold never really hurt anybody, you may be setting yourself up for a variety of problems, some of which can be fatal.

Desserts

A dessert is considered a happy ending to any meal, especially if it complements the rest of the menu. A heavy meal is best followed by a simple, light dessert, and, conversely, a heavier dessert will be more appropriate after a soup and salad supper. Also, a dessert can be planned to supply nutrients not provided in the rest of the meal. For example, if a vegetable plate is the main dish, then the dessert can be a cup custard which supplies missing protein.

Although quick and easy desserts require little preparation time, they, too, can provide a rich, glamorous ending to the meal. Cakes, pies, and some frozen desserts may be prepared the day ahead if time is a factor. However, nothing is enjoyed more by many people than a luscious topping on the all-American vanilla ice cream; or try a low calorie, brightly colored gelatin dessert prepared in a hasty fashion, but handsomely served in a sparkling clear compote.

The quick and easy desserts offered on the following pages will provide a new adventure in eating; they can be served with pride, eaten with pleasure.

EASY DAY CHOCOLATE CAKE

2 cups all-purpose flour
2 cups sugar
1 cup butter or margarine
3 tablespoons cocoa
1 cup water
½ cup buttermilk
1 teaspoon soda
2 eggs, slightly beaten
1 teaspoon vanilla extract
Easy Day Frosting (*see* Index)

Combine flour and sugar; set aside. Combine butter, cocoa, and water in a small skillet; bring to a boil and add to flour mixture. Stir well by hand. Do not use an electric mixer. Combine buttermilk, soda, eggs, and vanilla. Add to flour mixture and mix thoroughly. Spoon batter into a greased and floured 13- x 9- x 2-inch pan. Bake at 350° for 40 minutes. Prepare Easy Day Frosting 5 minutes before cake is done; frost cake while hot. Yield: about 15 servings.

QUICK DEVIL'S FOOD CAKE

1½ cups all-purpose flour
1 cup sugar
3 tablespoons cocoa
1 teaspoon soda
½ teaspoon salt
⅓ cup vegetable oil
1 tablespoon vinegar
1 teaspoon vanilla extract
1 cup cold water
Easy Day Frosting (*see* Index)

Combine and sift twice flour, sugar, cocoa, soda, and salt; sift into an ungreased 9-inch cakepan, and smooth flat. Make three depressions with back of tablespoon. Put oil in one, vinegar in the second, and vanilla in the third. Pour cold water over all. Stir with fork to mix. Bake at 375° for 30 minutes. Frost with Easy Day Frosting or serve plain. Yield: 6 servings.

WHITE CAKE WITH MAGIC FROSTING

1 (18½-ounce) package white cake mix
⅓ cup butter or margarine, melted
½ cup firmly packed brown sugar
¼ cup milk
Dash of salt
½ teaspoon vanilla extract
1 cup flaked coconut
½ cup chopped nuts

Prepare cake batter according to package directions. Spoon batter into a greased and floured 13- x 9- x 2-inch pan and bake according to package directions. Combine remaining ingredients; spread over hot cake. Broil slowly until bubbly. Yield: 12 to 15 servings.

QUICK ANGEL DESSERT

1 (1-pound) angel food loaf cake
½ cup butter or margarine, softened
½ cup firmly packed light brown sugar
1 tablespoon lemon juice
¼ teaspoon ground cinnamon
⅛ teaspoon ground nutmeg
1 cup commercial sour cream
1 cup fresh sliced strawberries or 1 (10-ounce) package frozen strawberries, thawed and drained

Cut cake into 6 slices. Combine butter, sugar, lemon juice, cinnamon, and nutmeg in a small bowl; mix until smooth. Toast one side of cake; turn and spread butter mixture generously on untoasted side. Toast under broiler. Serve warm topped with sour cream and strawberries. Yield: 6 servings.

CHOCOLATE FLUFF TOPPING ON ANGEL FOOD CAKE

 2 cups whipping cream
 1 cup sifted powdered sugar
 ½ cup cocoa
   Dash of salt
 1 angel food cake

Combine whipping cream, sugar, cocoa, and salt in mixing bowl; chill 30 minutes. Beat mixture until stiff. Serve on wedges of cake. Yield: 12 to 16 servings.

BAKED ALASKAN DREAM

 1 (1-pound) commercial pound cake
 1 pint ice cream, softened
   Meringue (recipe follows)

Cut 1-inch thick layer lengthwise from cake. Spread with ice cream. Freeze until ice cream is firm. Just before serving, place on foil-lined board or baking sheet. Cover top and sides completely with meringue. Bake at 500° for 3 to 5 minutes, or until lightly browned. Serve immediately or place back in freezer; slice as needed. Meringue does not freeze and therefore slices perfectly. Yield: 6 servings.

 Meringue:

 3 egg whites
 ½ cup sugar

Beat egg whites until foamy. Add sugar, 2 tablespoons at a time, beating thoroughly after each addition. Continue beating until mixture forms stiff, shiny peaks.

Note: Freeze remainder of pound cake for another quick dessert.

Baked Alaska can be stored in the freezer and sliced when ready to serve. Instant dessert!

NO CRUST CHEESE CAKE

 2 (8-ounce) packages cream cheese, softened
 ⅔ cup sugar
   Dash of salt
 3 eggs
 ½ teaspoon almond extract
 1 cup commercial sour cream
 3 tablespoons sugar
 1 teaspoon vanilla extract
   Dash of salt
   Toasted slivered almonds

Beat cream cheese until fluffy. Gradually beat in ⅔ cup sugar and salt. Add eggs, one at a time, beating well after each addition; beat until smooth. Add almond extract and pour into a buttered 9-inch piepan. Bake at 350° for 30 minutes. Remove from oven and let cool away from drafts for 20 minutes.

Combine sour cream, 3 tablespoons sugar, vanilla, and salt; beat until smooth. Spread over top of cake. Bake 10 additional minutes. Sprinkle with almonds; cool and serve. Yield: one 9-inch cake.

Note: To toast slivered almonds spread in shallow pan and bake at 350° for 5 minutes or until brown.

PEANUT BUTTER BRITTLE CAKE

 1 (16½-ounce) can ready-to-spread vanilla frosting
 ¼ cup peanut butter
 1 (1-pound) angel food loaf cake, halved crosswise
 1 cup finely crushed peanut brittle

Combine frosting and peanut butter and beat until smooth. Spread frosting over each cake half. Sprinkle peanut brittle over frosting. Yield: 6 servings.

Note: To crush peanut brittle, place brittle in plastic bag and tap gently with wooden mallet until desired fineness is reached.

Note: Freeze remainder of cake for another quick dessert.

PLUM GOOD CAKE

2 cups self-rising flour
2 cups sugar
1 teaspoon ground cloves
1 teaspoon ground cinnamon
3 eggs, beaten
1 cup vegetable oil
2 (4¾-ounce) jars plum baby food
1 cup chopped pecans

Combine flour, sugar, cloves, and cinnamon; set aside. Combine eggs, oil, and plum mixture; add to dry ingredients. Mix well. Stir in pecans. Pour into a greased and floured 13- x 9- x 2-inch pan. Bake at 325° for 1 hour. Serve warm. Yield: 15 servings.

Note: One cup of applesauce or 1 cup mashed bananas can be substituted for plum baby food.

STREUSEL CAKE

1 (9-ounce) package yellow cake mix
2 tablespoons butter or margarine
2 tablespoons sugar
¼ cup all-purpose flour
½ cup dry breadcrumbs or cereal crumbs
½ teaspoon ground cinnamon

Prepare cake mix according to package directions; pour into a greased and floured 9-inch cakepan. Blend butter and sugar; add flour, breadcrumbs, and cinnamon. Mix to consistency of coarse crumbs; sprinkle over cake batter. Bake according to cake package directions. Yield: 6 to 9 servings.

Note: One-half of 1 (18½-ounce) package butter cake mix may be substituted for 1 (9-ounce) package.

PRALINE CAKE SQUARES

1 (18½-ounce) package yellow cake mix
½ cup butter or margarine
1 (1-pound) package light brown sugar
2 tablespoons all-purpose flour
2 eggs, slightly beaten
1 teaspoon vanilla extract
1½ cups coarsely chopped pecans

Prepare cake mix according to package directions. Pour batter into two greased and floured 13- x 9- x 2-inch pans. Bake at 350° for 20 minutes. Melt butter in a 2-quart heavy saucepan. Combine sugar, flour, and eggs. Add to butter and bring to a boil over low heat; cook for 3 minutes stirring constantly. Remove from heat; add vanilla and pecans. Quickly spread mixture evenly over cooled cakes. Bake at 400° for 8 minutes. Cool before cutting. Yield: 30 to 40 squares.

QUICK CHEWY BROWNIES

1 (6-ounce) package semisweet chocolate morsels
½ cup butter or margarine
2 cups biscuit mix
1 (14-ounce) can sweetened condensed milk
1 egg, slightly beaten
1 cup chopped walnuts

Combine chocolate morsels and butter in large saucepan. Add biscuit mix, milk, and egg; stir well. Stir in nuts. Pour into a greased 9-inch square pan; bake at 350° for 20 to 25 minutes. Cut into squares. Yield: 9 servings.

Note: Two cups of Biscuit Mix may be used (*see* Index).

If you find yourself out of unsweetened chocolate, substitute 1 tablespoon of butter and 3 tablespoons of cocoa for each 1-ounce square of chocolate.

FUDGE NUT CLUSTERS

   3 tablespoons melted butter or
      margarine
   3 tablespoons milk
   1 (15.4-ounce) package chocolate
      fudge frosting mix
   1 (6½-ounce) can salted peanuts

Combine butter and milk in 2-quart sauce-pan. Stir in dry frosting mix. Cook over low heat, stirring constantly, about 5 minutes or until smooth and glossy. Remove from heat; stir in peanuts. Drop by rounded teaspoons onto waxed paper. If mixture becomes too thick, return to low heat to soften slightly. Yield: approximately 3 dozen.

CHOCOLATE PEANUT BARS

   2 cups Biscuit Mix (see Index)
   ½ cup milk
   ¼ cup sugar
   ¼ cup chunky peanut butter
   1 egg
   ½ cup semisweet chocolate morsels

Grease and flour an 8-inch square baking pan. Measure all ingredients except chocolate morsels into a large bowl. Beat at low speed with electric mixer until just mixed; increase speed of mixer to medium and beat 2 minutes, scraping bowl occasionally. Spread mixture evenly into a greased and floured 8-inch square pan. Bake at 350° for 25 minutes or until toothpick inserted in center comes out clean. Evenly sprinkle chocolate morsels over cake; bake 2 to 3 additional minutes until chocolate morsels are melted. Spread chocolate evenly to frost cake. Cool 10 minutes, and cut into bars. Yield: 8 servings.

CRUNCHY COOKIES

   1 (6-ounce) package semisweet
      chocolate morsels
   1 (6-ounce) package butterscotch
      morsels
   2 (3-ounce) cans chow mein noodles
   1 cup peanuts

Melt chocolate and butterscotch morsels in top of double boiler. Add noodles and nuts; stir until coated. Remove from heat. Drop by teaspoonfuls onto waxed paper. (For fast cooling, use aluminum baking sheet.) Yield: 60 pieces.

PEANUT BUTTER-COCOA MOUNDS

   2 cups sugar
   ⅓ cup cocoa
   ¼ cup butter or margarine
   ½ cup milk
   3 cups quick-cooking oats, uncooked
   ½ cup peanut butter
   2 teaspoons vanilla extract

Combine sugar and cocoa in a saucepan; add butter and milk. Bring to a boil, stirring constantly; boil 2 minutes. Remove from heat. Stir in oats, peanut butter, and vanilla. Drop by teaspoonfuls onto waxed paper. Let cool thoroughly before serving or storing. Yield: 4 dozen.

When baking an angel food cake from "scratch" or a mix, prepare mix in a 4-quart pyrex bowl. After mixing and before baking, wipe splatters from inside the bowl. Leave batter in mixing bowl and bake as directed. Bake 10 minutes longer than when using a tube pan. Cool by inverting bowl on 4 custard or coffee cups for support for 1½ to 2 hours. Loosen cake with knife.

GRAHAM CRISPIES

18 (2½-inch long) graham crackers,
    halved
1 cup butter or margarine
1 cup firmly packed dark brown
    sugar
1 cup chopped nuts

Line cookie sheet with aluminum foil.
Cover with graham crackers. Melt butter
in saucepan; stir in brown sugar. Bring
mixture to a boil and boil 2 minutes. Sprinkle nuts over crackers. Pour sauce over
nuts and bake at 375° for 10 minutes.
Break crackers apart before they cool.
Yield: about 3 dozen.

MASTER OATMEAL COOKIES

1 cup all-purpose flour
1 teaspoon baking powder
½ teaspoon salt
¾ cup shortening (room temperature)
1 cup firmly packed brown sugar
2 eggs
1 teaspoon vanilla extract
⅓ cup milk
3 cups quick-cooking oats, uncooked

Combine flour, baking powder, and salt.
Add shortening, sugar, eggs, vanilla, and
about half the milk. Beat until smooth,
about 2 minutes. Stir in remaining milk
and oats. Drop from a teaspoon onto
greased baking sheet and bake at 375° for
12 to 15 minutes. Yield: 4 dozen cookies.

Variations:

Chocolate Chip: Add 1 (6-ounce) package semisweet chocolate morsels to cookie
batter.

Peanut: Add 1 cup chopped peanuts to
cookie batter.

Date: Add 1 cup chopped dates to
cookie batter.

Coconut: Add 1 cup coconut to cookie
batter.

Raisin Spice: Add 1 teaspoon ground
cinnamon and ¼ teaspoon ground nutmeg
with dry ingredients. Omit vanilla. Add 1
cup raisins to cookie batter.

CHERRIES À LA MODE

3 tablespoons lemon juice
2 tablespoons brown sugar
⅛ teaspoon salt
1 (21-ounce) can cherry pie filling
    Commercial pound cake
1 quart chocolate ice cream

Combine lemon juice, sugar, salt, and pie
filling in a 1-quart saucepan; heat 5 minutes. Spoon sauce over pound cake slices,
add scoop of ice cream, and top with additional cherry sauce. Serve immediately.
Yield: 6 to 9 servings.

CRANBERRY CRUMBLE

1 (16-ounce) can whole cranberry
    sauce
½ cup quick-cooking oats, uncooked
¼ cup all-purpose flour
½ cup firmly packed brown sugar
¼ cup butter or margarine
    Whipped cream or vanilla ice cream

Spread cranberry sauce in a 9-inch piepan.
Combine oats, flour, and brown sugar; cut
in butter until crumbly. Sprinkle over
cranberries. Bake at 350° for 25 minutes.
Top with whipped cream or vanilla ice
cream. Yield: 5 to 6 servings.

CRANBERRIES JUBILEE

1 cup sugar
1½ cups water
2 cups fresh cranberries
¼ cup brandy
Vanilla ice cream

Combine sugar and water in a medium saucepan, stirring to dissolve sugar. Bring to a boil; boil 5 minutes. Add cranberries and bring to a boil again; cook 5 minutes. Turn into a heat-proof bowl or blazer pan of chafing dish. Heat brandy. Ignite brandy and pour over cranberry mixture. Blend into sauce and serve immediately over ice cream. Yield: 2½ cups.

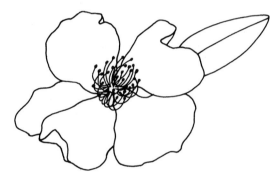

BAKED DRIED FRUIT

1 pound dried apricots
1 pound dried pitted prunes
1 (11-ounce) can mandarin orange sections, undrained
1 (15½-ounce) can pineapple chunks, undrained
1 (21-ounce) can cherry pie filling
½ cup sherry

Place apricots and prunes in a greased 2-quart casserole. Add orange sections and pineapple. Top with pie filling. Pour sherry over all. Bake at 350° for 1 hour. Serve hot or cold as a dessert, as a side dish, or as a topping for ice cream. Yield: 10 servings.

COLORFUL FRUIT COMPOTE

1 (16-ounce) can whole cranberry sauce
⅓ cup sugar
1 tablespoon lemon juice
¼ teaspoon ground cinnamon
¼ teaspoon ground ginger
1 (11-ounce) can mandarin orange sections, drained
6 fresh pears, pared, cored, and quartered

Combine cranberry sauce, sugar, lemon juice, cinnamon, and ginger in medium saucepan; bring to a boil. Combine orange sections and pears in a greased 1½-quart casserole. Pour cranberry mixture over fruit. Cover and bake at 350° for 40 minutes or until pears are tender. Spoon fruit mixture into sherbet dishes or compotes. Serve warm. Yield: 6 servings.

SPICY FRUIT COMPOTE

1 (16-ounce) can pear halves
2 medium apples, pared, cored, and cut into eighths
½ cup whole cranberry sauce
¼ teaspoon ground cinnamon
¼ teaspoon ground allspice

Place regular size (16- x 10-inch) baking bag in a 10- x 6- x 2-inch baking dish. Drain pears, reserving 1 tablespoon syrup. Combine all ingredients in bag; turn bag gently to mix. Close bag with twist tie; make 6 (½-inch) slits in top. Bake at 350° for 30 minutes or until apples are tender. Serve warm or chilled in compotes. Yield: 4 to 6 servings.

For an elegant dessert, just pour 1 to 2 tablespoons of crème de menthe on vanilla ice cream. It's great!

DELICIOUS GRAPE DESSERT

Seedless grapes
Commercial sour cream, whipped
Brown sugar

Alternate layers of grapes, sour cream, and a sprinkling of brown sugar in a compote. Repeat layers. Chill.

BAKED GRAPEFRUIT WITH RAISINS AND NUTS

2 grapefruits
2 tablespoons chopped raisins or figs
2 tablespoons chopped walnuts
3 tablespoons honey

Cut grapefruit in half crosswise. Run knife around each segment to loosen. Combine raisins and walnuts; place in center of each grapefruit half. Drizzle honey over grapefruit. Bake at 300° for 10 to 15 minutes or until heated through. Serve at once. Yield: 4 servings.

HAWAIIAN DESSERT PANCAKES

2 cups Biscuit Mix (*see* Index)
1 (8¾-ounce) can crushed pineapple, drained
1¼ cups milk
¼ cup vegetable oil
2 eggs
⅔ cup sweetened flaked coconut
¼ teaspoon ground nutmeg
Topping (recipe follows)

Combine all ingredients except topping until just blended. Preheat a lightly greased 10-inch skillet until small drops of water "sizzle." Drop pancake batter from spoon into skillet to make silver dollar-size pancakes. Cook until golden brown, about 3 minutes on each side. Keep warm until

served. Serve with topping. Yield: 6 servings.

Topping:

1 tablespoon powdered sugar
⅔ cup sweetened flaked coconut
⅛ teaspoon almond extract
1 cup whipping cream, whipped

Fold sugar, coconut, and almond extract into whipped cream. Yield: 1⅔ cups.

PEACH AND PUDDING PARFAIT

1 (3⅝-ounce) package vanilla pudding and pie filling mix
1½ cups milk
½ cup commercial sour cream
2 cups fresh or canned diced peaches

Combine vanilla pudding and milk in saucepan; cook over medium heat, stirring constantly, until mixture reaches boiling point. Remove from heat and stir in sour cream. Cool thoroughly, stirring frequently. Chill. When ready to serve, alternate layers of pudding and peaches in parfait glasses. Yield: 6 servings.

PEARS IN CARAMEL SAUCE

1 (16-ounce) can pear halves
2 tablespoons butter or margarine
2 tablespoons brown sugar
2 tablespoons corn syrup

Drain pears, reserving ¼ cup syrup. Combine butter, sugar, corn syrup, and ¼ cup pear syrup in a small saucepan; simmer until smooth and blended. Place pear halves in syrup. Heat, basting with syrup. Serve warm or chilled. Yield: 4 servings.

CHOCOLATE PECAN PIE

1 cup sugar
½ cup all-purpose flour
½ cup melted butter or margarine, cooled
1 egg, slightly beaten
1 teaspoon vanilla extract
1 (6-ounce) package semisweet chocolate morsels
1 cup chopped pecans
1 unbaked 9-inch pastry shell
Ice cream, whipped cream, or whipped topping

Combine first 7 ingredients and pour into pastry shell. Bake at 350° for 35 to 40 minutes. (If baked earlier in the day, reheat for 10 to 15 minutes.) Serve warm with ice cream, whipped cream, or whipped topping. Yield: one 9-inch pie.

CRANBERRY PUDDING PIE

1¼ cups fresh cranberries
¼ cup firmly packed brown sugar
¼ cup chopped walnuts
1 egg
½ cup sugar
½ cup all-purpose flour
⅓ cup melted butter or margarine
Vanilla ice cream

Spread cranberries in a greased 9-inch pie-plate. Sprinkle with brown sugar and walnuts. Beat egg until thick; gradually add sugar, beating until thoroughly blended. Add flour and butter; beat well. Pour batter over cranberries. Bake at 325° for 45 minutes. Cut in wedges. Serve warm with ice cream. Yield: 6 servings.

CUSTARD PIE

1½ cups milk
2 eggs
¼ cup plus 2 tablespoons sugar
½ teaspoon ground nutmeg
¼ teaspoon salt
½ teaspoon vanilla extract
1 unbaked 9-inch pastry shell

Heat milk to scalding; set aside. Beat eggs slightly; add sugar, nutmeg, salt, and vanilla. Slowly add milk, stirring constantly. (Avoid beating up a foam.) Fill pastry shell three-fourths full. Place pie on rack of oven and pour in remainder of custard. Bake at 425° for 10 minutes; lower heat to 325° and bake 20 to 25 minutes or until knife inserted in center comes out clean. Yield: one 9-inch pie.

MILLIONAIRE PIE

2 cups powdered sugar
½ cup butter or margarine, softened
1 egg
¼ teaspoon salt
¼ teaspoon vanilla extract
2 baked 9-inch pastry shells
1 cup whipping cream
1 cup well-drained crushed pineapple
½ cup chopped pecans

Cream sugar and butter until fluffy. Add egg, salt, and vanilla; beat well until light and fluffy. Pour mixture into pastry shells. Chill. Whip cream; blend in pineapple and pecans; spread over pie and chill again. Yield: two 9-inch pies.

Note: One (4½-ounce) container thawed frozen whipped topping may be substituted for whipping cream.

It's best not to wash berries or cherries before refrigeration. Wash them just prior to serving and use promptly.

OZARK APPLE PUDDING

1 egg
¾ cup sugar
3 tablespoons all-purpose flour
1¼ teaspoons baking powder
⅛ teaspoon salt
1 teaspoon vanilla extract
½ cup chopped nuts
½ cup pared, chopped apple
Whipped cream or whipped topping

Beat egg; gradually add sugar, beating thoroughly after each addition. Sift flour, baking powder, and salt; add to egg-sugar mixture. Stir in vanilla, nuts, and apple. Pour into a buttered 9-inch piepan. Bake at 350° for 20 to 25 minutes. Top with whipped cream. Yield: 6 servings.

CHOCOLATE VELVET

1 (4-ounce) package sweet cooking chocolate
¼ cup water
⅓ cup commercial sour cream
1 (9-ounce) container frozen whipped topping, thawed and divided
8 maraschino cherries, chopped

Combine chocolate and water in saucepan; cook over low heat, stirring constantly, until melted and smooth. Slowly add chocolate mixture to sour cream in mixing bowl. Set aside ½ cup whipped topping. Fold remaining whipped topping into chocolate mixture, blending well. Spoon into sherbet dishes. Chill until ready to serve. Garnish with topping and cherries. Yield: 6 servings.

CHARLOTTE RUSSE

5 envelopes unflavored gelatin
1¼ cups cold water
2 cups milk, scalded
1⅔ cups powdered sugar
2½ tablespoons vanilla extract
3½ cups whipping cream, whipped
Vanilla wafers
Commercial butterscotch sauce, chilled

Soften gelatin in cold water; dissolve gelatin mixture in scalded milk. Add powdered sugar and vanilla. Place bowl in a pan of ice water and stir mixture constantly until fluffy; fold in whipped cream. Line 10 to 12 sherbet glasses with vanilla wafers. Pour gelatin mixture into glasses; chill until ready to serve. Top with spoonful of cold butterscotch sauce. Yield: 10 to 12 servings.

CREAMY CRANBERRY PUDDING

1 (3¾-ounce) package instant vanilla pudding mix
1¼ cups cold milk
½ cup commercial sour cream
¼ teaspoon ground cinnamon
Dash of ground nutmeg
½ cup canned whole cranberry sauce
Flaked coconut

Combine pudding mix, milk, sour cream, and spices in a mixing bowl; beat until ingredients are well blended. Fold in cranberry sauce. Spoon into sherbet glasses; chill. Garnish with coconut. Yield: 4 servings.

If separating eggs seems like a difficult task, break the eggs into a small funnel. The egg whites will slip through; the yolks won't.

BLENDER FRENCH PUDDING

1½ tablespoons unflavored gelatin
 2 teaspoons instant coffee granules
 ¼ cup cold water
 ½ cup hot milk
 1 (6-ounce) package semisweet
     chocolate morsels
 1 tablespoon sugar
    Dash of salt
 ½ teaspoon vanilla extract
 2 egg yolks
1¼ cups finely crushed ice
 1 cup whipping cream

Combine gelatin, coffee, water, and milk in blender container. Cover and blend about 1 minute. Add chocolate morsels, sugar, salt, and vanilla; cover and blend about 10 seconds or until smooth. Keep motor running and add egg yolks, ice, and cream; blend 20 more seconds or until dessert begins to thicken. Pour into 6 cups or sherbet dishes; chill about 10 minutes or until ready to serve. Yield: 6 servings.

BLENDER VANILLA PUDDING

 2 packages unflavored gelatin
1½ cups cold milk, divided
 1 cup milk, heated to full boil
 2 eggs
 ½ cup sugar
 ⅛ teaspoon salt
 2 teaspoons vanilla extract
 1 cup ice cubes or crushed ice

Sprinkle gelatin over ½ cup cold milk in 5-cup container of electric blender; allow to stand until gelatin granules are moist. Add boiling milk; cover and process at low speed until gelatin dissolves, about 2 minutes. Stop blender. Add eggs, sugar, salt, vanilla, and remaining 1 cup cold milk (or cream). Cover and process at high speed for 1 minute. Remove cover and, with blender still running, add ice cubes one at a time. Continue to process until ice is melted. Pour immediately into individual serving dishes, 5-cup mold, or bowl. Chill until set. Individual servings may be served after 20 to 30 minutes; mold or bowl should be chilled about 2 hours. Yield: 6 to 8 servings.

Note: For richer dessert, use ½ cup cold milk and 1 cup whipping cream.

Chocolate Pudding:

Reduce vanilla to 1 teaspoon. After dissolving the gelatin, add 1 (12-ounce) package semisweet chocolate morsels; cover and process until smooth.

Mocha Pudding:

Prepare Chocolate Pudding, adding 1 tablespoon instant coffee granules with the chocolate morsels.

Orange Pudding:

Omit vanilla. Cut a thin rind from 1 orange with vegetable peeler and add to blender with gelatin. Add boiling milk, cover, and process at high speed until the gelatin is dissolved and the rind is in very tiny pieces. Peel the orange, remove the seeds, and add the orange to the blender with the eggs and sugar.

Strawberry Pudding:

Omit vanilla. Reduce cold milk or cream by ⅓ cup. Add 1 (10-ounce) package frozen strawberries, partially thawed, and 2 teaspoons lemon juice with the eggs and sugar.

Spirited Pudding:

Omit vanilla. Reduce cold milk or cream by ¼ cup and add ¼ cup brandy, créme de menthe, or coffee liqueur with eggs and sugar.

Top with dollop of marshmallow cream and fruit for color, or with whipped cream or whipped topping.

Egg whites hold air when beaten. The more sugar added to beaten egg white, the longer the cooking time required to reach a thick or firm stage.

FLUFFY DESSERT

1 (3-ounce) package fruit-flavored
    gelatin
1 cup boiling water
1 cup vanilla ice cream
3 ice cubes

Combine gelatin and boiling water in container of electric blender. Blend for 1 minute. Add ice cream and ice cubes one at a time. Blend 2 minutes. Pour into serving dishes. Refrigerate until ready to serve. Yield: 4 to 6 servings.

FRUIT COCKTAIL PUDDING

1 cup all-purpose flour
1 cup sugar
½ teaspoon salt
1 teaspoon soda
1 egg, well beaten
1 (16-ounce) can fruit cocktail,
    well-drained
¾ cup firmly packed brown sugar
½ cup chopped nuts
½ teaspoon ground cinnamon
    Sauce (recipe follows)

Combine flour, sugar, salt, and soda; add egg and fruit cocktail and mix well. Pour into a well-greased 13- x 9- x 2-inch pan. Combine brown sugar, nuts, and cinnamon; sprinkle over top. Bake at 350° for 45 minutes. Serve warm or cold with sauce or whipped cream. Yield: 8 to 10 servings.

Sauce:

1 cup evaporated milk
1½ cups sugar
⅔ cup butter or margarine
½ teaspoon rum or almond extract, or
    other flavoring

Combine first 3 ingredients in a saucepan; boil 1 minute. Add flavoring desired. Yield: about 2½ cups.

SMOOTH ORANGE DESSERT

1 (10½-ounce) package miniature
    marshmallows
2 cups orange juice
    Whipped topping
    Orange sections

Combine marshmallows and orange juice in top of double boiler; stir over medium heat until smooth, but do not cook. Spoon into compotes and chill until ready to serve. Garnish with whipped topping and orange sections. Yield: 6 servings.

STRAWBERRY BAVARIAN

1 (16-ounce) package frozen
    strawberries, thawed
¼ cup cold milk
2 envelopes unflavored gelatin
¼ cup sugar
2 egg yolks
    Red food coloring (optional)
1 cup whipping cream
1 cup crushed ice, drained

Drain strawberries, reserving ½ cup juice. Bring juice to a boil in a small saucepan. Combine milk, gelatin, and hot juice in container of electric blender; blend about 1 minute. When gelatin is dissolved, add sugar, strawberries, egg yolks, and food coloring, if desired; continue blending until strawberries are liquefied. Add cream and crushed ice; continue blending until ice is liquefied. Pour at once into serving dishes; let set 5 to 10 minutes before serving. Yield: 6 to 8 servings.

Smooth Orange Dessert (recipe above) is beautiful and luscious; definitely a party dessert, but surprisingly easy to prepare.

Overleaf: Cherries À La Mode, page 208, is a nice finale to a light meal. It combines cherries, chocolate ice cream, and pound cake for a real taste treat.

FESTIVE RICE

1 cup cooked rice
1 (16-ounce) can crushed pineapple,
   drained
2 tablespoons sugar
1 cup miniature marshmallows
1 cup whipping cream, whipped

Combine all ingredients except whipped
cream. Fold in whipped cream. Chill.
Yield: 6 servings.

CHOCOLATE MINT SUNDAE

12 chocolate-covered mint patties
2 tablespoons milk
1 pint vanilla ice cream

Melt patties in top of double boiler over
hot water; stir in milk. Serve warm over
ice cream. Yield: 4 servings.

HOT HONEY-FUDGE SUNDAE

2 (1-ounce) squares unsweetened
   chocolate
½ cup honey
   Dash of salt
1 pint vanilla ice cream
2 tablespoons chopped nuts

Combine chocolate and honey in top of
double boiler; cook over hot water until
chocolate is melted. Add salt and stir until
smooth. Put ice cream in serving dishes;
top with warm sauce and chopped nuts.
Yield: 4 servings.

MARSHMALLOW CREAM SUNDAE

1 pint chocolate ice cream
½ cup marshmallow cream
¼ cup commerical chocolate sauce

Put scoop of ice cream in serving dish. Dip
spoon into hot water then into marshmallow cream. Drop cream on top of chocolate ice cream. Lace with chocolate sauce
on top of cream. Yield: 4 servings.

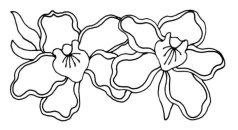

MARSHMALLOW MINT SUNDAE

½ cup marshmallow cream
2 tablespoons water
¼ cup mint jelly
   Green food coloring (optional)
1 quart chocolate ice cream
   Mint leaves (optional)

Combine marshmallow cream, water, and
jelly; beat until smooth and fluffy. Add
green food coloring, if desired. Spoon over
chocolate ice cream. Garnish with mint
leaves, if desired. Yield: 8 servings.

PEACH-GINGER SUNDAE

2 cups fresh or frozen peach slices,
   thawed
3 tablespoons orange juice
1 tablespoon lemon juice
1 tablespoon honey
2 tablespoons finely chopped
   crystallized ginger
1 pint vanilla ice cream

Combine peaches, orange juice, lemon
juice, honey, and ginger. Chill until ready
to serve. Scoop ice cream into individual
serving dishes. Spoon sauce over ice
cream. Yield: 4 servings.

RED RASPBERRY SUNDAE

1 cup red raspberry preserves
1 pint vanilla ice cream
¼ cup marshmallow cream

Put preserves in small bowl and stir vigorously until it is spooning consistency. Place 1 scoop of ice cream in each of 4 sherbets. Top ice cream with 2 tablespoons preserves. Dip spoon into hot water then into marshmallow cream; drop dollop of marshmallow cream on preserves. Serve immediately. Yield: 4 servings.

EASY DAY FROSTING

½ cup butter or margarine
¼ cup cocoa
¼ cup plus 2 tablespoons milk
1 (16-ounce) package powdered sugar
1 teaspoon vanilla extract
1 cup chopped pecans (optional)

Melt butter in medium saucepan; add cocoa and milk. Bring mixture to a boil; remove from heat. Add powdered sugar, vanilla, and pecans, if desired. Beat by hand until well blended. Yield: enough frosting for one 13- x 9- x 2-inch cake.

FLUFFY FROSTING

2 egg whites
1 cup light corn syrup
¼ cup sugar
½ teaspoon cream of tartar
Dash of salt
1 teaspoon vanilla extract

Combine first 5 ingredients in double boiler over medium heat. Begin beating immediately and beat until mixture stands in soft peaks (5 to 10 minutes). Remove from heat. Set in pan of ice water; continue beating as mixture cools. Add vanilla and stir well. Yield: frosting for 1 tube-pan cake.

LEMON CREAM SAUCE

¼ cup plus 2 tablespoons lemon juice
4 eggs, slightly beaten
1 cup sugar
2 tablespoons butter or margarine
Angel food cake or small tart shells

Combine lemon juice, eggs, and sugar in top of double boiler; cook over hot (not boiling) water until thick, stirring constantly. When spoon leaves a path in the sauce, remove from heat; add butter. Serve as topping over angel food cake or as filling for tart shells. Yield: 6 servings.

SPICED PEACH SAUCE

1 (28-ounce) can sliced peaches
¼ cup sugar
¼ teaspoon salt
2 tablespoons cornstarch
¼ cup water
1 tablespoon butter or margarine
¼ teaspoon ground nutmeg

Drain juice from peaches into a 1½-quart saucepan; heat juice to boiling. Combine sugar, salt, and cornstarch; stir in water. Add to juice, stirring constantly until liquid thickens. Remove from heat; add butter, nutmeg, and peach slices. Use as a topping for plain cake or ice cream. Yield: 6 to 8 servings.

BANANA TOPPING

1 egg white
¼ cup sugar
1 ripe banana, mashed

Beat egg white until frothy. Gradually add sugar and continue beating until smooth and stiff. Add mashed banana. Serve immediately on plain cake. Yield: 1 cup.

Note: Any mashed fruit can be substituted for banana.

Mixes

*P*lanning ahead is the best way to prepare meals at the last minute with ease and speed. This section on making your very own prepared mixes is designed to help you plan ahead so that quick and easy meals are a reality. By preparing the mixes of your choice, you will save not only time, but energy and money.

Today, the packaged mixes are frequently used because of lack of that precious commodity, time. However, commercial mixes are still costly; so the thrifty cook will take the time to prepare, label, and store her own. What a joy to decide to have a chocolate, white, spice, or whatever cake at the last minute with no thought of "do I have a mix on hand" or "do I have time to go to the store." Just reach for your very own mix.

Preparing your own convenience foods, when time permits, can be an innovation in meal management. Start with the many ideas given here, and then use these as a basis for creating your own. Just imagine serving a smooth white sauce, cookies, hot biscuits, fruit cobbler, or even turkey tetrazzini in a matter of minutes, and still within your budget, too.

BASIC MIX

For biscuits, muffins, shortcake, pancakes, coffee cakes, nut bread, etc., use the following basic mix:

> **12 cups all-purpose flour**
> **2 tablespoons salt**
> **¼ cup plus 2 tablespoons baking powder**
> **2 cups shortening**

Combine flour, salt, and baking powder; sift. Cut in shortening with pastry blender until mixture resembles coarse meal. Place in covered container. Store in refrigerator or any cool place. Yield: 14 to 14½ cups.

Uses for Basic Mix:

Biscuits:

Combine 2 cups Basic Mix and ½ cup milk. Roll out ½ inch thick and cut with biscuit cutter. Place on ungreased cookie sheet. Bake at 450° for 12 to 15 minutes. Yield: 10 to 12 biscuits.

Drop Biscuits:

Combine 2 cups Basic Mix and ¾ cup milk. Drop onto greased cookie sheet. Bake at 400° for 12 to 15 minutes. Yield: 10 to 12 biscuits.

Muffins:

Combine 2 cups Basic Mix, 2 tablespoons sugar, 1 well-beaten egg, and ¾ cup milk. Fill greased muffin pans two-thirds full. Bake at 425° for 15 to 20 minutes. Yield: 10 to 12 muffins.

Pancakes:

Combine 2 cups Basic Mix, 1¼ cups milk, and 2 well-beaten eggs. Drop in hot greased skillet. Cook over medium heat, browning both sides. Yield: 18 pancakes.

Quick Nut Bread:

Combine 3 cups Basic Mix, ¾ cup sugar, 1 well-beaten egg, 1 cup milk, and 1 cup finely chopped nuts. Pour in greased 9- x 5- x 3-inch loafpan. Bake at 350° for 1 hour or until done. Yield: 1 loaf.

BASIC MIX BEER MUFFINS

> **4 cups Basic Mix**
> **1 tablespoon sugar**
> **1 (12-ounce) can beer (at room temperature)**

Combine Basic Mix and sugar. Add beer and stir only until the flour is moist. Batter will be lumpy. Fill well-greased muffin pans two-thirds full. Bake at 375° for 20 minutes or until done. Yield: 24 muffins.

BISCUIT MIX

> **8 cups all-purpose flour**
> **1 cup nonfat dry milk powder**
> **¼ cup baking powder**
> **1 tablespoon salt**
> **1 cup shortening**

Sift dry ingredients together three times; cut in shortening until thoroughly mixed. Spoon mix lightly into 3-quart container. Do not pack. Close tightly and store on shelf. Needs no refrigeration. Yield: about 10 cups.

Variations:

Biscuits:

Combine 1 cup Biscuit Mix with about ⅓ cup water or milk—enough to make a soft dough. Turn onto a lightly floured board or pastry cloth and knead a few times. Pat or roll to ½-inch thickness, and cut with a floured biscuit cutter. Place on ungreased baking sheet. Bake at 450° for 12 to 15 minutes. Yield: 6 biscuits.

Shortcakes:

Combine 1 cup Biscuit Mix with 1 tablespoon sugar; cut in 1 tablespoon butter or margarine. Add about ⅓ cup water or milk to make a soft dough. Roll to ¼-inch thickness, and cut with floured biscuit cutter. Brush half the rounds with melted butter or margarine and cover each with one of the remaining rounds. Bake at 425° for 12 to 15 minutes. Yield: 6 shortcakes.

CURRIED PARTY BISCUITS

- 2 cups Biscuit Mix
- ⅔ cup milk or water
- 1 teaspoon curry powder
- 2 tablespoons melted butter or margarine
  Grated Parmesan cheese

Combine Biscuit Mix and enough milk or water to make a soft dough. Turn out onto a lightly floured board or pastry cloth and knead a few times. Pat or roll to ½-inch thickness and cut with a floured cutter. Roll each biscuit to about 6 inches in length. Combine curry powder and butter; mix well. Dip each biscuit in seasoned butter. Roll dough in Parmesan cheese. Twist. Place on ungreased baking sheet. Bake at 450° for 8 minutes. Yield: 10 to 12 biscuits.

ONION ROLLS

- 2 cups chopped onion
- ¼ cup butter or margarine, divided
- ⅔ cup milk or water
- 2 cups Biscuit Mix

Sauté onion in 2 tablespoons butter only until tender. Set aside. Add milk to Biscuit Mix and mix thoroughly. Turn out onto a lightly floured board. Knead a few times. Roll the dough into a rectangle ¼ inch thick. Melt remaining 2 tablespoons butter. Brush rectangle with butter and cover with onion. Roll lengthwise, as for jellyroll. Cut into 1-inch slices. Place cut side down in greased muffin pans. Bake at 400° for 15 minutes. Yield: 10 to 12 rolls.

PARTY SWIRLS

- 2 cups Biscuit Mix
- ⅔ cup milk or water
  Melted butter or margarine
  Marmalade or poppy seeds

Combine Biscuit Mix with about ⅔ cup water or milk—enough to make a soft dough. Turn onto a lightly floured board or pastry cloth and knead a few times. Roll or pat dough to form a a 5- x 10-inch rectangle. Brush with melted butter. Brush with marmalade or sprinkle with poppy seeds. Roll rectangle lengthwise, jellyroll fashion; cut into 1-inch slices. Place cut side down in greased muffin pan or ½ inch apart on greased baking pan. Bake at 425° for 8 minutes. Yield: 10 to 12 biscuits.

QUICK MIX

- 7 cups all-purpose flour
- 2 cups nonfat dry milk powder
- ¼ cup baking powder
- 1 tablespoon salt
- 1 cup shortening

Combine flour and nonfat dry milk powder and stir. Add baking powder and salt and stir. Cut shortening into mixture until it resembles coarse meal. Store Quick Mix in tightly covered 3-quart containers. Yield: 10 cups.

Note: If using self-rising flour, do not add baking powder and salt.

QUICK MIX BISCUITS

2 cups Quick Mix
½ cup water

Combine Quick Mix and water. Stir until dough is soft. Turn dough out onto a lightly floured surface and knead until smooth. Roll dough to ½-inch thickness and cut with floured biscuit cutter. Bake on ungreased baking sheet at 450° for 12 to 15 minutes or until light brown. Yield: 12 biscuits.

QUICK MIX SWEET MUFFINS

2 cups Quick Mix
½ cup sugar
2 eggs, well beaten
⅔ cup water

Combine Quick Mix and sugar and stir. Combine eggs and water; add to dry ingredients; mix until blended. Batter will have lumps. Fill greased muffin pans one-half full. Bake at 425° for 20 minutes or until light brown. Yield: 12 muffins.

QUICK MIX FRUIT COBBLER

¼ cup shortening
1 cup Quick Mix
1 cup sugar
1 cup water
1 (16-ounce) can fruit, undrained

Melt shortening in a 9-inch baking pan. Combine Quick Mix, sugar, and water. Pour batter in pan. Top with fruit, spreading over batter. Bake at 350° for 1 hour. Yield: 6 servings.

QUICK MIX PANCAKES

3 cups Quick Mix
2 eggs
1½ cups water

Combine all three ingredients just until flour is moistened (batter will be lumpy). Drop batter in hot greased skillet. Cook over medium heat, browning both sides. Yield: 12 pancakes.

QUICK MIX PEANUT BUTTER COOKIES

¼ cup shortening (at room temperature)
1 cup peanut butter
1 cup sugar
1 egg, slightly beaten
1 cup Quick Mix

Combine shortening, peanut butter, sugar, and egg; stir until creamy. Add Quick Mix a little at a time, stirring until smooth. Roll dough into small balls 1-inch in diameter and put on ungreased cookie sheet. Press balls with a fork to make a criss-cross pattern. (Dip fork in flour each time dough is pressed.) Bake at 375° for 5 to 7 minutes. Let cookies cool for about 3 minutes before removing from cookie sheet. Yield: 4 dozen cookies.

UNBELIEVABLE PIE

1¾ cups milk
¾ cup sugar
½ cup Quick Mix or any biscuit mix
4 eggs
   Rind of ½ orange or lemon, grated
¼ cup butter or margarine
1½ teaspoons vanilla extract
1 cup flaked coconut

Combine milk, sugar, Quick Mix, eggs, orange rind, butter, and vanilla in blender container. Blend slowly for 3 minutes. Pour into greased 9-inch piepan. Let stand for 3 minutes. Sprinkle coconut on top. Bake at 350° for 40 minutes. Serve warm or cool. Yield: 6 to 8 servings.

UPSIDE-DOWN CAKE

- 2 tablespoons butter or margarine
- 1 cup firmly packed brown sugar, divided
- 1 (16-ounce) can fruit
- 2 cups Quick Mix
- 1 egg

Melt butter in a 9-inch baking pan. Sprinkle ½ cup sugar over butter. Drain fruit, reserving liquid. Spread fruit over sugar. Add water to juice to equal 1 cup. Combine Quick Mix, remaining ½ cup sugar, egg, and juice in a large bowl; beat until smooth. Pour batter over fruit and bake at 350° for 30 minutes. Invert onto serving dish. Yield: 9 servings.

QUICK BREAD MIX

- 6 cups all-purpose flour
- 1 cup nonfat dry milk powder
- ¼ cup baking powder
- 2 teaspoons salt
- ½ cup sugar
- ¾ cup shortening

Combine first 5 ingredients; sift three times. Cut in shortening until thoroughly mixed. Spoon mix lightly into 2-quart containers. Do not pack. Close tightly and store on shelf or in refrigerator for lengthy storage. Yield: 8½ cups.

Note: For added milk value, add 1 additional cup of nonfat dry milk powder.

Variations:

Muffins:

To 1 cup Quick Bread Mix, add ⅓ cup water or milk and 1 beaten egg. Fill greased muffin pans two-thirds full. Bake at 400° about 20 minutes. Yield: 5 muffins.

Waffles:

To 1 cup Quick Bread Mix, add ¾ cup water or milk and 1 beaten egg yolk. Fold in 1 beaten egg white. Bake in hot waffle iron. Yield: 2 large waffles.

Griddlecakes:

To 1 cup Quick Bread Mix, add ⅔ to 1 cup water or milk and 1 beaten egg. Drop batter by spoonfuls onto a hot greased griddle. Cook slowly until surface is covered with bubbles; turn and brown on bottom. Yield: 7 cakes.

GENERAL PURPOSE MIX

- 8 cups all-purpose flour
- ⅓ cup baking powder
- 1½ tablespoons salt
- 2 tablespoons sugar
- 2 cups nonfat dry milk powder
- 1½ cups butter, margarine, or shortening

Combine flour, baking powder, salt, sugar, and nonfat dry milk powder. Add the butter and cut in with a pastry blender until the mixture resembles finely ground meal. Store the mix in a covered container or a large plastic bag. Yield: 11 to 12 cups.

Note: In preparing recipes, water may be used as the liquid, or milk may be used to increase the nutritive value.

BISCUITS

  2 cups General Purpose Mix
  ½ to ¾ cup water or milk

Combine ingredients. Knead 20 seconds.
Roll to ½-inch thickness. Cut with floured
biscuit cutter and bake on ungreased baking sheet at 425° for 12 to 15 minutes.
Yield: 10 to 12 biscuits.

MUFFINS

  2 cups General Purpose Mix
  1 tablespoon sugar
  ¾ cup water or milk
  1 egg, beaten

Combine all ingredients. Batter will be
lumpy. Pour into greased muffin pans.
Bake at 400° for 15 to 20 minutes. Yield:
10 to 12 muffins.

WAFFLES

  2 cups General Purpose Mix
  2 tablespoons sugar
  1 egg, separated
  1 cup water or milk

Combine General Purpose Mix and sugar.
Beat egg white until stiff, but not dry. Beat
egg yolk and mix with liquid. Add to dry
ingredients. Fold in beaten egg white and
bake in hot waffle iron. Yield: 4 large
waffles.

FREEZER BISCUITS

  2 packages dry yeast
  ¼ cup warm water (105° to 115°)
  5 cups all-purpose flour
  1 teaspoon soda
  1 teaspoon salt
  1 tablespoon plus 1 teaspoon baking
      powder
  ¼ cup sugar
  1 cup shortening
  2 cups buttermilk

Dissolve yeast in warm water. Sift dry
ingredients and cut in shortening. Add
yeast and buttermilk to dry ingredients,
mixing well. Knead quickly 20 to 30 times.
Cover and let rise in a warm place free
from drafts for 2 hours. Punch down, roll
½ inch thick, cut with biscuit cutter, and
place on cookie sheets. Freeze; then place
biscuits in freezer bags. When ready to
bake, place biscuits without thawing on
cookie sheet. Place in *cold oven*; set oven
at 400°. Bake until brown, 25 to 30 minutes. Yield: 30 biscuits.

Note: If baking in a preheated oven,
allow biscuits to thaw and rise at room
temperature for 1 to 1½ hours.

BRAN MUFFIN BATTER

  1 cup shortening
  3 cups sugar
  4 eggs, beaten
  2 cups shredded bran
  4 cups 100% bran
  1½ cups boiling water
  5 cups all-purpose flour
  1 tablespoon plus 2 teaspoons soda
  2 teaspoons salt
  4 cups buttermilk

Cream shortening and sugar. Add eggs;
mix well. Add shredded bran, 100% bran,
and boiling water. Combine flour, soda,

and salt; add to creamed mixture. Add buttermilk; mix thoroughly. Fill greased muffin pans two-thirds full. Bake at 400° for 20 minutes. Extra batter will keep a month if it is stored in a covered container in the refrigerator. Yield: about 3½ quarts.

CORNMEAL MIX

4 cups cornmeal
4 cups all-purpose flour
1½ cups nonfat dry milk powder
¼ cup baking powder
1 tablespoon salt
1½ cups shortening

Combine cornmeal, flour, nonfat dry milk powder, baking powder, and salt in large bowl. Add shortening to dry mixture; cut in until the mixture resembles coarse meal. Store the Cornmeal Mix in tightly covered container. Yield: about 11 cups.

Note: If using self-rising flour, do not add baking powder and salt.

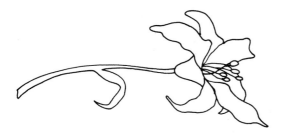

CORNMEAL MUFFINS

3 cups Cornmeal Mix
2 eggs, lightly beaten
1 cup water

Combine all ingredients and stir. Mixture will be lumpy; do not overbeat. Grease muffin pans and fill one-half full. Bake at 450° for 15 to 20 minutes or until brown. Yield: 12 muffins.

CORNBREAD

4½ cups Cornmeal Mix
2 eggs
1⅓ cups water

Combine Cornmeal Mix, eggs, and water; stir just enough to moisten dry ingredients. Batter will be lumpy. Pour batter into a greased 9-inch pan and bake at 425° for 15 to 20 minutes or until brown. Yield: 12 servings.

DROP CORNMEAL BISCUITS

2 cups Cornmeal Mix
½ cup water

Combine Cornmeal Mix and water; stir just enough to moisten dry ingredients. Drop dough by spoonfuls onto greased pan. Bake at 425° for 10 to 12 minutes or until brown. Yield: 12 biscuits.

CORNMEAL PANCAKES

2 cups Cornmeal Mix
1 egg, beaten
1 cup water

Combine all ingredients; stir just enough to moisten dry ingredients. Pour small amount of batter into hot greased skillet. Brown on both sides. Yield: 18 pancakes.

A great do-ahead idea: chop onions, green peppers, celery, and shred cheese. Wrap securely in ½ cup portions, label, and freeze. Place package in refrigerator the night before needed or thaw quickly by immersing wrapped food in water or heating in the microwave oven.

CORNMEAL GINGERBREAD

1 egg, well beaten
½ cup dark corn syrup
¾ cup buttermilk
½ cup melted butter or margarine
2¼ cups Cornmeal Mix
½ cup firmly packed brown sugar
¾ teaspoon ground cinnamon
¾ teaspoon soda
3 apples (optional)
Cornmeal

Combine egg, syrup, and buttermilk, mixing well. Add melted butter, stirring until all is well blended. Combine Cornmeal Mix, brown sugar, cinnamon, and soda. Make a well in the dry mixture and pour the liquid mixture in it, stirring until blended. If desired, peel and cut apples into small chunks and add to mixture. Sprinkle a little cornmeal in the bottom of a greased 9-inch cakepan to prevent gingerbread from sticking. Pour batter into pan and bake at 425° for 35 minutes or until done. Yield: one 9-inch cake.

ROLLED OATS MIX

4 cups regular oats, uncooked
4 cups all-purpose flour
1½ cups nonfat dry milk powder
¼ cup baking powder
1 tablespoon salt
1½ cups shortening

Combine oats, flour, nonfat dry milk powder, baking powder, and salt in large bowl. Stir. Cut in shortening until it resembles coarse meal. Store in tightly covered container. Yield: 11 cups of mix.

Note: If using self-rising flour, do not add baking powder and salt.

OATMEAL BISCUITS

2 cups Rolled Oats Mix
½ cup water

Combine Rolled Oats Mix and water until blended. Knead dough on lightly floured surface until smooth. Roll dough to ½-inch thickness. Cut biscuits with floured cutter and place on greased baking pan. Bake at 425° for 12 minutes or until light brown. Yield: 12 biscuits.

OATMEAL MUFFINS

2¼ cups Rolled Oats Mix
⅔ cup water
1 egg
¼ cup raisins

Combine all ingredients, but do not overbeat. Batter will have lumps. Fill greased muffin pans one-half full. Bake at 425° for 20 minutes or until light brown. Yield: 12 muffins.

OATMEAL COOKIES

2½ cups Rolled Oats Mix
¼ cup all-purpose flour
¾ cup sugar
1 teaspoon ground cinnamon
(optional)
1 egg, beaten
¼ cup water
1 teaspoon vanilla extract
⅓ cup raisins

Combine the first 4 ingredients, stirring well. Add egg and water; stir just until dry ingredients are moistened. Dough will have lumps and be stiff. Add vanilla and raisins. Drop dough by spoonfuls on greased baking sheet. Bake at 350° for 12 to 15 minutes or until cookies are light brown on bottom. Yield: about 2½ dozen cookies.

BANANA OATMEAL BREAD

3 cups Rolled Oats Mix
⅔ cup sugar
2 or 3 bananas, mashed
1 egg, beaten

Combine Rolled Oats Mix and sugar. Add mashed bananas, stirring well. Add egg to mixture. Stir well. Put dough in greased 9- x 5- x 3-inch loafpan and bake at 350° for 1 hour or until light brown. Yield: 1 loaf.

PEANUT BUTTER-OATMEAL COOKIES

1 cup peanut butter
¾ cup sugar
1 egg, beaten
¼ cup water
1 teaspoon ground cinnamon
1 teaspoon vanilla extract
1 cup Rolled Oats Mix

Combine peanut butter, sugar, egg, water, cinnamon, and vanilla; stir until mixture is smooth. Add Rolled Oats Mix a little at a time (dough will be stiff). Roll dough into small balls and place on greased baking sheet. Do not crowd. Mash flat with fork and bake at 350° for 8 to 10 minutes. Bottom will be a little brown. Yield: 4 dozen cookies.

PASTRY MIX I (Using Lard)

7 cups all-purpose flour
1 tablespoon salt
2 cups (1 pound) lard

Combine flour and salt. Cut lard into flour mixture with fork or pastry blender until mixture resembles coarse meal. Cover and place in refrigerator until ready to use.

Will keep at least a month in refrigerator. Yield: nine (9-inch) pastry shells.
Note: Lard makes a richer, flakier crust.

PASTRY MIX II (Using Shortening)

7 cups all-purpose flour
1 tablespoon plus 1 teaspoon salt
1¾ to 2⅓ cups shortening

Combine flour and salt. Cut in shortening with pastry blender until mixture resembles coarse meal. Store in a covered container in the refrigerator. Yield: nine (9-inch) pastry shells.

PASTRY SHELL

2 to 3 tablespoons cold water
1 cup Pastry Mix (I or II)

Add water 1 tablespoon at a time to Pastry Mix, mixing with a fork. Turn out onto waxed paper; press pastry firmly together to form a ball. Roll on lightly floured board. Place into 9-inch piepan and prick with a fork. Bake at 425° for 10 to 20 minutes.
Note: Double the recipe for a double-crust pie. Do not prick bottom of shell if filling is placed in unbaked single shell. Seal any breaks in shells.

HOME CAKE MIX

9 cups cake flour
5½ cups sugar
1 teaspoon salt
¼ cup baking powder
2 cups shortening

Sift dry ingredients together 3 times. Cut in shortening until consistency of fine meal. Store in a covered container at room temperature. Yield: approximately 15 cups dry mix.

Method:

Have ingredients at room temperature. Combine Home Cake Mix and additional dry ingredients in large mixing bowl. Add part or all of milk and flavoring. Beat with electric mixer on slow to medium speed 2 minutes. Scrape bowl frequently. Add any remaining liquid and eggs, one at a time, and continue beating 2 minutes longer, scraping bowl frequently. Bake at 375° for 20 to 25 minutes in two greased 8-inch pans. This method gives best results with this recipe only. Yield: two 8-inch layers.

Note: If using 13- x 9- x 2-inch pan, bake 35 to 40 minutes.

Home Cake Mix Variations:

Type of Cake	Amount of Cake Mix (cups)	Amount of Milk (cups)	Unbeaten Egg	Additions
Plain	3½	⅔	2	1 teaspoon vanilla extract
Chocolate	3½	¾	2	1 teaspoon vanilla extract; 2 squares melted unsweetened chocolate
Spice	3½	⅔	2	1 teaspoon vanilla extract; ½ teaspoon ground cinnamon; ¼ teaspoon each ground cloves, ground nutmeg, ground allspice
White	3½	⅔	4 whites	1 teaspoon almond extract
Yellow	3½	⅞	4 yolks	1 teaspoon lemon extract

CAKE MIX COOKIES

2 eggs
½ cup vegetable oil
1 teaspoon vanilla extract
3½ cups Home Cake Mix or a
    commercial cake mix

Beat eggs lightly; add oil, vanilla, and Home Cake Mix and mix well. Drop by spoonfuls on a greased cookie sheet. Bake at 350° for 15 to 20 minutes. Yield: 4 dozen.

BROWNIE MIX

4 cups all-purpose flour
1½ cups nonfat dry milk powder
4 cups sugar
1 cup cocoa
1½ tablespoons baking powder
1 tablespoon salt

Sift all ingredients three times. Store in tightly covered container. Yield: 6 recipes of brownies.

Brownies:

1¾ cups Brownie Mix
½ cup chopped nuts
1 egg, well beaten
⅓ cup water
½ cup melted butter or margarine
1 teaspoon vanilla extract

Place Brownie Mix in large mixing bowl. Stir in nuts. Beat egg in small bowl and add water, melted butter, and vanilla. Gradually add egg mixture to Brownie Mix, beating well after each addition. Turn into a well-greased 9-inch square pan and bake at 375° for 20 to 25 minutes. When cool, cut into squares. Yield: 16 squares.

HOT CHOCOLATE MIX

1 (16-ounce) package instant chocolate milk powder
1 (16-ounce) package powdered sugar
1 (6-ounce) jar instant non-dairy creamer
1 (1-pound 9.6-ounce) package nonfat dry milk powder

Combine all ingredients and mix thoroughly; store in a tightly covered container. Yield: about 9 cups dry mix.

Note: For a stronger chocolate flavor, add ¼ cup regular cocoa to the general mix.

Hot Chocolate:

3 tablespoons Hot Chocolate Mix
1 cup hot water

Stir mix into hot water. Yield: 1 cup.

INSTANT SPICED COCOA MIX

¼ cup cocoa
¾ cup sugar
1 teaspoon ground cinnamon
⅛ teaspoon ground allspice
Dash of salt
2 cups nonfat dry milk powder

Combine cocoa, sugar, spices, and salt in small bowl. Mix well. Add nonfat dry milk powder, and mix until well blended. Store in covered 1-quart container. Yield: 3 cups dry mix.

Instant Spiced Cocoa:

2 tablespoons Instant Spiced Cocoa Mix
¼ cup boiling water
Hot water

Blend Instant Spiced Cocoa Mix with boiling water. Then fill the cup with more hot water. Yield: 1 cup.

INSTANT SPICED TEA MIX

1¼ cups instant orange-flavored breakfast drink
⅓ cup instant tea with sugar and lemon
1 teaspoon ground cloves
1 teaspoon ground cinnamon
1 teaspoon ground allspice
¼ teaspoon grated lemon rind
¼ teaspoon grated orange rind

Mix above ingredients and store in tightly closed container. Yield: about 2½ cups dry mix.

Instant Spiced Tea:

1 to 1½ teaspoons Instant Spiced Tea Mix
1 cup boiling water

Put Instant Spiced Tea Mix in a cup and add boiling water. Correct sweetness as desired. Yield: 1 cup.

BASIC BARBECUE SAUCE

1 cup molasses
1 cup prepared mustard
1 cup cider vinegar

Blend together molasses and mustard. Add vinegar; mix well. Cover tightly; store at room temperature or in refrigerator. Sauce will keep a long time. Yield: 3 cups.

Variations:

Tomato Barbecue Sauce:

Add ¼ cup catsup to 1 cup Basic Barbecue Sauce.

Herb Barbecue Sauce:

Add a dash each: dried leaf marjoram, ground oregano, and ground thyme to 1 cup Basic Barbecue Sauce.

Curry Barbecue Sauce:

Add 1 tablespoon curry powder, 1 tablespoon Worcestershire sauce, and ½ teaspoon hot sauce to 1 cup Basic Barbecue Sauce.

BARBECUED HAMBURGERS

Place hamburgers on grill; set 4 to 6 inches from heat. Brush with one of the barbecue sauces. Broil 4 to 8 minutes on each side, depending on desired degree of doneness. Turn once during broiling and brush with barbecue sauce.

VERY QUICK CHEESE SAUCE

1 cup evaporated milk
1 cup (4 ounces) shredded sharp
   Cheddar cheese

Combine milk and cheese in 1-quart saucepan. Place over low heat; cook until cheese melts, stirring constantly. (Do not boil.) Serve over vegetables or fish. Yield 1¼ cups.

Variations using 1 cup sauce:

Cheese Sauce for Cabbage:

Add 2 teaspoons caraway seeds and ½ teaspoon Worcestershire sauce to 1 cup Cheese Sauce.

Cheese Sauce for Broccoli:

Add 1 teaspoon Worcestershire sauce, ¼ teaspoon whole oregano, and ⅛ teaspoon cayenne pepper to 1 cup Cheese Sauce.

Cheese Sauce for Asparagus:

Add 1 (2-ounce) can sliced mushrooms, drained, ½ teaspoon dry mustard, and dash of pepper to 1 cup Cheese Sauce.

Cheese Sauce for Potatoes:

Add 4 strips bacon, cooked and crumbled, to 1 cup Cheese Sauce.

FRENCH DRESSING

2 teaspoons sugar
1 teaspoon salt
1 teaspoon dry mustard
1 teaspoon paprika
   Dash of cayenne pepper
¼ cup lemon juice
¼ cup vinegar
1 cup vegetable oil

Place all ingredients in a covered jar. Shake well before using. Yield: 1½ cups.

Variations:

Chiffonade Dressing:

To ¾ cup French Dressing, add ½ hard-cooked egg, sieved; ½ teaspoon finely chopped parsley or green pepper; and ½ tablespoon finely chopped pimiento or pickled beet.

Cream Cheese Dressing:

Slowly blend ¾ cup French Dressing into 1½ ounces (one-half 3-ounce package) softened cream cheese.

Blue Cheese Dressing:

Add 1 tablespoon crumbled blue cheese to ¾ cup French Dressing and shake.

Currant Dressing:

To ¾ cup French Dressing, add 1 tablespoon currant jelly, whipped with a fork.

Cream Dressing:

To ¾ cup French Dressing add 1 tablespoon sweet or sour cream.

Savory Dressing:

To ¾ cup French Dressing, add catsup or chutney and ⅛ teaspoon Worcestershire sauce.

Piquant Dressing:

To ¾ cup French Dressing, add 1½ tablespoons sugar, ¼ teaspoon dry mustard, ¼ teaspoon paprika, 1 tablespoon plus 1 teaspoon chili sauce, and 1 tablespoon grated onion.

INSTANT MAYONNAISE, BLENDER-STYLE

  1 egg
  2 tablespoons lemon juice
  ½ teaspoon salt
  ¼ teaspoon paprika
  ¼ teaspoon dry mustard
    Cayenne pepper to taste
  ¾ to 1 cup vegetable oil

Put first 6 ingredients in blender container. Cover, switch on motor for just a few seconds, stop, and remove cover. Start motor and add oil gradually, with motor running. If mixture thickens adequately, stop with ¾ cup of oil. If still fluid, add the full cup. *Blend only until thick and smooth, and then stop the motor.* Yield: 1 cup.

Note: To achieve a real taste of elegance, use olive oil or at least ⅓ cup olive oil—the rest can be vegetable oil.

Variations: Use ½ cup of Instant Mayonnaise to prepare each of the variations listed below. Gently fold the ingredients for each variation into the mayonnaise. Avoid excess agitation.

Russian Mayonnaise:

Fold in ¼ cup chili sauce, ¼ hard-cooked egg, sieved, and 1 tablespoon finely chopped green pepper. Yield: 1 cup.

Thousand Island Mayonnaise:

Fold in ¼ cup chili sauce, ¼ chopped hard-cooked egg, 1 tablespoon finely diced green pepper, 1 tablespoon finely chopped pimiento-stuffed olives, 2 tablespoons diced pimiento, and 1 teaspoon minced onion or chives. Yield: 1 cup.

Cucumber Mayonnaise:

Fold in ¼ cup finely diced cucumber. Yield: ¾ cup.

Creamy Mayonnaise for Fruit Salads:

Fold in ¼ cup whipping cream, whipped. Yield: 1 cup.

Tartar Sauce Mayonnaise:

Fold in 1 tablespoon minced dill pickle, 1 teaspoon minced capers, and 1 teaspoon minced onion. Yield: ½ cup.

Green Goddess Mayonnaise:

Blend ½ tablespoon anchovy paste with 2 tablespoons heavy cream. Fold in anchovy mixture, 2 teaspoons lemon juice, 1 tablespoon finely chopped chives, and 1 tablespoon minced parsley. Yield: ¾ cup.

For freshness, buy graded eggs in cartons at a store that keeps them in refrigerated cases.

FREEZER ONION-CHEESE SAUCE

    2 to 3 medium onions, chopped
    ½ cup melted butter or margarine
    ½ cup all-purpose flour
    4 cups milk
    2 chicken bouillon cubes (optional)
    2 teaspoons salt
    ¼ teaspoon pepper
    3 cups (12 ounces) shredded sharp
        Cheddar cheese

Sauté onion in butter until tender but not brown. Blend in flour. Gradually add milk and bouillon cubes, if desired. Cook, stirring constantly, until thickened and smooth. Blend in seasonings and cheese. Heat until cheese melts. Cool. Store in 1-cup covered plastic containers in the freezer. Yield: 8 cups.

To Serve Onion-Cheese Sauce:

Topping: Heat sauce and serve as a topping for baked potatoes, hamburgers, or salmon loaf.

Casseroles: Use in place of white sauce, onion, and cheese in casseroles.

Vegetables: For creaming vegetables, combine defrosted sauce with cooked vegetables and heat through.

Make bread or cracker crumbs ahead of time from old bread and crackers. Roll with rolling pin or run crisp dry bread or crackers through food chopper or blender until reduced to crumbs. Store in tightly covered container in refrigerator.

FREEZER ONION-TOMATO SAUCE

    3 large (about 3 pounds) onions,
        chopped
    3 cloves garlic, crushed
    ½ cup olive or vegetable oil
    5 pounds tomatoes, peeled and
        quartered
    ½ cup chopped parsley
    1 medium-size green pepper, seeded
        and chopped
    1 tablespoon leaf oregano
    2 teaspoons paprika
    ¾ teaspoon rosemary
    1½ teaspoons salt
    ¾ teaspoon pepper
    1 cup dry red wine
    ½ cup water

Sauté onion and garlic in oil until tender. Add tomatoes, parsley, green pepper, seasonings, wine, and water. Simmer until thick, 1½ to 2 hours. Cool and pour into freezer containers, leaving ½-inch head space. Freeze. Yield: about 2½ quarts of sauce.

QUICK VEGETABLE SOUP

    2 cups Onion-Tomato Sauce, thawed
    2 (10½-ounce) cans beef broth,
        undiluted
    1 cup water
    1 cup sliced carrots
    1 cup chopped celery
    1 teaspoon salt
    ¼ teaspoon pepper
    ½ cup elbow macaroni

Combine Onion-Tomato Sauce, broth, and water in large saucepan. Heat to boiling. Add carrots, celery, salt, and pepper. Cover and simmer 15 minutes. Add macaroni. Cover and simmer 15 minutes longer. Correct seasonings. Yield: 6 servings.

MEDITERRANEAN BAKED FISH

2 cups Onion-Tomato Sauce, thawed
    and divided
1½ to 2 pounds fish steaks or fillets
    Salt and pepper
¼ cup grated Parmesan cheese

Place 1 cup Onion-Tomato Sauce in bottom of shallow baking dish. Sprinkle fish with salt and pepper. Arrange in baking dish. Spoon remaining 1 cup sauce over fish. Sprinkle with Parmesan cheese. Bake at 350° for 25 minutes, or until fish flakes when tested with fork. Yield: 6 servings.

BASIC SPAGHETTI SAUCE

1 large onion, chopped
¼ cup chopped green pepper
3 tablespoons vegetable or olive oil
3 (8-ounce) cans tomato sauce or 2
    pounds peeled fresh tomatoes
1 (6-ounce) can tomato paste
1 (6-ounce) can water
2 cloves garlic, finely crushed, or 2
    teaspoons garlic powder
1 teaspoon fennel seeds (optional)
2 bay leaves
2 teaspoons dried parsley flakes
1½ teaspoons sweet basil
1 teaspoon whole oregano
1 teaspoon salt
1 teaspoon sugar
½ teaspoon pepper
1 (4-ounce) can sliced mushrooms,
    undrained

Sauté onion and green pepper in vegetable oil until tender. Add remaining ingredients. Simmer gently 1 hour. Cool; remove bay leaves, pour into ice cube tray with divider, and freeze. Remove from tray when frozen; wrap desired number of cubes for a meal in freezer storage bags or freeze in 1-quart container. Yield: 4¼ cups sauce.

Note: Recipe may be doubled or tripled.

CHICKEN CACCIATORE

4 chicken breasts, split and boned
2 tablespoons olive or vegetable oil
3½ cups Basic Spaghetti Sauce, thawed
½ cup dry white wine
1 (16-ounce) package spaghetti,
    cooked and drained
    Grated Parmesan cheese

Sauté chicken breasts on all sides in oil. Add Basic Spaghetti Sauce. Simmer 30 to 45 minutes. Remove chicken from sauce. Add wine to sauce. Simmer 10 minutes longer, uncovered. Serve sauce over spaghetti; top with chicken and cheese. Yield: 8 servings.

NEW-STYLE LASAGNA

1 pound ground beef
1 teaspoon salt
¼ teaspoon pepper
    Lasagna noodles
3½ cups Basic Spaghetti Sauce, thawed
1 pound cottage cheese or ricotta
1 (8-ounce) package sliced Swiss
    cheese
¼ cup Parmesan cheese

Brown ground beef and season with salt and pepper. Drain. Line bottom of a greased 13- x 9- x 2-inch casserole with uncooked lasagna noodles. Spread with 1 cup Basic Spaghetti Sauce. Add a layer of ground beef, a layer of cottage cheese, and a layer of Swiss cheese slices. Continue process until pan is full. End with sauce. Cover tightly and bake at 350° for 1 to 1½ hours, depending on number of layers. Top with Parmesan cheese while hot. Yield: 8 servings.

POLENTA

4 chicken bouillon cubes
3 cups boiling water
1 teaspoon salt
1½ cups cornmeal
½ cup grated Parmesan cheese
1 pound ground beef, cooked
    (optional)
3½ cups Basic Spaghetti Sauce, thawed

Dissolve bouillon in boiling water. Bring bouillon and salt to a boil in a heavy saucepan. Stir cornmeal in slowly to avoid lumping. Cook, stirring constantly, until mixture is thick and smooth and rather dry. Remove from heat; stir in cheese. Add beef, if desired, to Basic Spaghetti Sauce and add ½ of the sauce to cornmeal mixture. Pour cornmeal mixture into a shallow serving dish and top with the remaining sauce. Yield: 6 servings.

MACARONI CASSEROLE

1 pound ground beef
1 teaspoon salt
¼ teaspoon pepper
3½ cups Basic Spaghetti Sauce, thawed
1 (12-ounce) package shell or elbow
    macaroni
    Grated Parmesan cheese

Brown ground beef; add salt and pepper. Drain excess drippings. Add Basic Spaghetti Sauce and simmer 20 minutes. Cook macaroni according to package directions. Drain and add to sauce. Pour into a lightly greased 2-quart casserole. Top with Parmesan cheese. Bake at 350° for 15 minutes. Yield: 6 servings.

Looking for a quick way to give barbecue fare a garlic flavor? Just toss garlic cloves on the coals while meat grills.

TAGLIOLINI CON POLLO (NOODLES WITH CHICKEN)

5 cups water
1 (10½-ounce) can condensed chicken
    broth, undiluted
1 (12-ounce) package tagliolini noodles
    or other thin noodles
4 cups cooked chopped chicken
3½ cups Basic Spaghetti Sauce, thawed
    Grated Parmesan cheese

Combine water and broth. Bring to a boil; add noodles. Cook 8 minutes or until almost done (less than al dente). Drain and turn into a lightly greased 2-quart casserole. Arrange chicken over noodles. Spoon heated sauce over all. Cover and bake at 350° for 30 minutes. Top with Parmesan cheese. Yield: 6 servings.

BASIC WHITE SAUCE MIX

1 cup all-purpose flour
1 cup butter or margarine
1 tablespoon salt
2½ cups nonfat dry milk powder

Blend all ingredients with a fork or pastry blender until the mixture resembles coarse meal and is crumbly. Store in a covered container in the refrigerator. Yield: 4 to 4½ cups dry mix.

Medium White Sauce:

Blend ⅓ cup Basic White Sauce Mix with 1 cup water in a saucepan, adding the liquid slowly. Heat to boiling, stirring constantly over low heat until mixture is smooth. For a thicker sauce, stir in more mix dissolved in a little cold water. Yield: 1 cup.

Variations to yield 1 cup sauce:

Béchamel:

Combine ⅓ cup Basic White Sauce Mix and 1 cup chicken stock.

Cheese:

Combine ⅓ cup Basic White Sauce Mix and 1 cup water; add 1 cup (4 ounces) shredded cheese when sauce is cooked.

Curry:

Combine ⅓ cup Basic White Sauce Mix, 1 cup water, and 1 teaspoon curry powder.

Green Pea:

Combine ⅓ cup Basic White Sauce Mix and 1 cup water; add ⅓ cup frozen, cooked green peas after sauce thickens.

Horseradish:

Combine ⅓ cup Basic White Sauce Mix, 1 cup beef bouillon, and ¼ cup grated fresh horseradish.

Parsley:

Combine ⅓ cup Basic White Sauce Mix, 1 cup water, and 1 tablespoon minced fresh parsley.

Pimiento:

Combine ⅓ cup Basic White Sauce Mix, 1 cup water, and 1 tablespoon finely chopped pimiento.

Mushroom Sauce:

Combine ⅓ cup Basic White Sauce Mix, 1 cup water, and ½ cup canned or fresh sliced mushrooms browned in butter.

Newburg Sauce:

Add dash of cayenne pepper to 1 cup prepared Medium White Sauce and pour over 1 beaten egg yolk. Cook over low heat, stirring constantly until thickened. Add shrimp, lobster, or other ingredients, using about 2 cups of fish to 1 cup of sauce. Can use part white wine for water in making the sauce.

À la King Supreme:

Brown 1 tablespoon chopped green pepper, 1 tablespoon chopped onion, and ½ cup sliced mushrooms in butter or margarine. Add to 1 cup prepared Medium White Sauce. When the sauce is cooked, add 1 tablespoon chopped pimiento.

Shrimp Sauce:

To 1 cup Medium White Sauce, add ½ cup canned shrimp; ½ tablespoon finely chopped parsley may be added for additional flavor and color.

Tomato Sauce:

Combine ⅓ cup Basic White Sauce Mix and 1 cup tomato juice. Brown 1 tablespoon chopped onion in butter and add to sauce.

When making a mix-in-one main dish, stir it up in the greased casserole. This saves an extra bowl and cuts down on after-dinner cleanup.

To save time, bone and flatten chicken breasts and thighs ahead of time and refrigerate or freeze them. The flattened meat will cook in only 35 to 40 minutes, about half the usual time.

BASIC SWEET SAUCE MIX

½ cup cornstarch
1 cup butter or margarine
4 cups sugar
½ teaspoon salt

Blend all ingredients with a fork or pastry blender until the mixture is uniform and crumbly. Store in a covered container in the refrigerator. Yield: 5½ cups.

Sweet Sauce:

Pack the Basic Sweet Sauce Mix to measure. Blend with the cold liquids indicated below; heat to boiling, stirring constantly.

Variations to yield 1 cup sauce:

Cherry Sauce:

Combine ⅓ cup Basic Sweet Sauce Mix and juice from 1 (16-ounce) can red sour cherries and water to make ⅔ cup liquid; add ½ cup red sour cherries and red food coloring after the mixture thickens.

Chocolate Sauce:

Combine ⅓ cup Basic Sweet Sauce Mix, ⅔ cup milk, and ½ ounce unsweetened chocolate, melted.

Lemon Sauce:

Combine ⅓ cup Basic Sweet Sauce Mix, ½ cup water, and 3 tablespoons lemon juice.

Orange Sauce:

Combine ⅓ cup Basic Sweet Sauce Mix and ⅔ cup orange juice.

Pineapple Sauce:

Combine ⅓ cup Basic Sweet Sauce Mix and juice from 1 (8¼-ounce) can crushed pineapple plus water to make ⅔ cup liquid; add ½ cup crushed pineapple.

Raisin Sauce:

Combine ⅓ cup Basic Sweet Sauce Mix, ⅔ cup water, and ¼ cup raisins.

CHILI SEASONING MIX

1 cup plus 2 tablespoons all-purpose flour
¾ cup instant minced onion
3 tablespoons chili powder
1 tablespoon ground cumin
1 tablespoon crushed red pepper
2 tablespoons salt
1 tablespoon instant minced garlic
1 tablespoon sugar

Combine all ingredients. Put in tightly covered container. Yield: about 2¼ cups.

RANCH-STYLE CHILI

1 pound ground beef
3 tablespoons plus 1 teaspoon Chili Seasoning Mix
½ cup water
1 (16-ounce) can tomatoes
1 (15-ounce) can kidney beans, undrained

Brown ground beef in large skillet; drain off excess drippings. Stir in Chili Seasoning Mix, water, tomatoes, and kidney beans. Bring to a boil; reduce heat and simmer, covered, for 10 minutes. Yield: 4 to 6 servings.

COAT AND COOK MIX
(For Chicken or Pork Chops)

2 cups fine breadcrumbs
½ cup all-purpose flour
2 tablespoons plain or seasoned salt
1 tablespoon poultry seasoning
1 tablespoon paprika
1 teaspoon pepper
½ teaspoon monosodium glutamate
   (optional)
1 tablespoon onion powder
1 tablespoon hickory smoke salt

Combine all ingredients. Store in covered container in pantry or in refrigerator for lengthy storage. Yield: about 3 cups.

To Use: Place ¼ cup mixture at a time in a plastic bag. Add meat, one piece at a time; shake vigorously. Place on greased pan. Do not allow pieces to touch. Bake at 350° for 1 hour or until done. For variety, add ¼ cup grated Parmesan cheese to 1 cup Coat and Cook Mix.

POTATO FINGERS

3 medium baking potatoes, unpeeled
¼ cup water
½ teaspoon hot sauce
½ cup Coat and Cook Mix
¼ cup grated Parmesan cheese
   Salt

Cut potatoes in strips as for French fries. Mix water and hot sauce in small piepan. Combine Coat and Cook Mix with Parmesan cheese in plastic bag. Roll potato fingers in water mixture. Shake in plastic bag to coat well, adding a few at a time. Remove and place on a foil-lined baking sheet. Bake at 425° for 30 minutes. Sprinkle with salt and serve hot. Yield: 4 servings.

SALAD HERBS MIXTURE

2 tablespoons sweet basil
1 tablespoon dried celery flakes
1 tablespoon dried parsley
1 tablespoon dried tarragon leaves

Combine and store in tightly covered container. Sprinkle liberally over tossed salad. Yield: about ⅓ cup.

SEASONING SALT

¼ cup garlic salt
¼ cup celery salt
¼ cup onion powder
1 teaspoon pepper
2 teaspoons monosodium glutamate
   (optional)
2 teaspoons sugar

Combine and store in tightly covered container. Yield: ¾ cup.

To give a tangy flavor to your meat patties, add 1 teaspoon of salt per pound of meat and a little barbecue or Worcestershire sauce to the pan before you complete cooking the meat.

GROUND BEEF MIX

4 medium onions, chopped
3 cloves garlic, crushed
2 cups chopped celery
1 large green pepper, chopped
¼ cup melted butter or margarine
4 pounds ground beef
1 tablespoon plus 1 teaspoon salt
1 teaspoon pepper
¼ cup Worcestershire sauce
2 (14-ounce) bottles catsup

Sauté onion, garlic, celery, and green pepper in butter in large skillet. Add ground beef and cook until all redness of the beef disappears. Add salt, pepper, Worcestershire sauce, and catsup. Simmer 20 minutes. Skim off excess fat. Cool quickly. Spoon the mixture into five 1-pint containers and freeze. Mix can be stored up to three months. Yield: 10 cups.

Uses for Ground Beef Mix:

Beefburger on Buns:

Heat 1 pint Ground Beef Mix in skillet. Spread on hot buttered buns. Yield: 4 servings.

Chili Con Carne:

Heat 1 pint Ground Beef Mix with 1 (15-ounce) can red kidney beans, drained. Season with chili powder. Yield: about 4 servings.

Spaghetti:

Heat 1 pint Ground Beef Mix. Add a dash each of cayenne pepper, hot sauce, and garlic salt. Cook 1 (8-ounce) package spaghetti according to package directions. Top with meat sauce and grated Parmesan cheese. Yield: 4 servings.

Beef and Noodles:

Heat 1 pint of Ground Beef Mix. Add 2 cups cooked noodles and 1 cup canned mixed vegetables. Stir. Pour into greased 1-quart casserole. Sprinkle ½ cup shredded Cheddar cheese and ½ teaspoon chopped parsley over top. Bake at 350° for about 15 minutes. Yield: 4 servings.

Beef and Rice:

Heat 1 pint Ground Beef Mix. Add 2 cups cooked rice and ½ cup chopped green pepper. Simmer to blend flavors and cook pepper. Yield: 4 servings.

Peppers Stuffed with Beef:

Prepare Beef and Rice above. Cut top off 6 green peppers; remove seeds and membrane. Cook in boiling water 4 minutes. Stuff peppers with beef mixture. Bake in a shallow pan at 375° about 50 minutes. Yield: 6 servings.

Beef Stroganoff:

Heat 1 pint Ground Beef Mix in large skillet. Add 1 (8-ounce) can sliced mushrooms and 1 (10¾-ounce) can cream of mushroom soup, undiluted. Stir and simmer 5 minutes. Carefully spoon 1 cup commercial sour cream over surface. Sprinkle with chopped parsley. Do not stir. Simmer 1 minute more. Serve over hot cooked rice. Yield: 4 servings.

If steak is your favorite barbecue fare, vary the flavor by rubbing the meat with garlic before broiling; then brush it with butter occasionally while the meat cooks over the hot coals. Or top that steak with fresh sliced mushrooms and green onions that have been sautéed in butter.

Pan-fried fruit (such as apples, bananas, peaches, or pineapple) lend a delicious accompaniment for meat. You can also broil the fruit if you're careful not to scorch them. Brush them with lemon juice.

SAVORY CHEESE SPREAD

¼ cup butter or margarine, softened
2 cups (8 ounces) shredded Cheddar
  cheese (at room temperature)
¼ cup (1 ounce) crumbled blue cheese
2 tablespoons chopped fresh parsley
1 teaspoon lemon juice
⅛ teaspoon cayenne pepper

Blend all ingredients together until smooth. Store in tightly covered container in refrigerator for several days, using as needed. Yield: approximately 1½ cups.

To Use: Spread on sizzling steaks, chops, hamburgers, or use as a spread for sandwiches, crackers, and toast, broiling just until spread melts.

FROZEN FRENCH-FRIED ONION RINGS

2 large onions
1¼ cups all-purpose flour
1 teaspoon baking powder
¼ teaspoon salt
1 egg, beaten
1 cup beer (at room temperature)
1 tablespoon vegetable oil
  Oil for deep-fat frying
  Salt

Peel onions and cut into ⅜-inch thick slices. Separate into rings. Combine flour, baking powder, salt, egg, beer, and 1 tablespoon oil. Blend until smooth. With fork, dip onion rings into batter and coat well. Fry in oil heated to 375° until light brown on both sides, turning once. Drain on paper towels. Spread out on baking sheet to freeze. When frozen, package desired quantities in foil and store in freezer. To reheat, spread onion rings on baking sheet and bake at 400° for 5 to 7 minutes. While hot, sprinkle with salt. Yield: about 5 dozen rings.

VANILLA PUDDING MIX

2½ cups nonfat dry milk powder
1½ cups sugar
1¼ cups all-purpose flour
1 teaspoon salt

Combine all ingredients. Store in a tightly covered container in a cool place until ready to use. Yield: 24 servings.

Variations:

Chocolate Pudding Mix:

Add ¾ cup cocoa to the other ingredients of Vanilla Pudding Mix before stirring.

Caramel Pudding Mix:

Substitute firmly packed brown sugar for granulated sugar in Vanilla Pudding Mix.

PUDDING FROM HOMEMADE MIX

1¼ cups Vanilla, Chocolate, or Caramel
  Pudding Mix
2½ cups warm water
1 tablespoon butter or margarine
1 egg, beaten
¾ teaspoon vanilla extract

Combine Pudding Mix with warm water in the top of a double boiler. Place over boiling water and stir constantly until thickened. Cover and cook 10 minutes longer. Add 1 tablespoon butter or margarine. Remove from heat and slowly blend half of mixture with egg. Add egg mixture to remaining pudding mixture, stirring constantly. Cook over hot water 1 minute longer. Remove from heat and stir in vanilla. Chill. Yield: 6 servings.

Appendices

Handy Substitutions

Even the best of cooks occasionally runs out of an ingredient she needs and is unable to stop what she is doing to go to the store. At times like those, sometimes another ingredient or combination of ingredients can be used. Here is a list of substitutions and equivalents that yield satisfactory results in most cases.

Ingredient called for	Substitution
1 cup self-rising flour	1 cup all-purpose flour plus 1 teaspoon baking powder and ½ teaspoon salt
1 cup cake flour	1 cup sifted all-purpose flour minus 2 tablespoons
1 cup all-purpose flour	1 cup cake flour plus 2 tablespoons
1 teaspoon baking powder	½ teaspoon cream of tartar plus ¼ teaspoon soda
1 tablespoon cornstarch or arrowroot	2 tablespoons all-purpose flour
1 tablespoon tapioca	1½ tablespoons all-purpose flour
2 large eggs	3 small eggs
1 egg	2 egg yolks (for custard)
1 egg	2 egg yolks plus 1 tablespoon water (for cookies)
1 cup commercial sour cream	1 tablespoon lemon juice plus evaporated milk to equal 1 cup; or 3 tablespoons butter plus ⅞ cup sour milk
1 cup yogurt	1 cup buttermilk or sour milk
1 cup sour milk or buttermilk	1 tablespoon vinegar or lemon juice plus sweet milk to equal 1 cup
1 cup fresh milk	½ cup evaporated milk plus ½ cup water
1 cup fresh milk	3 to 5 tablespoons nonfat dry milk powder in 1 cup water
1 cup honey	1¼ cups sugar plus ¼ cup liquid
1 square (1 ounce) unsweetened chocolate	3 tablespoons cocoa plus 1 tablespoon butter or margarine
1 clove fresh garlic	1 teaspoon garlic salt or ⅛ teaspoon garlic powder
1 teaspoon onion powder	2 teaspoons minced onion
1 tablespoon fresh herbs	1 teaspoon ground or crushed dry herbs
¼ cup chopped fresh parsley	1 tablespoon dehydrated parsley
1 teaspoon dry mustard	1 tablespoon prepared mustard
1 pound fresh mushrooms	6 ounces canned mushrooms

Equivalent Weights and Measures

Food	Weight or Count	Measure
Apples	1 pound (3 medium)	3 cups, sliced
Bacon	8 slices cooked	½ cup, crumbled
Bananas	1 pound (3 medium)	2½ cups, sliced, or about 2 cups, mashed
Bread	1 pound	12 to 16 slices
Bread	About 1½ slices	1 cup soft crumbs
Butter or margarine	1 pound (4 sticks)	2 cups
Butter or margarine	¼ pound (1 stick)	½ cup
Butter or margarine	Size of an egg	About ¼ cup
Candied fruit or peels	½ pound	1¼ cups, cut
Cheese, American	1 pound	4 to 5 cups, shredded
cottage	1 pound	2 cups
cream	3-ounce package	6 tablespoons
Chocolate morsels	6-ounce package	1 cup
Cocoa	1 pound	4 cups
Coconut, flaked or shredded	1 pound	5 cups
Coffee	1 pound	80 tablespoons
Cornmeal	1 pound	3 cups
Cream, heavy or whipping	½ pint	2 cups, whipped
Dates, pitted	1 pound	2 to 3 cups, chopped
Dates, pitted	7¼-ounce package	1¼ cups, chopped
Eggs	5 large	About 1 cup
Egg whites	8 large	About 1 cup
Egg yolks	12 large	About 1 cup
Flour		
all-purpose	1 pound	4 cups, sifted
cake	1 pound	4¾ to 5 cups, sifted
whole wheat	1 pound	3½ cups, unsifted
Graham crackers	16 to 18 crackers	1⅓ cups crumbs
Lemon juice	1 medium	2 to 3 tablespoons
Lemon rind	1 medium	2 teaspoons, grated
Macaroni	4 ounces (1 cup)	2¼ cups, cooked
Milk		
evaporated	6-ounce can	¾ cup
evaporated	14½-ounce can	1⅔ cups
sweetened condensed	14-ounce can	1¼ cups
sweetened condensed	15-ounce can	1⅓ cups
Miniature marshmallows	½ pound	4½ cups
Nuts, in shell		
almonds	1 pound	1 to 1¾ cups nutmeats
peanuts	1 pound	2 cups nutmeats
pecans	1 pound	2¼ cups nutmeats
walnuts	1 pound	1⅔ cups nutmeats

Food	Weight or Count	Measure
Nuts, shelled		
almonds	1 pound, 2 ounces	4 cups
peanuts	1 pound	4 cups
pecans	1 pound	4 cups
walnuts	1 pound	3 cups
Orange, juice	1 medium	⅓ cup
Orange, rind	1 medium	2 tablespoons, grated
Potatoes	2 pounds	6 medium
Raisins, seedless	1 pound	3 cups
Rice	1 cup	About 4 cups, cooked
Spaghetti	7 ounces	About 4 cups, cooked
Sugar		
brown	1 pound	2¼ cups, firmly packed
powdered	1 pound	3½ cups, unsifted
granulated	1 pound	2 cups
Whipping cream	1 cup	2 cups, whipped

Equivalent Measurements

Use standard measuring cups (both dry and liquid measure) and measuring spoons when measuring ingredients. All measurements given below are level.

3 teaspoons	1 tablespoon
4 tablespoons	¼ cup
5⅓ tablespoons	⅓ cup
8 tablespoons	½ cup
16 tablespoons	1 cup
2 tablespoons (liquid)	1 ounce
1 cup	8 fluid ounces
2 cups	1 pint (16 fluid ounces)
4 cups	1 quart
4 quarts	1 gallon
⅛ cup	2 tablespoons
⅓ cup	5 tablespoons plus 1 teaspoon
⅔ cup	10 tablespoons plus 2 teaspoons
¾ cup	12 tablespoons
Few grains (or dash)	Less than ⅛ teaspoon
Pinch	As much as can be taken between tip of finger and thumb

Metric Measures

Approximate Conversion to Metric Measures

When you know . . .	Multiply by mass (weight)	To find . . .	Symbol
ounces	28	grams	g
pounds	0.45	kilograms	kg
	Volume		
teaspoons	5	milliliters	ml
tablespoons	15	milliliters	ml
fluid ounces	30	milliliters	ml
cups	0.24	liters	l
pints	0.47	liters	l
quarts	0.95	liters	l
gallons	3.8	liters	l

Cooking Measure Equivalents

Metric Cup	Volume (Liquid)	Liquid Solids (Butter)	Fine Powder (Flour)	Granular (Sugar)	Grain (Rice)
1	250 ml	200 g	140 g	190	150 g
¾	188 ml	150 g	105 g	143 g	113 g
⅔	167 ml	133 g	93 g	127 g	100 g
½	125 ml	100 g	70 g	95 g	75 g
⅓	83 ml	67 g	47 g	63 g	50 g
¼	63 ml	50 g	35 g	48 g	38 g
⅛	31 ml	25 g	18 g	24 g	19 g

HERB CHART

For:	Appetizers & Garnishes	Soups	Fish	Eggs or Cheese	Meats	Poultry & Game	Vegetables	Salads	Sauces
Use: **Basil**	Tomato Juice Seafood Cocktail	Tomato Chowders Spinach Minestrone	Shrimps Broiled Fish	Scrambled Eggs Cream Cheese Welsh Rarebit	Liver Lamb Sausage	Venison Duck	Eggplant Squash Tomatoes Onions	Tomato Seafood Chicken	Tomato Spaghetti Orange (for Game) Butter (for Fish)
Bay Leaves	Tomato Juice Aspic	Stock Bean	Court Bouillon Poached Halibut Salmon		Stews Pot Roast Shish Kabob Tripe	Chicken Fricassee Stews	Tomatoes	Aspic Marinades for Beet Onion	All Marinades Espagnole Champagne
Dillweed	Cheese Dips Seafood Spreads Pickles	Borscht Tomato Chicken	Halibut Shrimp Sole	Omelet Cottage Cheese	Beef Sweetbreads Veal Lamb	Chicken Pie Creamed Chicken	Cabbage Beets Beans Celery	Coleslaw Cucumber Potato	White (for Fish) Tartare
Fines Herbs			Baked or Broiled Cod or Halibut Dressings	Omelet Scrambled Eggs Cheese Sauce Soufflés	Broiled Liver and Kidneys Roast Pork Pot Roast, Stews Meat Loaf Hamburgers	Dressings Broiled Chicken	Peas Mushrooms Tomatoes		
Marjoram	Liver Pâté Stuffed Mushrooms Butters	Spinach Clam Mock Turtle Onion	Crab, Tuna Clams Halibut Salmon	Omelet Scrambled Eggs	Pot Roast Pork Beef Veal	Creamed Chicken Dressings Goose	Carrots Zucchini Peas	Chicken Mixed Green	White Brown Sour Cream
Oregano	Guacamole Tomato	Tomato Bean Minestrone	Shrimp Clams Lobster	Huevos Rancheros	Sausage Lamb Meat Loaf	Marinades Dressings Pheasant Guinea Hen	Tomatoes Cabbage Lentils Broccoli	Vegetable Bean Tomato	Spaghetti Tomato

HERB CHART — Continued

For:	Appetizers & Garnishes	Soups	Fish	Eggs or Cheese	Meats	Poultry & Game	Vegetables	Salads	Sauces
Peppermint*	Fruit Cup Melon Balls Cranberry Juice	Pea	Garnish for Broiled Shrimps Prawns	Cream Cheese	Lamb Veal		Carrots New Potatoes Spinach Zucchini	Fruit Coleslaw Orange Pear	Mint
Rosemary	Fruit Cup	Turtle, Pea Spinach Chicken	Salmon Halibut	Omelet Scrambled Eggs	Lamb, Veal Beef Ham Loaf	Partridge Capon, Duck Rabbit	Peas Spinach Potatoes	Fruit	White Barbecue Tomato
Saffron		Bouillabaisse Chicken, Turkey	Halibut Sole	Cream Cheese Scrambled Eggs	Veal	Chicken Rabbit	Risotto Rice	Seafood Chicken	Fish Sauce
Sage	Sharp Cheese Spreads	Chicken Chowders	Halibut Salmon	Cheddar Cottage	Stews Pork Sausage	Goose Turkey Rabbit Dressings	Lima Beans Eggplant Onions Tomatoes		
Salad Herbs	Fruit Cup Vegetable and Tomato Juices Seafood Cocktail Sauce		All Fish		Meat Loaf			All Salads	
Savory	Vegetable Juice Cocktail	Lentil Bean Vegetable	Crab Salmon	Scrambled or Deviled Eggs	Pork Veal	Chicken Dressings	Beans, Rice Lentils Sauerkraut	Mixed Green String Bean Potato	Horseradish Fish Sauce
Tarragon	Tomato Juice Cheese Spreads Liver Pâtés	Chicken Mushroom Tomato Pea	All Fish	All Egg Dishes	Veal Sweetbreads Yorkshire Pudding	Chicken Squab Duck	Salsify Celery Root Mushrooms	Mixed Green Chicken Fruit Seafood	Bearnaise Tartare Verte Mustard
Thyme	Tomato Juice Fish Spreads Cocktails	Borscht Gumbo, Pea Clam Chowder Vegetable	Tuna Scallops Crab Sole	Shirred Eggs Cottage Cheese	Mutton Meat Loaf Veal Liver	Dressings Venison Fricassee Pheasant	Onions Carrots Beets	Beet Tomato Aspics	Creole Espagnole Herb Bouquets

*Use ½ teaspoon for 6 servings

Courtesy of Spice Islands

SPICE CHART

For: / Use:	Appetizers & Garnishes	Fish	Eggs or Cheese	Meats	Poultry & Game	Vegetables	Sauces	Desserts & Beverages
Allspice		*Marinades		Pot Roast Stew Braised Veal Pork, Lamb	*Marinades (for Game)	*Pickling liquids for all vegetables	Chili, Catsup Barbecue Spaghetti Brown	Apple Pie Pumpkin Pie Fruit and Spice Cakes Mincemeat
Beau Monde Seasoning	Dips Spreads	Broiled Baked	All Egg Dishes	Steaks Chops Roasts	Chicken Duck Turkey		White Tomato Barbecue	
Cardamom				Spareribs Ham Pork			Barbecue	Coffee Cakes Breads Fruitcake Cookies	Hot Fruit Punches *Mulled Wines
Chili Con Carne Seasoning	Cheese Dips Spreads		Welsh Rarebit Soufflés Baked or Scrambled Eggs	Marinades for Pork Lamb Beef	Marinades for Chicken	Corn Rice Kidney Pink or Lima Beans	Barbecue Cheese	
Cinnamon	Cranberry Sauce Pickled or Spiced Fruits Broiled Grapefruit *Pickles *Chutney Catsup	*Court Bouillon for all Fish and Shellfish		Ham Lamb Pork Chops Beef Stews *Stock for Pickled or Smoked Meats	Dressing for Goose			All Milk Drinks Custard, Fruit or Rice Puddings Pumpkin, Apple, Peach, Cream or Custard Pies	*Mulled Wine *Hot Tea *Coffee *Chocolate *Spiced and Pickled Fruits
Cloves		*Court Bouillon Baked Fish	Scrambled or Creamed Eggs	*Marinades for Beef, Pork Lamb, Veal *Stock for Boiling Meat Loaf	*Marinades for Game *Stock for Boiling Poultry	Harvard Beets Sweet Potatoes Tomatoes	Spaghetti Chili Wine Barbecue	*Hot or Cold Fruit Punches *Mulled Wines	All spice cakes, cookies, and puddings
Curry Powder	Dips	Broiled Baked	Deviled Eggs Egg Salad Cheese Spreads	Lamb Pork Beef	Chicken	Cooked Vegetables	Curry Marinades for Lamb, Beef Chicken Fish, Game White Sauce	
Ginger	*Pickled or Spiced Fruits *Preserves Jams Jellies	Broiled Baked		Pot Roast Steak Lamb *Marinades for Beef, Lamb	Dressing for Poultry *Marinades for Chicken, Turkey	Candied Sweet Potatoes Glazed Carrots or Onions Winter Squash	For Pork Veal Fish	Canned Fruit Gingerbread Gingersnaps Ginger Cookies	Steamed Puddings Bread or Rice Puddings

For: Use:	Appetizers & Garnishes	Fish	Eggs or Cheese	Meats	Poultry & Game	Vegetables	Sauces	Desserts & Beverages
Mace	Pickles Fruit Preserves Jellies	Trout Scalloped Fish	Welsh Rarebit	Lamb Chops Sausage		Buttered Carrots Cauliflower Squash Swiss Chard Spinach Mashed or Creamed Potatoes	Fish Veal Chicken	Cooked Apples Cherries Prunes Apricots Pancakes Chocolate Pudding	Fruit Cottage or Custard Puddings
Mustard (Hot)	Butter for Vegetables Seafood Cocktail	Crab		Stew Pot Roast Ham Pork	Fried Chicken	Creamed Asparagus Broccoli Brussels Sprouts Cabbage Celery Green Beans Pickled Beets	French Dressing Mustard Sauce Gravies Cream Cheese and Newburg Sauces	
Mustard (Mild)		Fried Broiled		Beef Stew Swiss Steak		Scalloped & Au Gratin Potatoes Steamed Cabbage Brussels Sprouts Asparagus Broccoli	French Dressing Cooked Salad Dressing Mayonnaise Raisin, White Sauces	
Nutmeg	Garnish for milk, chocolate, and spiced drinks	Baked Croquettes Broiled	Welsh Rarebit	Swedish Meat Balls Meat Loaf Meat Pie	Chicken	Glazed Carrots Cauliflower Squash Swiss Chard Spinach	White Sauce for Chicken Seafood Veal	Ice Cream Cakes	Cookies Puddings
Paprika	Pâtés Canapes Hors d'oeuvres		All Cheese Mixtures	Ground Beef Dipping Mixture for Pork Chops Veal Cutlets	Dipping Mixture for Fried Chicken	Baked Potatoes	Cooked French Sour Cream Salad Dressings White Sauce	
Tumeric		Marinades for Broiled Salmon, Lobster, or Shrimp	Scrambled or Creamed Eggs	Curried Beef or Lamb	Marinades for Chicken		White Mustard	
Vanilla Beans							Fruit	Ice Cream Cakes	Custards Puddings

Note: All spices are ground except those indicated by an asterisk (*), which indicates whole spice

Courtesy of Spice Islands

D

E

Notes